3ds Max Basics
for Modeling Video Game Assets

Volume Two

Model, Rig and Animate Characters for Export to
Unity or Other Game Engines

3ds Max Basics
for Modeling Video Game Assets

Volume Two

Model, Rig and Animate Characters for Export to Unity or Other Game Engines

Bill Culbertson

CRC Press
Taylor & Francis Group
Boca Raton London New York

CRC Press is an imprint of the
Taylor & Francis Group, an **informa** business

First Edition published 2021
by CRC Press
6000 Broken Sound Parkway NW, Suite 300, Boca Raton, FL 33487-2742

and by CRC Press
2 Park Square, Milton Park, Abingdon, Oxon, OX14 4RN

ISBN: 978-0-367-70781-1 (hbk)
ISBN: 978-0-367-70780-4 (pbk)
ISBN: 978-1-003-14796-1 (ebk)

Typeset in Myriad Pro
by codeMantra

Contents

Contents

Acknowledgments

Writing this book was an adventure in finding ways to create characters that would be basic in their construction, yet be appropriate for meeting the project goals. Thanks go to my colleagues for their feedback and reviews. Special thanks to Jordan Dubreuil for his help with creating the Unity Environment Package and the ThirdPersonCharacter Package with scripts for importing the characters into Unity.

Thanks again to Autodesk for creating some amazing software. Thanks to New England Tech for the opportunity to teach and work with their students and the Video Game Department faculty.

Thanks to Focal Press and Sean Connelly for this opportunity.

A special thanks to my amazing wife and family for putting up with and allowing me to go on a bizarre and wild career path, from sculpting toys to monumental public art, from designing theme park amusement rides to creating video games. Somehow it all fits together, a truly great adventure.

Author

Bill Culbertson, Creative Director/Owner Whooplah LLC, has traveled along several diverse paths that crisscrossed, overlapped and eventually merged together. He is a Fine Artist, Commercial Artist, Corporate Director, Freelancer, Entertainment Media Producer and Professor.

A graduate in Fine Art at Towson University in Maryland, Culbertson earned a Master of Arts degree from the Rhode Island School of Design, Providence, RI, USA. Commercially, he began his career at Hasbro, Inc., as an industrial designer in Research & Design. Within a short time, he was the Director of the Sculpture Department, guiding the sculpting of the company's popular toy lines such as G.I. Joe and My Little Pony. Moving into the freelance community, he developed an international clientele including manufacturers, theme parks and cruise lines. Specializing in licensed characters, he worked extensively with The Walt Disney Company, Jim Henson Company, Sesame Street Workshop, Nickelodeon and others. As an inventor, Culbertson is responsible for a number of manufactured toy concepts. Additionally, he created and produced the award-winning puppet show, "Li'l Rhody!" for Rhode Island PBS.

As a fine artist, Culbertson has been recognized nationally and internationally for his work through numerous large-scale public art works. He has been distinguished as a Copley Master by the Copley Society of Boston.

As the founder of Whooplah LLC, Culbertson is committed to creating family-fun entertainment that helps parents meet and exceed their parenting goals. The company's first game released, "Pollywog Pond," is an early learner portal to reading, music, videos, games and more. In 2019, Pollywog Pond was nominated for a Kidscreen Award for Best Video Game – Original. In 2021, Pollywog Pond is scheduled to be released as a children's television series co-production between Whooplah and RI PBS for national distribution.

As a Professor at the New England Institute of Technology in Rhode Island, Culbertson is a member of the nationally ranked Video Game Development and Design Department. With over 18 years of post-secondary teaching experience, his teaching emphasis is in 3D modeling, animation and game development.

For more information, please visit: Whooplah.com and PollywogPond.com

Introduction

Welcome to Volume II of this book series. In volume I, we covered the basic workflow pipeline for modeling and the basic tools in 3ds Max. In doing so, we modeled and textured modules to assemble a castle. The modules were all based on geometric forms. We created the models for the environment using "hard modeling." We then exported the completed the castle to the Unity game engine and moved around our creation.

In Volume II, we will be modeling some basic characters for our medieval castle environment using "soft modeling" techniques, models that are more organic in construction. We will use a couple of different types of bone rigging methods to allow us to animate the characters. When the characters are complete, we will import them into our Unity Castle scene from Volume I. Completing these projects in the order they are presented is recommended, as the concepts and techniques are organized in a progressive order, building your skills and knowledge in a step-by-step lesson format. As in Volume I, during the process of creating these objects, you will repeatedly use the tools and techniques to reinforce and gain mastery of them.

Please remember that, while using 3ds Max, you will find that there are typically two or three different ways to do the same or similar procedure that yield the same result. Some procedures may be easier or more efficient to use than others. Personal preference can come into play. For example, some people prefer hotkeys, some people prefer floating menus, some like using the toolbar menus. 3ds Max is a flexible software in that almost everything in 3ds Max is customizable. We will use certain methods, so you will be familiar with them.

Note:

> If you have not completed the project chapters in Volume I of this series, I would recommend you stop here and complete the lessons in that book. We will not be covering many of the tool basics that were covered in Volume I in this text. The projects in this book were created assuming you have completed those projects and are ready to build on your acquired skills. If you find yourself getting lost or confused while working on the projects presented here, that may be the cause of the problem.

The main target audience for this book is the potential modeler for video game assets. In the current state of the hardware available, video game assets need to be on the low end of the Polygon count spectrum to keep the game running with a minimum of lag. We will be striving to keep the models low poly: using as few polygons is necessary to create the assets. Although the text targets video games, the same principles of modeling will apply for other industries: simulation, film, animation, architecture and others.

Another goal of both volumes of this series is to give the reader a taste of what it might be like to work in a game studio as a modeler. In Volume I, we worked with our imaginary video game company's Game Design Document (GDD) to guide our design decisions for the castle modules. In this volume, we will return to the GDD as a guide for modeling our characters.

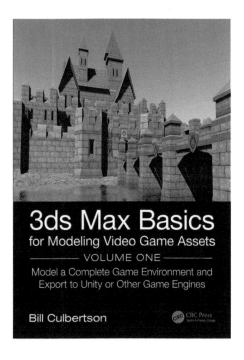

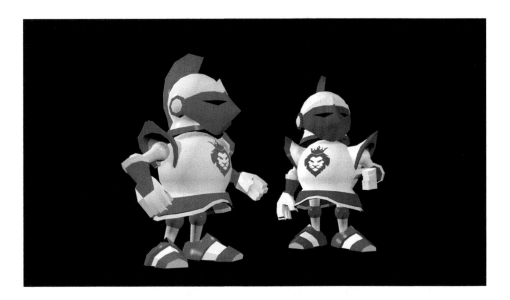

Character Design

Topics in This Chapter

- Game Design Document
- Sourcing Reference Materials
- Developmental Sketches

Concepts/Skills/Tools Introduced in This Chapter

- Character Sheet – Turnaround
- Scene Set-Up with Templates

Where to Start?

There have been tons of references written on character design and development. They all start with an idea that establishes the direction the character development will take. As designers at our fictitious game company, we too need a starting point for creating characters for our game. In most cases, there is a definite starting point for our process. That would be the Game Design Document (GDD). We referenced it in the creation of our castle modules in Volume I. From it, we gleaned the parameters that the game designers for our game defined. The GDD gave us the style, tone, size and look desired for the modules as well as the polygon and other limiting parameter required.

For our characters, we will also need to first reference our game's GDD. In our role in the company as modelers it is typically not our responsibility to define the character for the game, our role is to translate the character's defined characteristics provided in the GDD into a visual model. In some books, chapters similar to this one might discuss character development: what makes the character "tick," their wants and desires, etc. As modelers, we are interpreting an already defined character description. Sometimes reference to work from will be provided, sometimes not.

Referring to our company's GDD information about characters, I have summarized the following as a refresher of our game and what we modeled in Volume I:

Game Name: Castle Keep: Red vs. Blue	
• General Features	3D Medieval Environment, Multiplayer, FPS
• Gameplay	"Capture the Flag," Two Kingdoms, the Red and the Blue
• Game Engine/Editor	Unity 3d
• Player Characters	King, Queen, Knight on Horseback, Knight, Dragon
• Environment	Hand-painted, medieval fantasy
• Castle Modules	Curtain Wall, Fixed Bridge, Gate House, Turrets, Keep
• Castle Accessories	Wooden Table and Chair, Wall Torch, Wine Barrel, etc.

Look specifically at the character information. The GDD lists five characters: The King, the Queen, the Knight on Horseback, the Knight and the Dragon. We will be modeling and rigging the Knight on Horseback, the Knight and the Dragon together in this book. The King and Queen will be assignment exercises you can complete on your own.

Let's use the Knight as our first figure to design, model and rig. Referring to the GDD for character parameters for this character, we find the following:

Game Castle Keep, Blue vs. Red	
• Who	Character: Knight In the game, the male Knight serves as the main infantry soldier. The Knight has the ability to attack other characters and objects by swinging/slashing a hand-held sword. His movement is strong, skilled and confident. He's not hesitant, ready to fight on command.
• What	The Knight is a biped figure. The character has a cartoonish look. For his proportions, he stands three "heads" high. He wears a stylized suit of armor (creating an air of confidence/tough guy) that allows free movement for running, jumping and swinging his sword for attack. The character has markings that can be used to assign the character to either the Blue or Red team (one character used for both teams with different skins).

• When	The character is middle to late medieval time period, refined armor and weapons, appropriate to the modeled environmental castle modules.
• Where	The Knight will fight at the ground or surface level (regular gravity). • Movement: WASD movement with jump, arm sword swing • Animations: Idle, walk, run, jump, attack (sword swing), die
• Model	
	Poly limit: 4000 poly limit (low poly)
	Height limit: 1.5 m (scaled to castle environment: fits through doorways)
	Complexity: Can be simple, non-deformation

There is some key information in the above character description. We have been given the impression the character is a short, feisty guy who is comfortable in his armor. He will be a low poly character of 4000 polygons. His proportions of three heads high give him a cartoony look. Because he can be a non-deformable character, we can design him with multiple parts that can be rigged using just linking. I will be creating our design based on this information.

References

Our next step would be to start gathering some references for the character design. We want to be sure our reference includes some actual armor, so we are not just working from someone's interpretation of armor, like a 3d model. The following are some of the images I found.

IMAGE 1.1 © Shutterstock. Used with Permission.

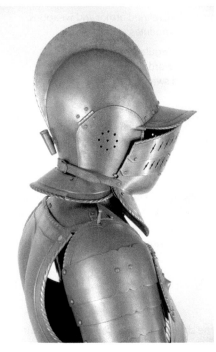

IMAGE 1.2 © Shutterstock. Used with Permission.

The images above show typical medieval armor construction. The torso and waist areas are covered with armor pieces. The helmet visors on these two samples are different styles: one opens in the up direction and one in the downward. The elbow and knee areas are covered with separate, spherical cover pieces. The leg pieces shown in Image 1.3 of reproduction armor shows similar knee shapes. Note the separate toe covering pieces that allow foot movement.

IMAGE 1.3 © Shutterstock. Used with Permission.

The armor image to the right shows the shoulder flairs for jousting. The shapes echo the shapes used on the helmet. The pointed shapes add a sense of flair to the image, adding some visual flair and movement.

These are just a few images of the several dozen I collected as reference for designing this character. The ones here appealed to me as a collection that I could envision coming together to form our Knight. The next step is to start sketching to explore some possibilities. As you can see, I started with some loose sketching, exploring different possible directions to go. I am working on both three-quarter views and orthographic views (front and side), exploring different proportions and looks.

IMAGE 1.4 © Shutterstock. Used with Permission.

Design

IMAGE 1.5

Reviewing initial sketches, I then start refining the design in a single direction. Tightening up to a true three head height (using three stacked circles) helps to ensure the design will be within the specs of the GDD.

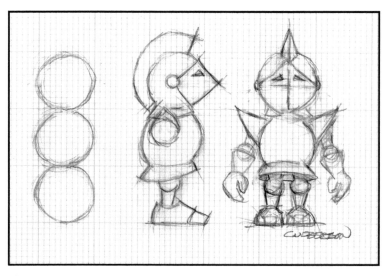

IMAGE 1.6

Further refinement brings us closer to a finished design. Note how the features of the reference were incorporated into the design. Our character looks like it could be a real armored soldier because it has the features of real armor. It is really important that designs be based on real-world features that the player can relate to. At this point, I have transitioned from paper sketching to drawing in the computer (Photoshop) using a drawing tablet (Wacom Cintiq). The reason for switching is, in the end of this process, I will need digital images to import into 3ds Max as template guides. Notice that I purposely aligned the features in the front and side views, so they align horizontally. At this point, you would want to check with our supervisor and other designers in our company for suggestions and comments on our design to make sure we are heading in a good direction.

IMAGE 1.7

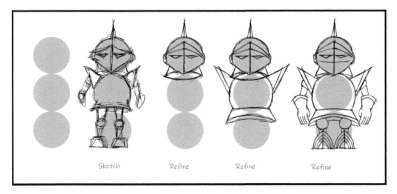

IMAGE 1.8

We are effectively creating a Character Model Sheet. Companies that license their characters usually create Character Model Sheets for their characters. The Model Sheet ensures that their characters will have a consistent look across the marketplace. Notice that I purposely aligned the features in the front and side views, so they align horizontally. This is very important. When we are modeling the mesh using these drawings as templates, the features must align or there will be problems.

IMAGE 1.9

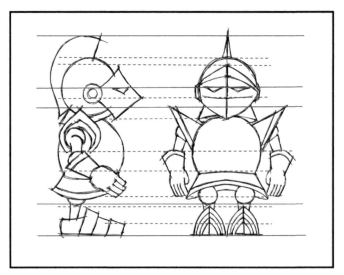

IMAGE 1.10

We are at the stage where we would seek out approvals at our company to proceed to the modeling stage. Once everyone has had the opportunity to add their comment, we would make the necessary tweaks to reach the approved stage. Next, we would break the single image we have created (Image 1.8) into separate front and side views in Photoshop or another image editing software. The two images would be used as textures on planes in 3ds Max to serve as modeling guides.

Image 1.12 shows the front and side images applied to planes in the Perspective Viewport in 3ds Max. Note where they are positioned, away from the X, Y, and Z-axis intersection at 0,0,0. The side view plane is parallel to the X-axis, and the front is parallel to the Y-axis.

IMAGE 1.11

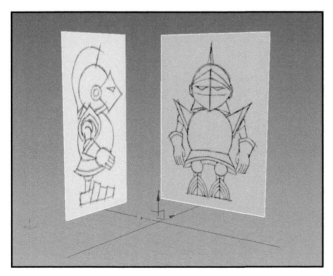

IMAGE 1.12

Image 1.13 shows a blue cylinder to represent the area where we would create the model. Setting the mesh to "see-through" in the Object Properties we can adjust the vertices to match the images on the planes. In the next chapter, we will start to model the Knight character.

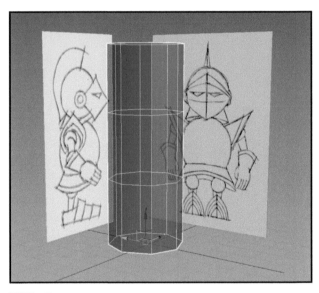

IMAGE 1.13

Chapter 1 Exercise: Design a King or Queen

In this chapter, the design for the Knight was developed through a process of researching medieval knights, gathering imagery and developing design concepts based on the reference. For this exercise, you need to design a King or Queen for the game.

The character styling should complement the Knight character, utilizing similar styling. Follow the same process as used for the Knight. You do not need to model the character; you need to just design the character and create a turnaround drawing (see Image 1.10) that can be used to make the front and side view templates for modeling as in Image 1.12.

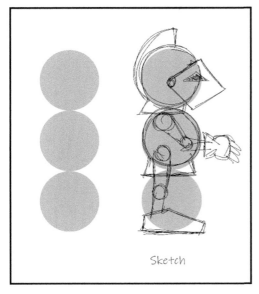

Sketch

IMAGE 1.14

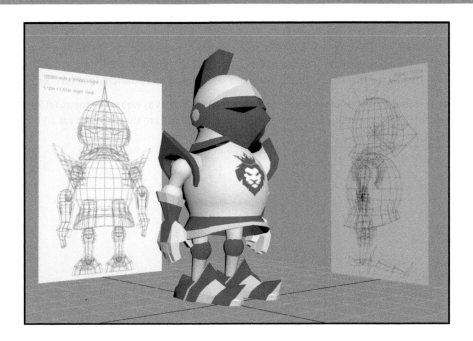

Character Modeling:
The Knight

Topics in This Chapter

- Preparing the scene: Template planes
- Template images
- The Slate Editor

Concepts/Skills/Tools Introduced in This Chapter

- Creating and assigning materials with the Slate Editor
- Review of using the basic tools from Volume I

Preparing the Scene in 3ds Max

Now that our character model sheet with front and side views is complete, we can start modeling the character. Our first step would be to create individual images of the front and the side views to be used as templates in the scene as shown in Image 1.12

In preparing to write this chapter of the book, I went ahead and modeled the character using the two hand-drawn templates in the scene. I made some slight design changes along the way, refining the process and making better design decisions. Having completed the character model, I was able to create new template images using wireframe screenshots of the completed model. The advantage in this case, you will be able to more accurately model the character with less "guessing" as to the correct positioning of vertices.

Additionally, I created a number of templates to isolate the mesh parts as we model them. All you will need to do is swap out the texture images. The first two images we will use are shown in Images 2.1 and 2.2.

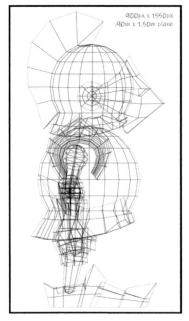

IMAGE 2.1

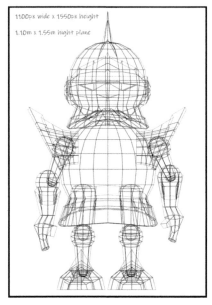

IMAGE 2.2

To start, open 3ds Max to a new scene. As in the previous book volume, we need to provide our programmers with a place holder to use in the game program as they develop the game on their end. First, we will set up the scene.

Setting Up the Scene

Begin by saving the scene. Using the Save As, save the file to a location of your choosing using the same naming convention as we used when modeling the castle environment, *lastname_knight_01*. As before, let's create a folder using the Scene Explorer for the objects we will be creating. Select the Toggle Scene Explorer Button if the Scene Explorer is not open already. Make sure the "Sort by Layer" button at the bottom of the window is active, not the "Sort by Hierarchy" one.

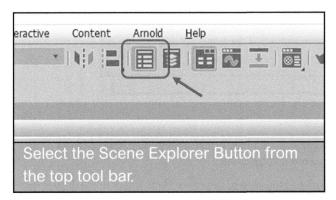

IMAGE 2.3

When the Sort by Hierarchy button is active, the window does not allow layers to be added. Add a new layer to the list by selecting the "add a New Layer" icon. Name the new layer "knight." Add three layers within the knight layer: templates, placeholder and knight model.

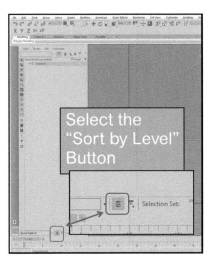

IMAGE 2.4

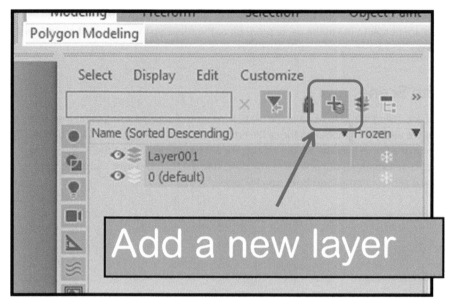

IMAGE 2.5

Select the "templates" layer. We will bring in our two image templates into this layer. This will allow us to turn the images on and off easily to review the modeling progress.

Check to make sure we are using the metric units of measure by selecting "Units Setup" in the drop-down menu of the "Customize" tab on the top toolbar. Select the Metric radio button and Meters and the units of measure.

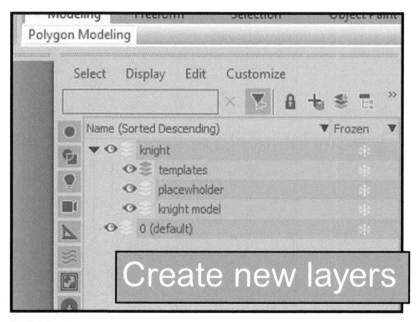

IMAGE 2.6

Check to make sure we are using the metric units of measure by selecting "Units Setup" in the drop-down menu of the "Customize" tab on the top toolbar. Select the Metric radio button and Meters and the units of measure.

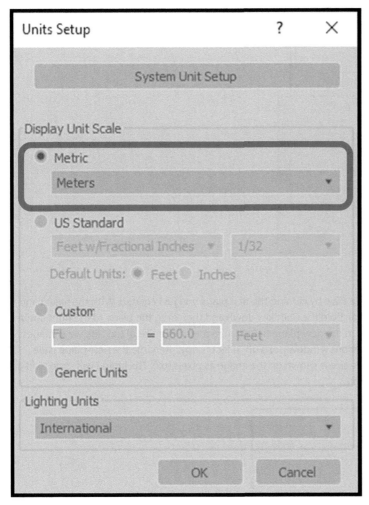

IMAGE 2.7

Creating the Template Planes

Next, create a plane in the Front Viewport with a size of 1.55 m height and 1.10 m width, length Segs and Height Segs set to 1. If you are not sure how to create a plane using the 3ds Max interface tools, it probably means you have not completed the tutorials in Volume I of this book series. Please step back to complete these tutorials. Successfully completing this volume of tutorials is dependent on having learned the skills taught in Volume I. All the front view images we will be using as templates for this model will fit this plane and register in alignment with each other. Change the X-, Y-, and Z-axis settings on the bottom tool bar to X=0.0, Y=0.0, and Z=0.785. Rename the plane "front_template."

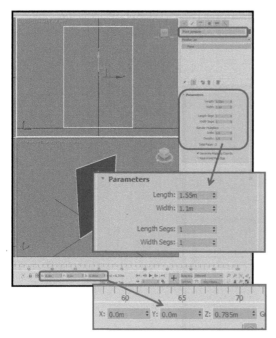

IMAGE 2.8

Now create another plane for the side view by cloning the first plane you just created. With the Select and Move Tool selected on the top toolbar, hold the Shift key down and then drag the plane to the right about 1.55 m. Change the width parameter in the new plane to 0.90 m to match the size of the side view images we will be using. When the Clone Options window pops up, select "Copy." Rename the new plane "side_template." Please note that the image size is shown on the image as pixels (px). The image will scale to fit a plane in 3ds Max shown in meters (m).

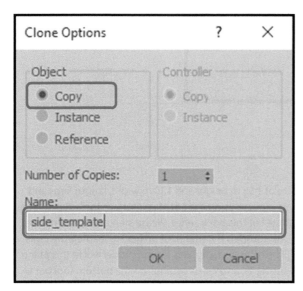

IMAGE 2.9

This plane needs to be rotated 90 degrees to orient it for the side view. Switch to the Select and Rotate tool. In the Coordinate Display boxes on the lower tool bar, change the Z-axis setting to –90 degrees.

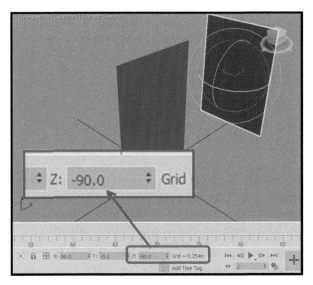

IMAGE 2.10

Next, move to the front_template plane back from the Y-axis line. Select the front template again and change the Z coordinate value in the Coordinate Display to 1.50 m. Now we will be able to create our model at the 0, 0, 0 coordinates, away from our two template planes.

Setting up the template planes in this orientation is a fairly standard practice for modeling objects. This orientation allows us to model, move vertices, so they follow the template reference image without the template intersecting the model, causing problems.

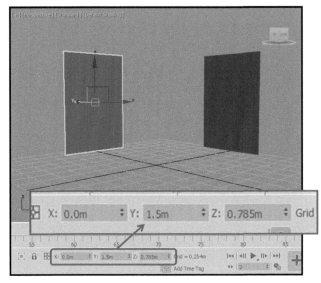

IMAGE 2.11

Next, assign the "knight wireframe-00-front" image from the companion files (located on the companion web site page, www.3dsMaxBasics.com) to the front_template plane and the "knight wireframe -00 side" to the "side_template."

We are ready to assign texture maps to the two planes. In Volume I, we created materials in the Material Editor using the Compact Editor mode. In this volume, we will use the Slate Editor mode to expand your skill set.

The Slate Editor

To open the Slate Editor, either hover the mouse over the Material Editor icon on the Top Tool Bar to expose the drop-down button for the Slate Editor and select it or click on the Material Editor icon to open the editor.

In the window that opened is in Compact Editor mode, click on the "Modes" tab on the tool bar and select the Slate Editor. The Slate Editor has the same functions as the Compact Editor but has some enhanced tools for creating and tweaking more complex material textures. Using the Compact Editor is more convenient when using existing materials, the Slate Editor more practical for creating new materials.

If we take a quick look at the two editors, we will find a lot of similarities and tools in common. In fact, the tools with similar names have the same functions for both. On the left side of the Slate Editor is the same menu list that appears when you select the "Get Material" icon button on the Compact Editor. To create a new material, we go through the same process as with the Compact Editor, just a little differently procedurally.

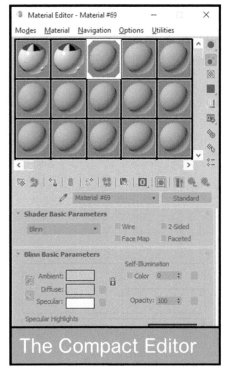

IMAGE 2.12

20

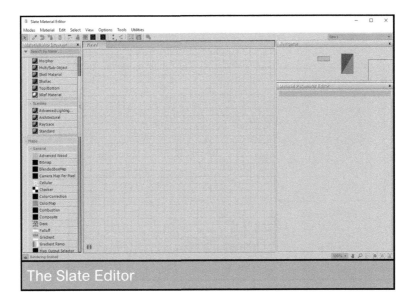

The Slate Editor

IMAGE 2.13

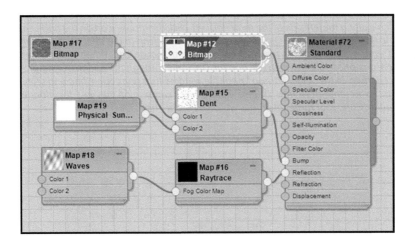

IMAGE 2.14

If we take a quick look at the two editors, we will find a lot of similarities and tools in common. In fact, the tools with similar names have the same functions for both. On the left side of the Slate Editor is the same menu list that appears when you select the "Get Material" icon button on the Compact Editor. To create a new material, we go through the same process as with the Compact Editor, just a little differently procedurally. The Slate Editor create material, map, and shader tree hierarchies by wiring together material, map or shader, and controller nodes. To create the tree hierarchies, you connect the object nodes with wires, like spaghetti connecting meatballs.

> Step 1) Select a Standard material in the Scanline material section by double-clicking on "Standard" or by right-clicking anywhere in the View 1 window area to open a flyout menu. Navigate to "standard" and select it.

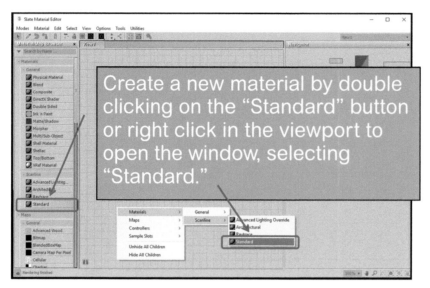

IMAGE 2.15

Step 2) A material slot will be created in the active View window. There are a number of node endings available along the left side of the material. Left-click the mouse icon on the node ending (the circle) next to the "Diffuse" option. Drag the depressed mouse icon to the side, away from the material. A red "wire" will stretch from the node ending to your mouse icon. When you release the mouse button, an option rollout menu will appear. Navigate through the options: General > Bitmap. Select Bitmap. In the Select Bitmap Image file window that pops open, find and select the "knight_wireframe-frontview_01.png" image in the companion files you downloaded to your computer. Note: your material names will be different, that's OK.

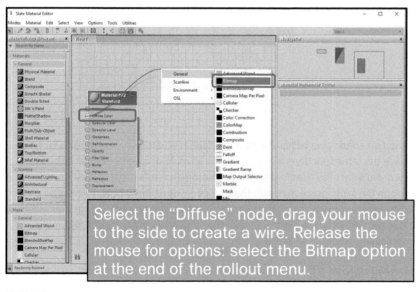

IMAGE 2.16

In the next image, note that I rearranged the elements orientation in the active view to make a clearer view of the relationships of the connected nodes.

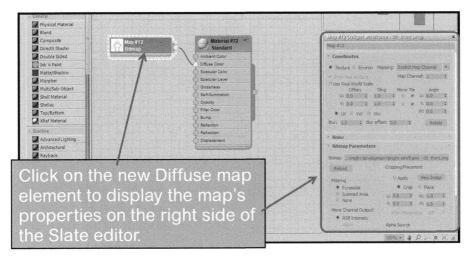

Click on the new Diffuse map element to display the map's properties on the right side of the Slate editor.

IMAGE 2.17

If you double-click on the map, the map's properties will appear in the Parameter Editor on the right-side column of the editor. These properties appear in the same orientation as they do in the Compact Editor. All that is left to do is to assign the material to the front template. You will find the same icon buttons we used in the Compact Editor on the Top Tool Bar of the Slate Editor. First, select the object you want to have the material, in this case the front template, then left-click on the "Assign Material to Selection" button and then left-click on the "Show Material in Viewport" button. The knight wireframe image should appear on the front template plane. Make sure the Right, Left and Perspective Viewports are set to "Default Shading" so you can see the images (in the upper Left Viewport corner menus).

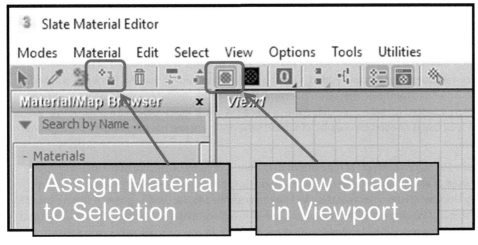

Assign Material to Selection

Show Shader in Viewport

IMAGE 2.18

We are ready to begin modeling the character. We have our template images in place, and they are aligned vertically so the features on both images are aligned horizontally.

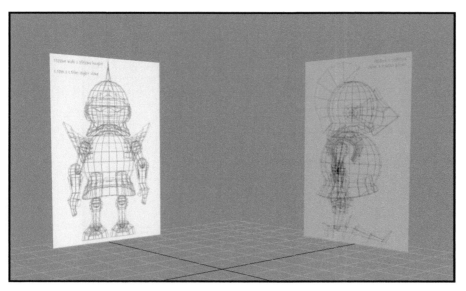

IMAGE 2.19 (Max File Save 2.1)

Making a Place Holder

As explained in the previous volume, it is our responsibility as modelers to provide the programmers with placeholder models they can use until the finished models are completed. This way they can keep working without needing to wait for us. For this character placeholder, we can use basic shapes to make a facsimile of the completed model. We could add some basic animations but will hold off this time as that is what we will be learning to do once we complete this model. By adding the basic animations, the placeholder could be used in the game in a more developed way.

With your current modeling skill set, model a quick placeholder mesh using Standard Primitives and the two template images. Be sure to select the "Placeholder" layer in the Scene Explorer, so your model is in the correct layer.

The next image shows the placeholder I quickly made in a few minutes. It is composed of ten spheres, nine cylinders, two boxes and a cone. I added a Taper modifier to the boxes used for the feet. I also added a taper to the cone used for the helmet visor. The comb on top of the helmet is a short cylinder with the Slice parameters adjusted to make a pie shape with a piece cut out. It looks more like a chicken than a knight, but it is all that is needed for our placeholder. It's the right size and has joints where the final one will have them.

Note too I added a "dummy object" at the bottom of the fire. A dummy object is a non-rendering object that is often used as an animation helper. To access it, go to: Create panel > (Helpers) > Standard > Object Type rollout > Dummy. All the objects in this placeholder are linked to the center sphere. It then is linked to the dummy object. If you move the dummy object, the whole placeholder will move with it as one object. The programmers can move the placeholder using just the dummy object, making their job easier to manage the model.

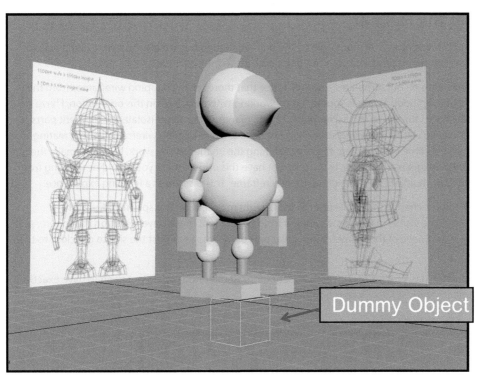

Dummy Object

IMAGE 2.20 (Max File Save 2.2)

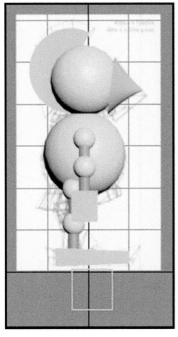
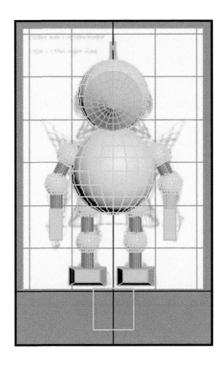

IMAGE 2.21

Modeling the Helmet

The first part of the knight we will model will be the helmet. Remember, we are modeling all the parts of the knight character separately as opposed to one single mesh for the model.

Looking at the images on our templates, you will notice that there are overlapping wireframes from the different parts of the model. As this is your first time working with templates in this orientation, I have made multiple images for you to use as templates on the planes. The images isolate the different parts of the model that you will be modeling so you will not have the overlapping wireframe issues creating confusion. It will be a little inconvenient to keep switching the images as you work, but it will make the modeling more manageable. Typically, you would not have this opportunity; you would be working from a single image that would not be a pre-done mesh wireframe. This is setup as a learning experience.

In the Scene Explorer, change the active layer to the "knight model." Create a sphere in the Front Viewport. It should be visible in the scene explorer inside the knight model layer. Position the sphere, so it is centered over the image of the helmet, the circular part of the image. Adjust the size to get close to the image size.

The sphere I created has a radius of .215, with 20 segments. Remember, you do not need to have exactly the same number values as I do. Close is good.

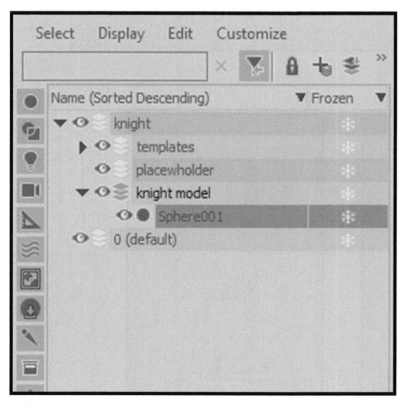

IMAGE 2.22

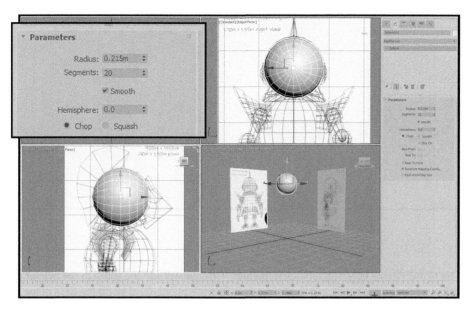

IMAGE 2.23

Next, rotate the sphere 90-degrees, so the two pole vertices are vertically aligned. Left-click on the Select and Rotate tool on the top toolbar to get into the rotation mode. In the Coordinate Display, change the X-axis value to 0.0, which will rotate the sphere.

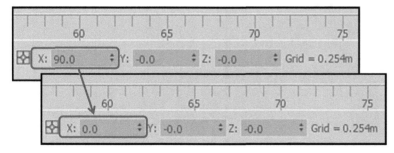

IMAGE 2.24

Note the position of the sphere and the two template planes in the Perspective Viewport. In the Front and Left viewports, it appears that the sphere is right on top of the template image. Remember, in all but the Perspective Viewport, every point in the viewport is seen from 90 degrees to the viewport plane. In the Perspective Viewport, we see the true orientation. Image 2.24 demonstrates this.

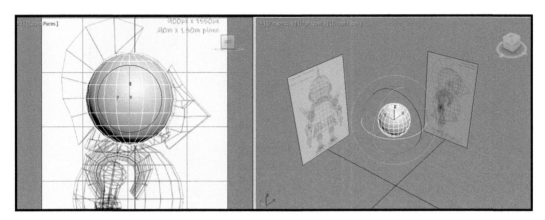

IMAGE 2.25 (Max File Save 2.4)

Convert the sphere to an Editable Poly, and rename it "helmet." First, we will add the comb to the helmet, the raised fin along the top and back side. In polygon mode, select the 14 polygons along the back of the mesh as shown in Image 2.26.

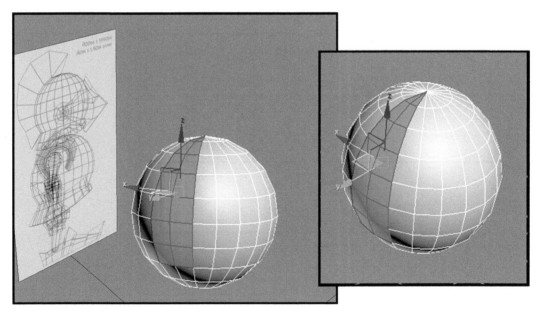

IMAGE 2.26

Use the Extrude Caddy to extrude the selected polygons 0.05 m. It is a small extrusion, but it will help to define the change of direction in the mesh construction.

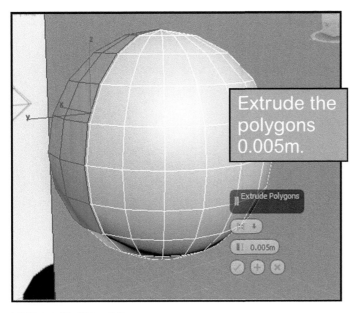

IMAGE 2.27 (Max File Save 2.5)

Select the center row of vertices along the center row of the polygons we just raised.

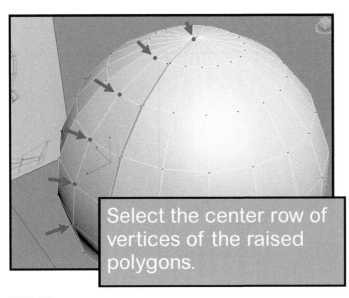

IMAGE 2.28

Using the Select and Move toll in the Left Viewport, move the vertices up and to the left as shown. This will roughly create the comb shape. Using the Select and Move toll in the Left Viewport, move the vertices up and to the left as shown. This will roughly create the comb shape.

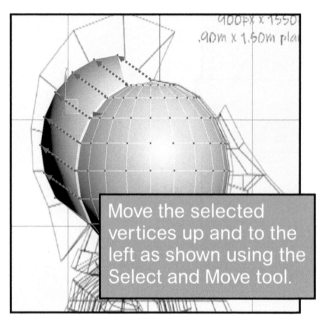

IMAGE 2.29

To complete the comb, move the selected vertices individually to the corresponding vertices on the template image. Remember, your mesh might not match the image exactly.

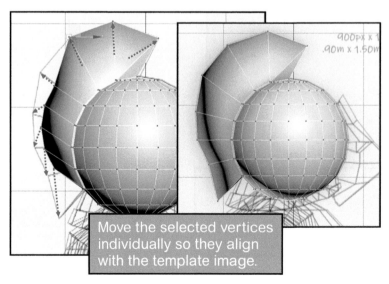

IMAGE 2.30 (Max File Save 2.6)

Next, we will model the bottom flared neck guard. In Vertex mode, select the bottom row of vertices on the sphere and the bottom vertex. Delete the selected vertices to create an opening.

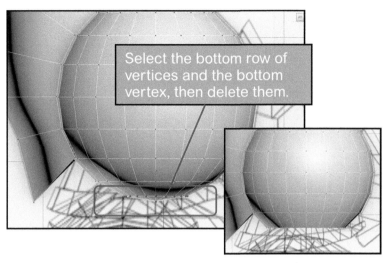

IMAGE 2.31

Create the curving bottom edge of the helmet by moving the individual vertices of the sphere to match the template image vertices, as you did to create the comb on top of the helmet. We are moving the vertices to the row mid-way to the bottom of the helmet. The vertices might be difficult to discern. Remember, they do not need to be exactly like in the images here. Look at the overall shape and work to create a nice smooth curve with the vertices.

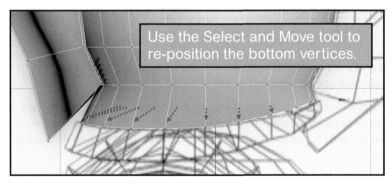

IMAGE 2.32

Switch to the Border tool again and select the bottom edge. We will be creating a small lip/shelf to create a raised border around the bottom of the helmet as trim. We will be recreating this Border trim on other parts of the character model as a unifying design element. With the Border selected, click on the Extrude Caddy to open it. Enter an extrusion setting of 0.01 m, and accept it by clicking the green check mark.

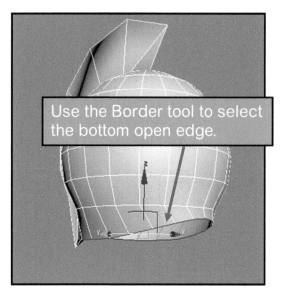

IMAGE 2.33

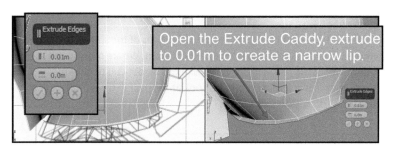

IMAGE 2.34

The edges are extruder at 90-degrees to the original Edge's plane, so the lip around the bottom of the helmet has some interesting angles as it goes around the perimeter.

Next, we need to create the vertical wall of the trim section. If you use the Extrude Caddy again, the edge will be extruded in a direction we do not want. Instead, using the Select and Move tool with the Border still selected, hold down the Shift key and click on the Z-axis of the gizmo. Drag it down a short distance as shown to establish the extrusion.

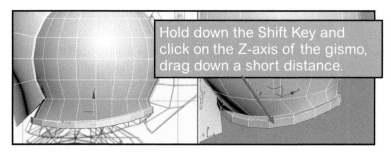

IMAGE 2.35

Now, switch to Vertex mode and move the vertices again to approximately match the vertices in the template image, creating the bottom edge of the helmet.

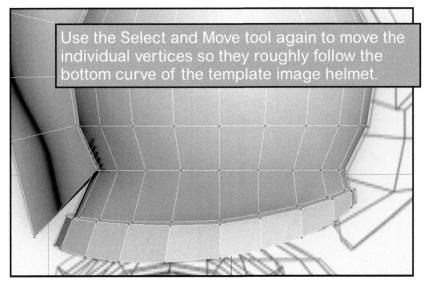

IMAGE 2.36 (Max File Save 2.7)

Use the Border mode to select the bottom row of vertices. Looking at the Front view of the model, the new trim section at the bottom of the helmet that we just created is too narrow compared to the template image. Switch to Vertex mode and select the vertices as shown. Using the X-axis of the Select and Uniform Scale tool gismo, click and drag it to angle the vertical walls closely matching the template image.

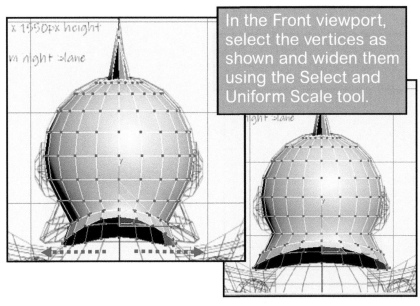

IMAGE 2.37

Next, we need to finish the underside of the helmet. We can complete this in a few steps. Rotate the view of the helmet in the Perspective Viewport using the View Cube so you can see the underside of the model.

With the Border edge still selected, use the Extrude caddy to extrude the edge −0.03 m to create a bottom edge.

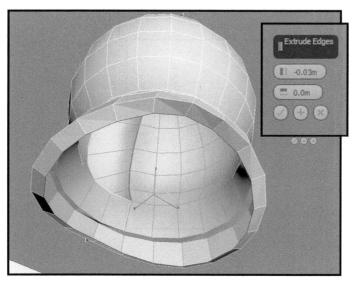

IMAGE 2.38

Create the inner wall of the helmet holding down the Shift key and dragging the Z-axis of the Select and Move gizmo in the positive direction as shown.

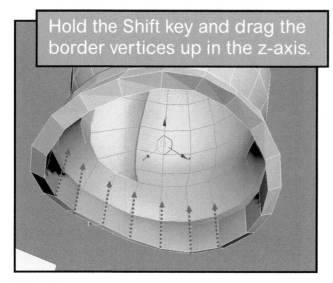

IMAGE 2.39

Switch to the Select and Uniform Scale tool and scale the Border edge inward to create a small oval shape.

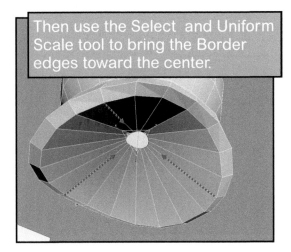

IMAGE 2.40 (Max File Save 2.8)

The Helmet Visor

The helmet visor is three pieces: the visor and the two pivot hinges. We will model the visor first. Create a cylinder with the parameters as shown in Image 2.41. Rename the cylinder to "helmet visor." The object should appear in the Scene Explorer inside the helmet layer. Position the new cylinder as shown over the helmet mesh.

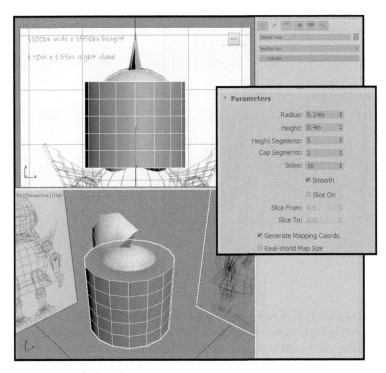

IMAGE 2.41 (Max File Save 2.9)

Convert the cylinder to an Editable Poly. In Vertex mode, select all the vertices to the left of the center row of vertices in the Left Viewport and then delete them. This cuts down the mesh to a usable shape for our visor.

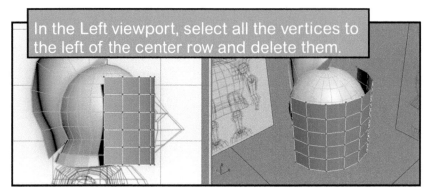

IMAGE 2.42

Next, in the Front Viewport, select all the vertices to the right of the center row and then delete them. We will model half the visor and use the Symmetry Modifier to complete it when we are done modeling it.

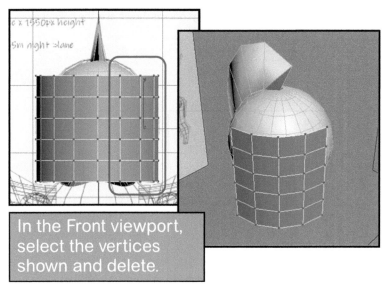

IMAGE 2.43 (Max File Save 2.10)

While modeling the helmet, there were a few times in the process of moving vertices it was difficult to see the template image. The helmet mesh is going to make seeing the template image almost impossible. To see better, go up to the Scene Explorer on the left margin of the interface, and turn off the helmet visibility by clicking on the "open eye" icon in the helmet layer row.

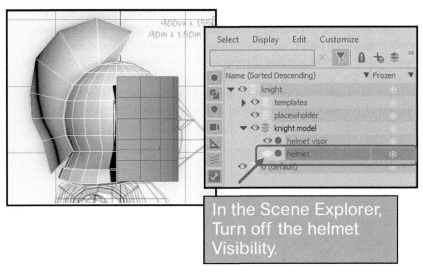

IMAGE 2.44

We can make the visibility even better by making the visor mesh see-through. To do this, right-click on the visor mesh. In the pop-up Quad Menu, select "Object Properties." A new Object Properties window will pop open. On the left side column, click on the see-through tick box. Click OK to close the window.

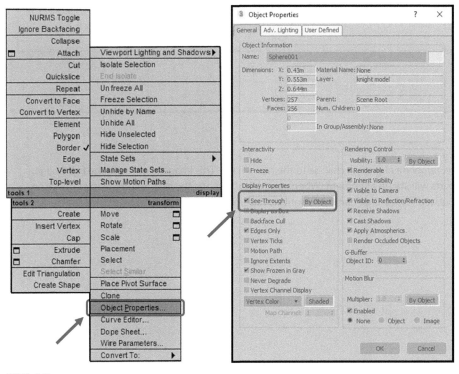

IMAGE 2.45

Normally, we would start modeling the mesh, using the template image as a guide. For this model, I have taken extra steps to create additional texture maps that isolate the model parts, so there will not be confusion deciding which lines are the correct ones. Using these additional template images will help to ensure that you will develop an understanding of modeling organic shapes in 3d. Open the Slate Editor from the Top Tool Bar or use the "m" hot key. Double-click on the Front texture map to open the properties window on the right-hand side of the editor. Change the Bitmap image to "knight_wireframe-frontview_02a" that can be found in the companion file folder where you located the first image.

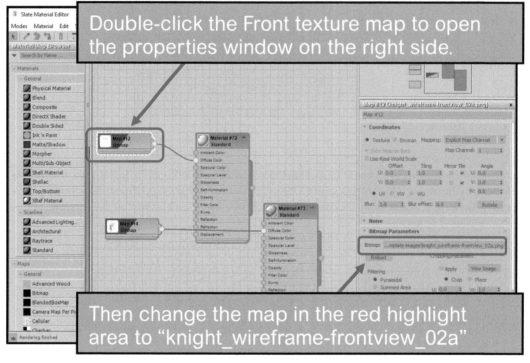

IMAGE 2.46

The image on the template plane will change to the new image. This image aligns with the first image, so your model parts will stay in alignment. When completed, change the side texture map in the same manner to the isolated visor image named "knight_wireframe-sideview_02a."

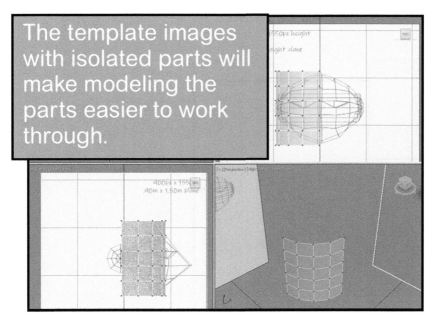

The template images with isolated parts will make modeling the parts easier to work through.

IMAGE 2.47 (Max File Save 2.11)

Begin shaping the visor by moving the vertices along the centerline to match the template image vertices. It might be easiest to *select* the vertex in the Perspective Viewport and then right-click in the Left Viewport to *move* the vertex. First, select the column of vertices farthest to the left. Use the Select and Uniform Scale to move them close together as shown. They will eventually be within the visor hinge. Continue moving the columns, getting them in the rough area where they match up with the template image.

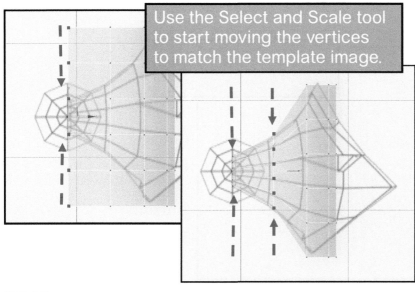

Use the Select and Scale tool to start moving the vertices to match the template image.

IMAGE 2.48

Image 2.49 shows the vertices moved into the proper positions.

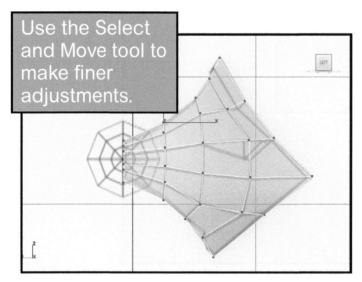

IMAGE 2.49

We have been working in the Left Viewport. This is 3D modeling, so we need to do the same procedure in another viewport, in this case, the Front Viewport. Adjust the vertices as need be, moving the vertices close to the template image as a guide.

When you are satisfied with the vertex positions, it is time to symmetry the mesh toward completion. Select an edge along the centerline that we want to be the symmetry axis. Add a Symmetry Modifier from the Modifier List in the Command Panel. Adjust the Mirror Axis parameters in the Command Panel, "Flip" if necessary.

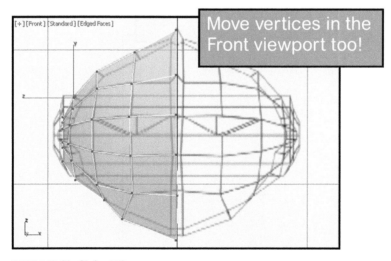

IMAGE 2.50 (Max File Save 2.12)

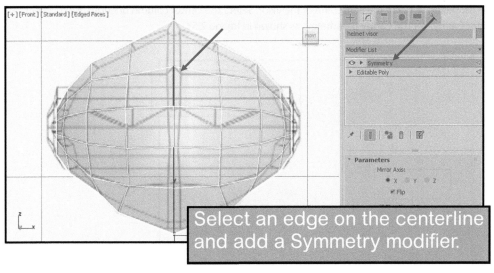

Select an edge on the centerline and add a Symmetry modifier.

IMAGE 2.51

Next, simplify the mesh equation. Remember, when the program calculates each object, it starts at the bottom of the Modifier Stack and calculates each modifier as an additional calculation going up the stack. Collapsing the Modifier Stack when possible helps to make the calculations run faster. Right-click in the Modifier Stack and select Collapse All from the menu list. When the Warning pop-up window appears, click on "Yes." The mesh will become an Editable Poly again without the added symmetry equation added to it.

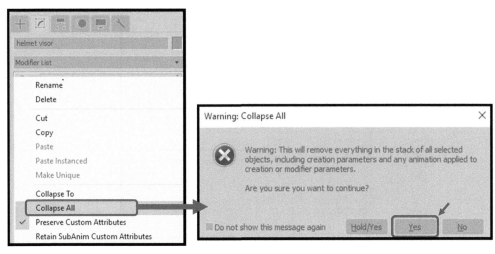

IMAGE 2.52

Add some modeling detail to the centerline of the visor. Select the center column of edges. Next, select the Chamfer Caddy. Set the Caddy parameters as shown in Image 2.53.

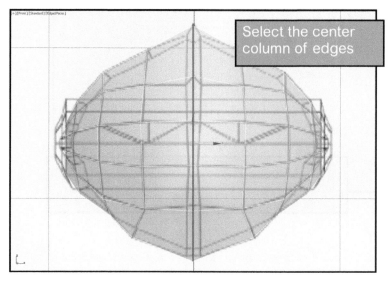

IMAGE 2.53

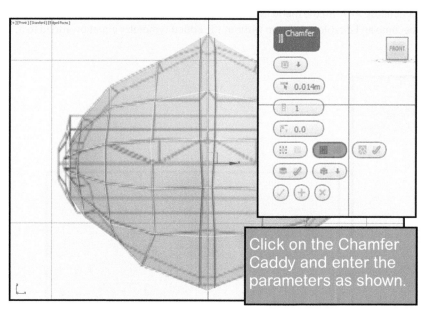

IMAGE 2.54

The Chamfer adds a spline on either side of the centerline. To accentuate the ridge, select the four vertices as shown in the next image and move them down in the Y-axis. This will create a raised edge along the centerline.

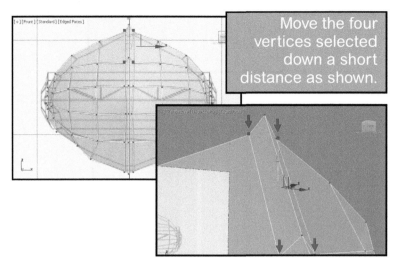

Move the four vertices selected down a short distance as shown.

IMAGE 2.55 (Max File Save 2.14)

In the next steps, we will model the triangular eye slits in the visor. We will make recessed areas that will be textured solid black. To create the shapes in the mesh, we will use the Cut tool. Remember using the Cut tool on the castle modules in Volume I? First, we need to set the 3d Snaps to ensure the Cut tool selects vertices. On the Top Tool Bar, right-click on the 3d Snaps icon button. This opens the Grid and Snap Settings window. In the list of Snap items, select only the Midpoint and Endpoint tick boxes. Close the window and make sure the 3d Snaps icon is turned on.

Click on the "Cut" button in the Vertex mode in the Command Panel to activate it. On the mesh, in the Front Viewport, make four cuts, first clicking on a corner vertex as shown (number 1), then the midpoint of the vertical edge (number 2) and then the opposite corner vertex (number 3). Complete the second eye in the same manner.

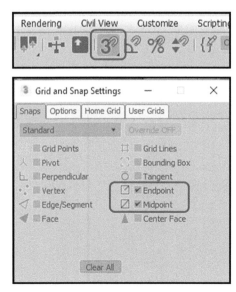

IMAGE 2.56

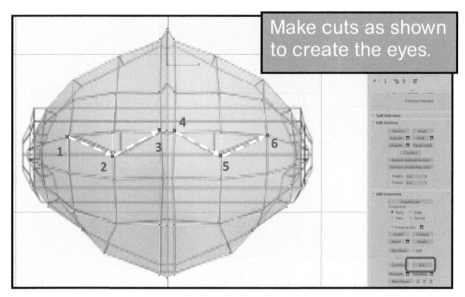

IMAGE 2.57

Next, select the four polygons created by the cuts, then delete them. Using the Border mode, select the edges of the two holes you just created. Click on the Cap button in the Command Panel to create new, single polygons.

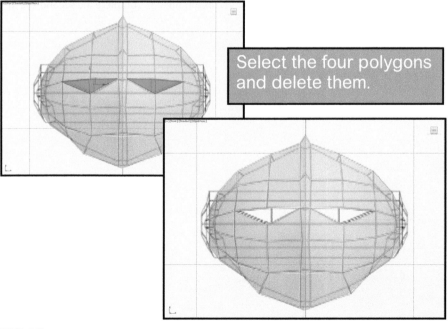

IMAGE 2.58

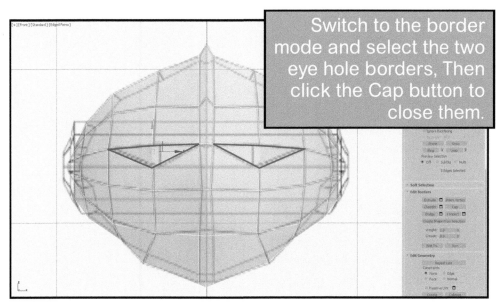

Switch to the border mode and select the two eye hole borders, Then click the Cap button to close them.

IMAGE 2.59

Now that the eye openings are single polygons, they will extrude nicely to create the eye slits in the visor. As two polygons each, they would have created an issue when extruded at the centerlines. Select the two polygons and extrude them −0.015 m with the Extrude Caddy

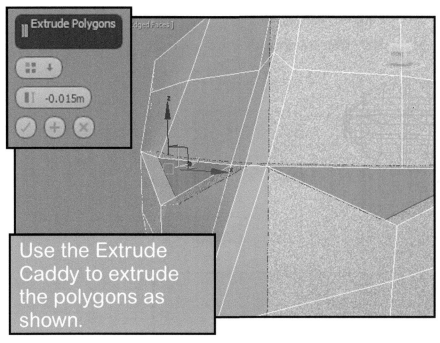

Extrude Polygons

-0.015m

Use the Extrude Caddy to extrude the polygons as shown.

IMAGE 2.60 (Max File Save 2.15)

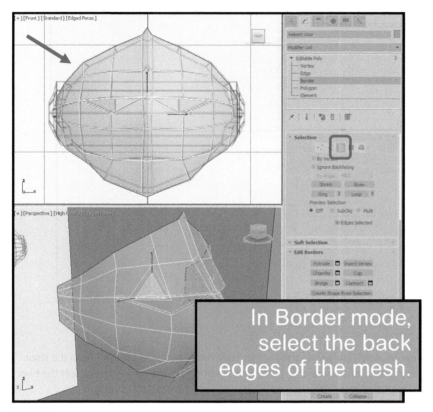

IMAGE 2.61

Open the Extrude Caddy, and set the extrusion parameter to −0.03 m to create the lip on the backside of the visor.

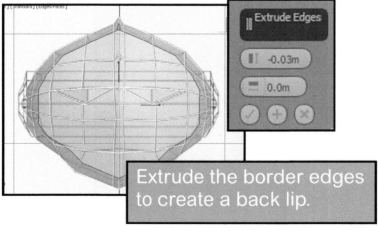

IMAGE 2.62

Select the top row of polygons along the top edge of the front of the visor. We will add a trim piece here by extruding as a group, 0.005 m.

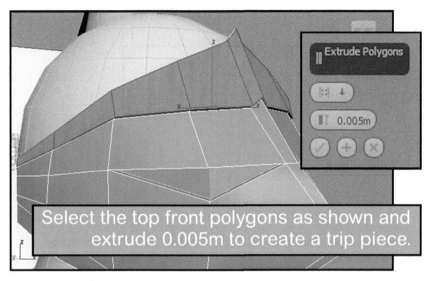

IMAGE 2.63 (Max File Save 2.16)

On the inside of the top lip of the visor, there are three vertices that are crossed up due to the extrusion. Select the three vertices and use the Weld Caddy to weld them into a single vertex. The same thing happened at the bottom inside lip. Weld them together to one vertex too.

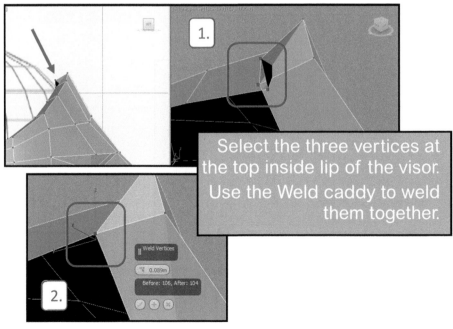

IMAGE 2.64

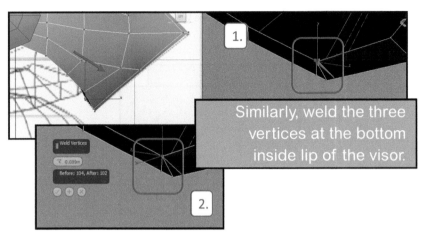

IMAGE 2.65

The last part of the visor is the visor hinge. To create it, we will use a single cylinder that extends from one side of the visor to the other. Make the cylinder length long enough, so the ends of the capsule are the visible. We could create two separate visor hinges, but, using a single cylinder will use less polygons. Remember, we are making low-poly objects for video games.

Convert the cylinder to an Editable Poly. Select the inner cap segment ring of vertices on both ends of the cylinder, and use the Select and Uniform Scale tool to widen them using the X-axis arm of the gizmo. This will add some modeling detail to the hinges for visual interest.

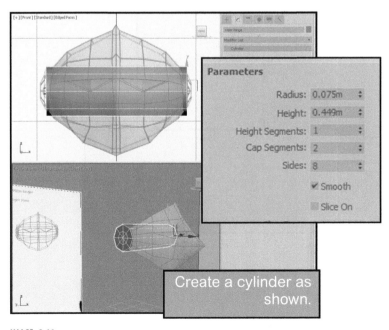

IMAGE 2.66

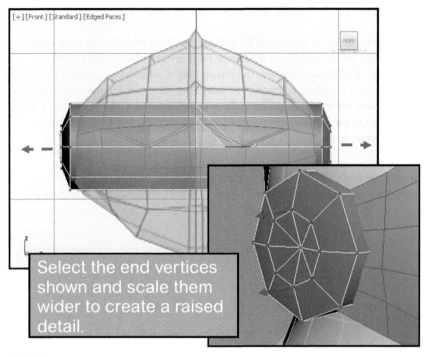

Select the end vertices shown and scale them wider to create a raised detail.

IMAGE 2.67

That completes the helmet for our knight character. We will create the rest of his Body in the same manner as we made the helmet. I have created isolated Body part images for use as template images to allow you to focus on the modeling.

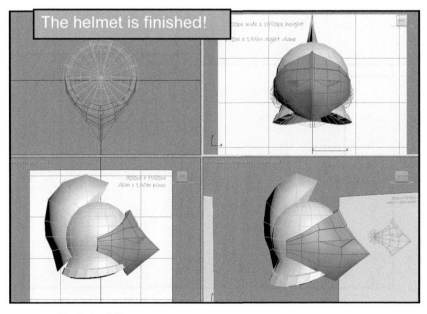

The helmet is finished!

IMAGE 2.68 (Max File Save 2.17)

Modeling the Body

Before we start modeling the Body section of the knight, let's change the front and side template images. Open the Material Editor to change the images as you did before. For the Front plane, use the texture map: knight_wireframe-frontview_03. For the Side View, use image: knight_wireframe-sideview_03. The images should align on the templates as before. Normally, you would not have all the various template images. You would likely be working off one front and one side view, making design decisions as you work. Remember the reason I have gone to the trouble of making all the templates is to ensure that through repetition you will become accustom to the process without needing to have the additional issue of making design decisions.

Create a sphere for the start of the Body. Change the parameters to match the ones in Image 2.69. Align the sphere with the Body on the image template in both the Front and the Left Viewports. Rename the sphere as "Body."

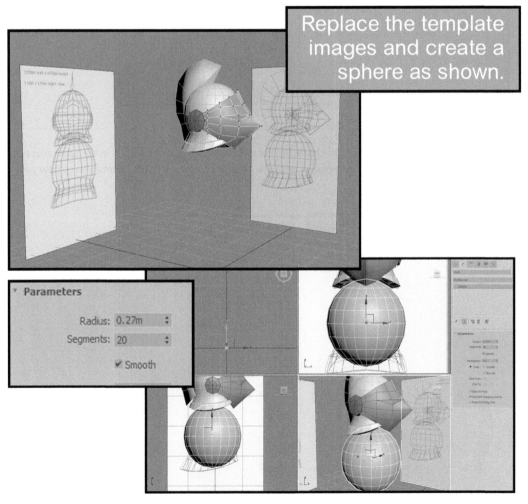

IMAGE 2.69 (Max File Save 2.19)

We will model the bottom of the Body first. Convert the sphere to an Editable Poly. Select the bottom row of vertices and the very bottom one. Delete these vertices to create a hole in the bottom of the sphere.

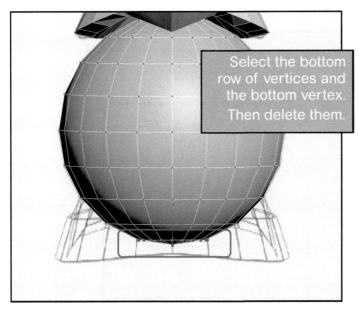

IMAGE 2.70

Create the flared shape at the bottom of the Body by selecting the new bottom row of vertices of the sphere. Use the Select and Uniform Scale tool to widen the ring of vertices. Be sure to use the yellow triangular area of the gizmo to ensure you are scaling in both the X- and Y-axis directions.

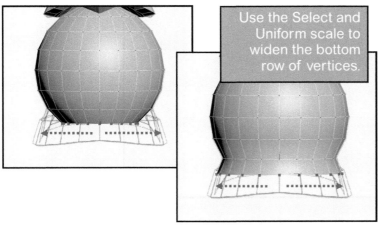

IMAGE 2.71

Now use the Select and Move tool to move the bottom row of vertices to match the bottom row of the template images in the Front and Left Viewports. Be sure to select the front and back vertices when working in the Left Viewport. Take your time and get them as close as you can to Image 2.72 shown. If you are off a bit, it is not critical.

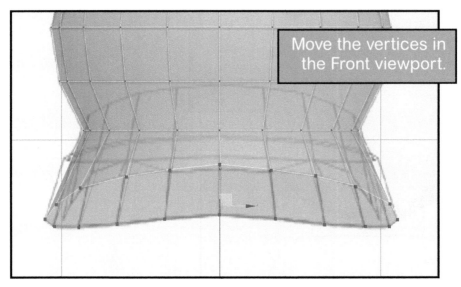

Move the vertices in the Front viewport.

IMAGE 2.72

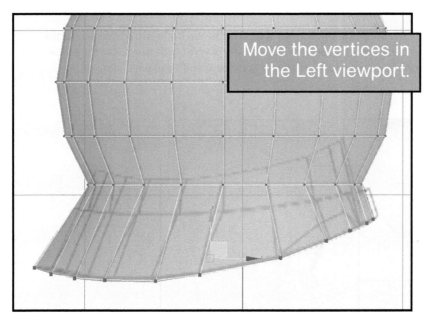

Move the vertices in the Left viewport.

IMAGE 2.73 (Max File Save 2.20)

The next thing to do is to create a lip on the bottom edge like we did with the helmet. In the Border mode, select the bottom ring of edges. Extrude them with the Extrude Caddy as shown in Image 2.74.

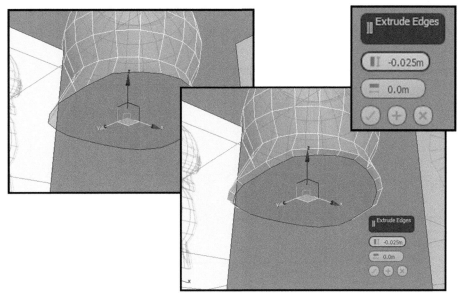

IMAGE 2.74

The extrusion created a lip that projects below the bottom row of vertices. With the Border still selected, use the Select and Move tool to raise the Border edges up to the height of the bottom row of vertices as shown here.

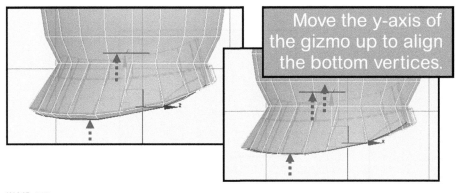

IMAGE 2.75

Next, create the inside of the bottom like you did with the helmet. With the Border edges still selected, hold down the Shift key and drag the gizmo Y-axis in the positive, up direction. Raise it high enough to be inside the spheres. Then, use the Select and Scale tool to bring the edges close to the center enough that the entire Border edge selection is within the mesh. Do not try to match the template image in this case. That would be difficult to replicate exactly. As long as the border is inside the sphere shape, it cannot be seen poking through the outer mesh surface.

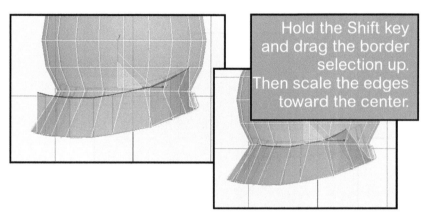

Hold the Shift key and drag the border selection up. Then scale the edges toward the center.

IMAGE 2.76

We are going to cap the open hole in the mesh. If we cap it now, there will be a plane created that has convex curves in multiple directions. Not a great thing to do when modeling. We can fix the issue by aligning the vertices along the border hole first. In the Left Viewport, use Vertex mode to select all the vertices along the border hole. Right-click in the Top Viewport to keep the selection set and to move to a view 90 degrees to the plane we want to be parallel to. Click on the View Align button in the Edit Geometry section of the Control Panel.

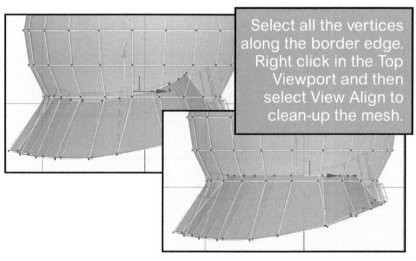

Select all the vertices along the border edge. Right click in the Top Viewport and then select View Align to clean-up the mesh.

IMAGE 2.77

Next, switch to Border mode and select the Border edges of the hole. Click on the Cap button to close the mesh. We are capping this hole because we will want a texture on this surface. There might be times in the game play that the player might be able to view the character from below. Having a surface here will avoid the possibility of a "nodraw" occurring where the player would see into the mesh to the back side of the polygon normals, which do not render.

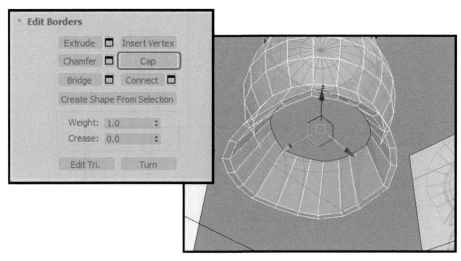

IMAGE 2.78 (Max File Save 2.21)

The bottom of the Body flared section has a raised trim detail like on the helmet. When we added it to the helmet, we created it as we modeled. This time we will add it to the existing model. First, select the bottom edges of the mesh as shown. Click on one segment in Edge mode, then hover the mouse over an adjacent edge in line with the first. The ring of edges will turn yellow. Click to accept the selection. If it is not working for you, just hold down the Ctrl key and manually select each one.

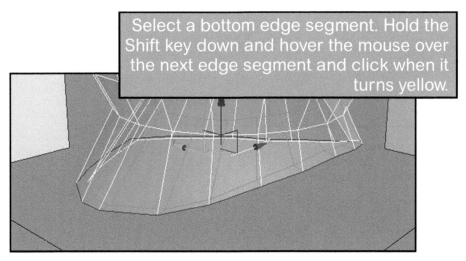

IMAGE 2.79

Next, in the Ribbon bar below the Top Menu Bar, click on the Modeling tab. In the Edit drop-down menu, click on the Swift Loop tool. Move your mouse to the approximate position of the new Swift Loop line segments in the next image and click to set it.

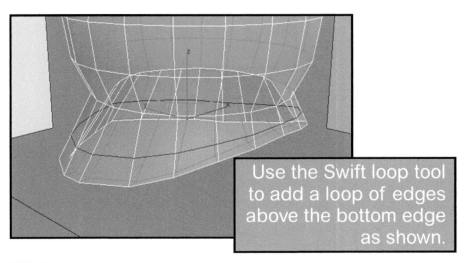

IMAGE 2.80

Select the ring of polygons at the bottom of the mesh that we just created. Select one of the polygons, then hold down the Shift key and select an adjacent polygon to select the entire ring of polygons as shown.

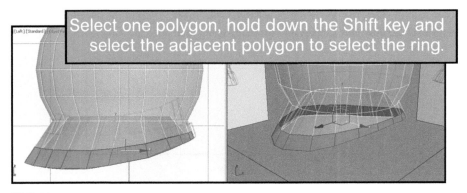

IMAGE 2.81

Open the Extrude Caddy and extrude 0.01 m. Make sure the second button from the top of the Caddy is set to "Local Normal."

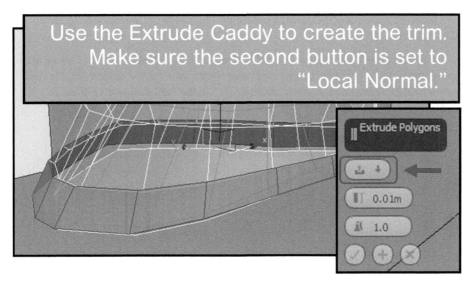

IMAGE **2.82** (Max File Save 2.22)

Make one more alteration to the Body. Select the top row of vertices and the top vertex. Use the Select and Move tool to move these vertices up a little and toward the back of the mesh as shown. This will create a neck area that will prevent a visual gap between the helmet and the Body should the head rotate to an extreme up or down position when it is animated.

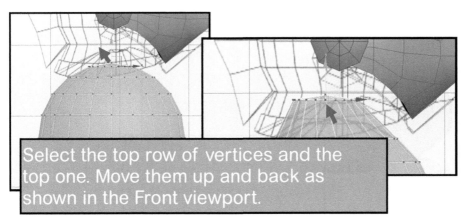

IMAGE **2.83** (Max File Save 2.23)

Modeling the Pauldrons

The pauldrons are the components of a knight's armor developed in the 15th century that cover the shoulders. They are a bit larger than pauldrons, an earlier version of the component protecting the shoulder. Pauldrons provided more coverage down to the armpit. Our pauldrons are exaggerated with flaring edges and trim detail.

Open the Material Editor to change the images as you did before. For the Front plane, use the texture map: knight_wireframe-frontview_03a. For the Side View, use image: knight_wireframe-sideview_03a. To start the pauldron, create a tube as shown and rename it "pauldron_rt" for the right shoulder. Locate it as shown in Image 2.84.

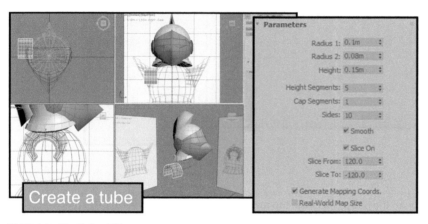

IMAGE 2.84 (Max File Save 2.24)

We can create the shape of the pauldron from the tube by adding modifiers. In the Modifier List drop-down menu, add a Taper modifier. Set the parameters to those shown in Image 2.85.

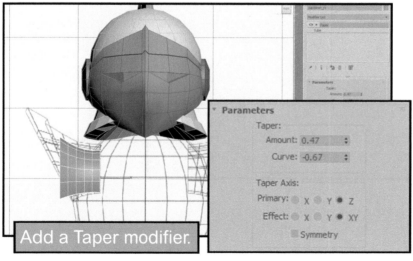

IMAGE 2.85

That gets us part way there. Add another Taper modifier to the Stack. Adjust the parameters to the ones in Image 2.86.

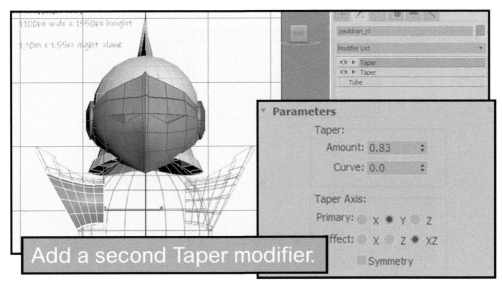

IMAGE 2.86 (Max File Save 2.25)

Right-click in the Modifier Stack and collapse the stack. Convert the Editable Mesh to an Editable Poly.

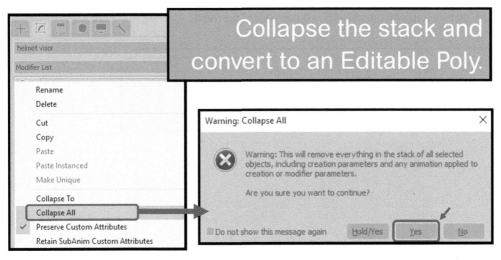

IMAGE 2.87 (Max File Save 2.25)

The template shows the pauldron having a taller profile. Right-click on the mesh to open the Quad Menu, then to go to Object Properties and turn on "See-Through." We need to move the top row of vertices higher to match the vertices in the template image. Move them one-by-one. Try to get them close to the template image and create a nice curve at the same time.

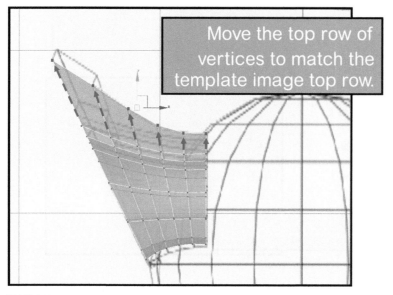

Move the top row of vertices to match the template image top row.

IMAGE 2.88

Next, move the second row of vertices from the top edge higher as shown in the next image. Make sure you drag a selection box over the targeted vertex to ensure you are selecting the vertex on the other side of the mesh that lines up with the visible one on this side of the mesh.

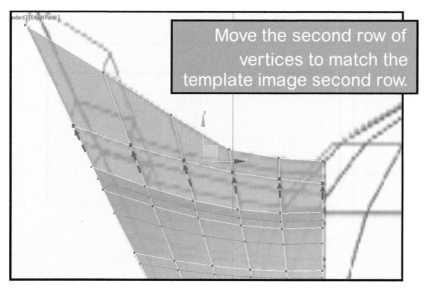

Move the second row of vertices to match the template image second row.

IMAGE 2.89 (Max File Save 2.26)

Right-click on the mesh to open the Quad Menu to go to Object Properties and turn off "See-Through." The last part of modeling the pauldron is to add the detail trim to the outside edge to go with the trim on the Body and Helmet. In Polygon mode, select one of the polygons along the edge and hold down the Shift key. Click on an adjacent polygon to auto-select the ring of polygons.

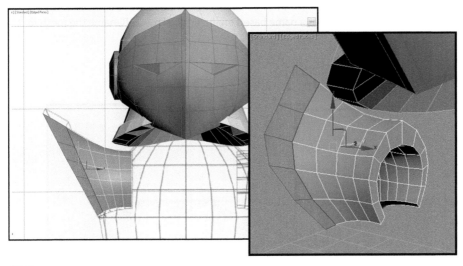

IMAGE 2.90

Use the Extrude Caddy to extrude the polygons to create the trim band. Be sure the second button from the top in the Caddy is set to "Local Normal" for the correct extrusion. Use the parameters as shown in the next image.

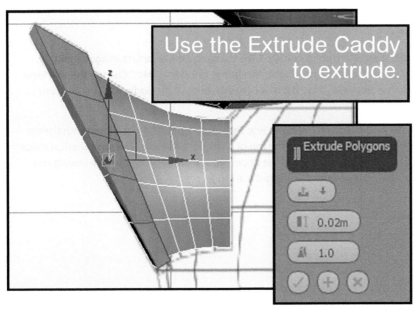

IMAGE 2.91

That completes the modeling of the pauldron. Click in the Front Viewport if it is not active and select the Pauldron. Hold shift and drag them to the right (the character's left). Select the Copy option in clone. Click on Modifier List, and add a Mirror modifier. Do not use the Mirror Tool on the Top Tool Bar. Using the Mirror Tool will add a negative value to the mesh that will flip the faces when imported to Unity. The Mirror Modifier will not do this. Use the settings shown in the image. Position the mesh to the Body accordingly. Select the cloned mesh, right-click in the Modifier Stack and collapse the stack back to an Editable Poly (Collapse All). The new mesh has a name based on the original mesh. Rename the mesh to "pauldron_lt."

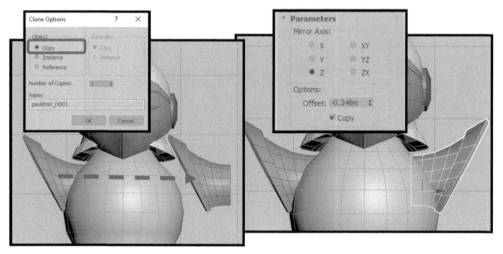

IMAGE 2.92 (Max File Save 2.27)

Modeling the Legs

We will model the legs next. They will happen quickly. Time to change the template images again. In the Front view template, change the image to "knight_wireframe-frontview_04a." Change the side view template to "knight_wireframe-sideview_04a." If it is not already, turn off the Body mesh in the Scene Explorer.

The legs are two meshes, the upper leg and the lower leg. The upper leg will be positioned with the top of it inside the Body. When it is static or animated, the top of it will not be visible. The top spherical shape of the lower leg mesh will cover the bottom part of the upper leg, concealing it. We will be linking and adjusting pivot points later. For now, we want to just get the model right.

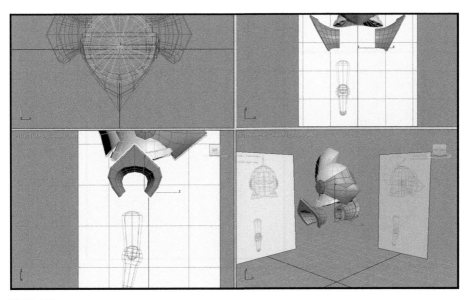

IMAGE 2.93

To start the upper leg, create a Capsule from the Extended Primitives menu in the Command Panel. Start in the Top Viewport to start the capsule. Click and drag the mouse to create the radius, release the mouse button and move the mouse to create the height. After you create it, enter the parameters shown below into their respective boxes. Once you have established the size, use the Select and Move tool to position the mesh over the template image properly. Be sure to position it in both the Left and Front Viewports.

Next add a Taper modifier from the Modifier List to the capsule with the parameters as shown in Image 2.94. That will finish the upper leg. Time to move on to the lower leg.

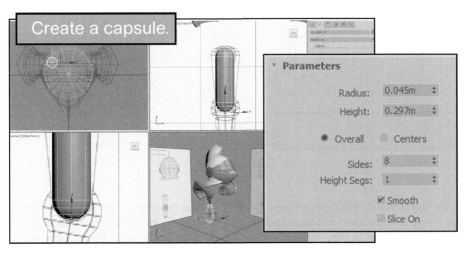

IMAGE 2.94 (Max File Save 2.28)

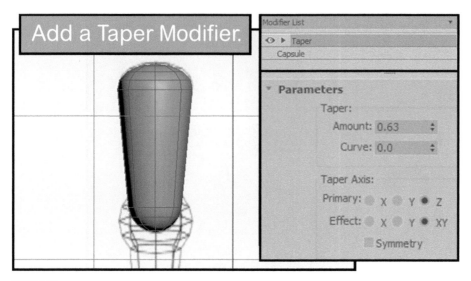

IMAGE 2.95

Create another capsule in the Top Viewport with the parameters shown in Image 2.96. Rename the capsule "leg_lower_rt." In the Front Viewport, positioned the capsule over the lower leg shape in the template image.

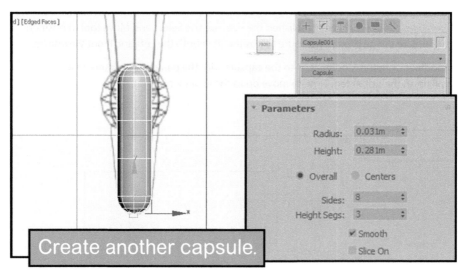

IMAGE 2.96 (Max File Save 2.29)

Convert the capsule to an Editable Poly. Next, move each row of vertices separately to approximately align with the template image. Use the Select and Move tool. Be sure to move the third row from the bottom too. The mesh will not perfectly align with the image template; that is OK. The image in the template is rotated slightly as you can see in the side view in the Left Viewport, creating curved lines in the Front Viewport. When we finish the mesh and rotate it, it will align more closely.

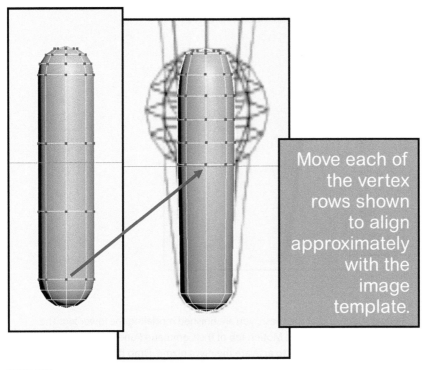

Move each of the vertex rows shown to align approximately with the image template.

IMAGE 2.97

Create the spherical shape at the top of the mesh by scaling the horizontal rows of vertices. Again, close is acceptable. Use the Select and Uniform Scale tool to individually widen the diameter of the vertex rows. Follow the template image to make the spherical shape. Be sure you click in the yellow area of the gizmo to scale uniformly. Do not create ovals.

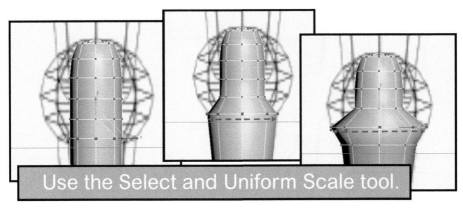

Use the Select and Uniform Scale tool.

IMAGE 2.98

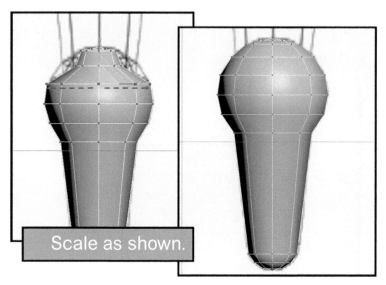

IMAGE 2.99

Once you complete the spherical shape end of the mesh, you are finished modeling the lower leg. The only thing left to do is to position it correctly. In the Motion tab of the Command Panel, click on the "Pivot" button. Then, select the "Affect Pivot Only" button to activate the pivot gizmo. Drag the Pivot Gizmo up the Y-axis to the approximate center of the spherical shape. Click the "Affect Pivot Only" button to turn it off.

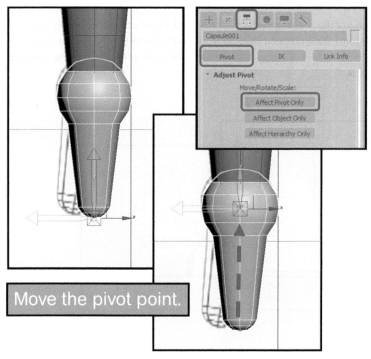

IMAGE 2.100

Now you can rotate the lower leg in the Left Viewport clockwise to match the template image using the Select and Rotate tool.

Our Knight character is coming along. The feet are next. They will be made with three separate meshes that will allow the feet to flex when animated.

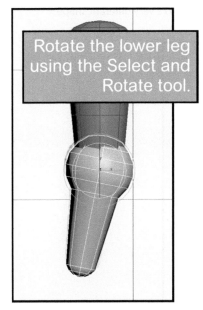

IMAGE 2.101

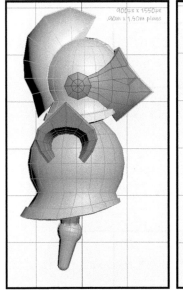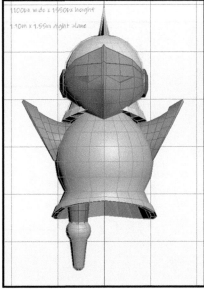

IMAGE 2.102 (Max File Save 2.30)

Modeling the Foot

As before, change the template images so we can see the feet. Open the Slate Material Editor. For the side view, use "knight_wireframe-sideview_04b." For the front view, use the image file "knight_wireframe-frontview_04b."

Start the foot shoe by creating a capsule with the parameters shown in Image 2.103. We will create this capsule with a flat side on the bottom. We will be changing this capsule into a very different shape.

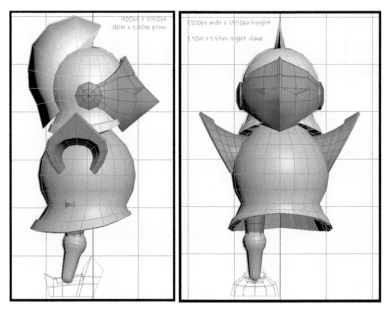

IMAGE 2.103

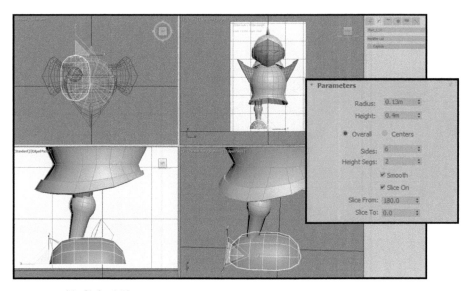

IMAGE 2.104 (Max File Save 2.31)

Rotate the Perspective Viewport to show the bottom of the capsule mesh. In Vertex mode, make two cuts as shown at the heel end of the foot. Doing this will minimize the hole that will happen when we delete the end vertex in the next step. Make sure you turn on the 3D Snaps on the top toolbar with the Midpoint and Endpoint selected before you make the cuts to ensure you select the desired vertices. Turn off the 3d Snaps when finished making the cuts.

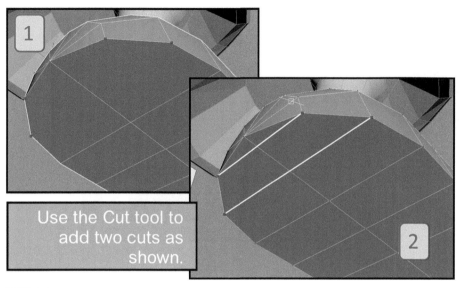

> **1**
>
> Use the Cut tool to add two cuts as shown.
>
> **2**

IMAGE 2.105

Next select the vertex at the end of the capsule and delete it. We are creating the end of the shoe. When deleted, it will create a hole as all the polygons radiating from the vertex will be eliminated.

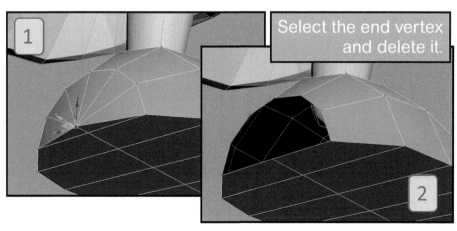

> **1**
>
> Select the end vertex and delete it.
>
> **2**

IMAGE 2.106

To close the hole created by deleting the end vertex, switch to Border mode and select an edge along the opening. Click on the Cap button in the Command Panel to create a polygon.

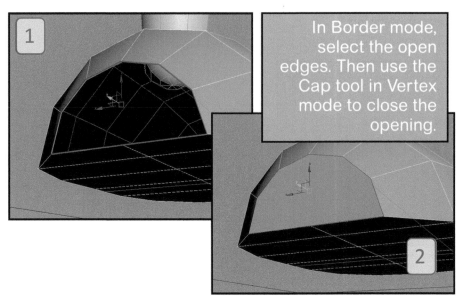

IMAGE 2.107

Switch back to Vertex mode, and make cuts across the new polygon as shown in Image 2.108. Doing this will define polygons consistent with the mesh. If we did not create these cuts, 3ds Max might divide the polygon into an odd arrangement of triangles.

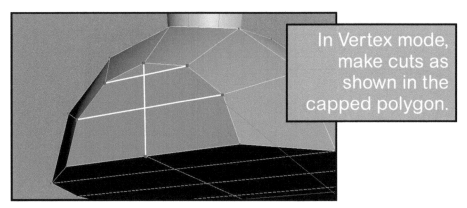

IMAGE 2.108

In the Left Viewport, select the two columns of vertices as shown in the next image. We will be shaping the front part of this section of the shoe. This will create a hole in the front of the mesh.

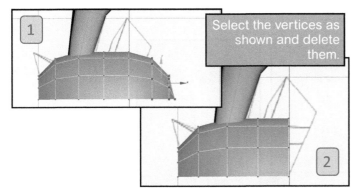

IMAGE 2.109

Close the mesh with the cap tool and then make the appropriate cuts with the Cut tool as before with the heel end of the mesh.

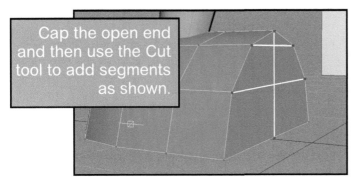

IMAGE 2.110 (Max File Save 2.32)

The next step will require you to move the individual vertices to align with the vertices in the template image. Try to get them as near as possible to the positions as possible; they will not be exact matches.

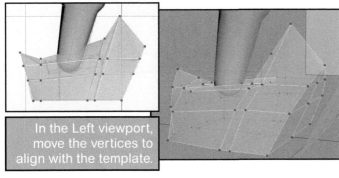

IMAGE 2.111

The lower leg is inserted into the mesh. To make it look more like an ankle inserted into a shoe, make a depressed area where the ankle would go into the shoe. Select the two polygons shown here. Select the inset tool, and set the parameters as shown in the image. Click the green Check mark to accept the setting.

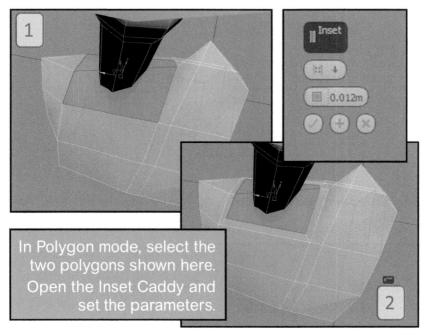

In Polygon mode, select the two polygons shown here. Open the Inset Caddy and set the parameters.

IMAGE 2.112

Switch to the Select and Move tool, and move the new inset polygons slightly down toward the bottom of the mesh to start creating the depressed area.

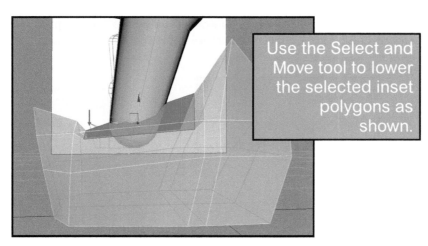

Use the Select and Move tool to lower the selected inset polygons as shown.

IMAGE 2.113

Switch to Vertex mode and move the vertices highlighted in red in Image 2.114, so they create a relatively flat plane, representing the inside of the shoe. The lower leg is still visibly inserted into it.

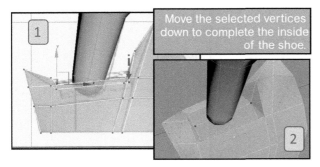

IMAGE 2.114 (Max File Save 2.34)

The next few steps will be easier to do if we turn off the see-through property. Open the Object Properties window by right-clicking on the mesh and selecting it from the Quad Menu.

Add a trim band to the side polygons along the front edge of the mesh. This will tie-in with the trim pieces we made on the helmet and Body. Select the polygons along the front edge sides of the mesh on both sides. Do not select the bottom polygons. With those polygons selected, open the Extrude caddy and extrude as shown. Click on the green check mark icon to set the extrusion.

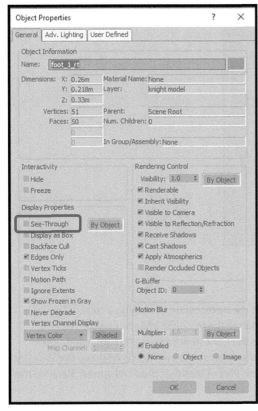

IMAGE 2.115

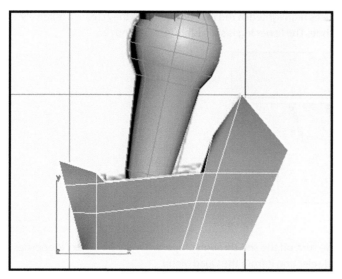

IMAGE 2.116

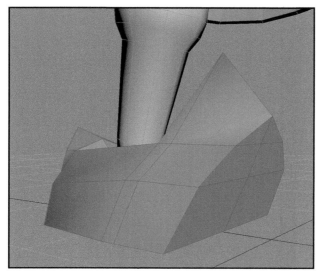

IMAGE 2.117

That completes the first section of the foot. We will create the next section by making a copy of the front side of this mesh. To model the mid-foot section, Change the template images. Change the side view image to "knight_wireframe-sideview_04c." Change the front view image to "knight_wireframe-frontview_04c." Select the polygons on the front side of the mesh as shown. Then hold down the Shift key and drag the Select and Move tool gizmo forward. A "Clone Part of Mesh" pop-up will appear. Rename the part "foot_2_rt" and Clone to Object.

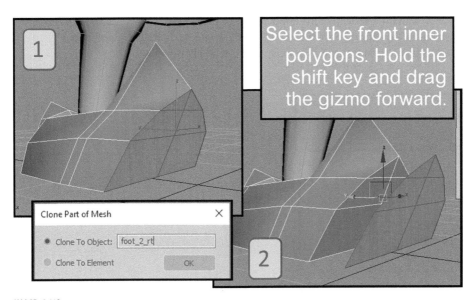

IMAGE 2.118

In the Scene Explorer, turn off the foot_1_rt layer to isolate the new mesh better against the template image. When you select the new mesh, the gizmo is located back where the original mesh's was. Go to the Hierarchy tab of the Command Panel and select "Pivot," then "Affect Pivot Only." Move the Pivot gizmo forward to meet up with the new mesh. Turn off the "Affect Pivot Only" button and switch back to the Modify panel tab.

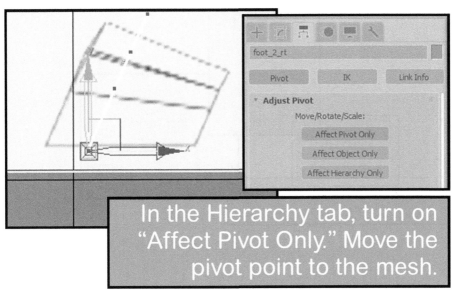

IMAGE 2.119

Move the mesh to align with the back end of the template image mesh to start the modeling process for this section. Next, in the Left Viewport, move the vertices to align with the template image. Image 2.120 shows the before and after of the first step in two viewports: Left and Perspective.

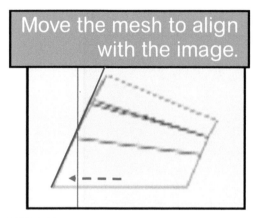

IMAGE 2.120

Select the polygons of the mesh, and open the Extrude Caddy. Set the extrusion as Local Normal and to the parameters shown in Image 2.121. Click the green check mark to accept.

As shown in Image 2.121, move the vertices in the Left Viewport, so they align with those of the template image. Again, they probably will not line up exactly; that is acceptable.

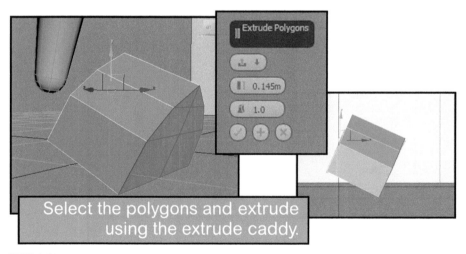

IMAGE 2.121

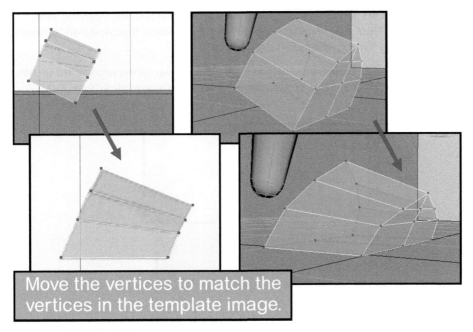

Move the vertices to match the vertices in the template image.

IMAGE 2.122 (Max File Save 2.35)

When the vertices are all lined-up, switch to the Front Viewport and, using the Select and Scale tool, scale the width of the front row and then the back row. Select the row of vertices, and drag the Z-axis of the gizmo to adjust them.

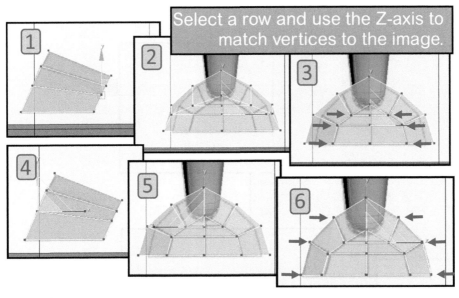

Select a row and use the Z-axis to match vertices to the image.

IMAGE 2.123

To start modeling the third, end, section of the foot, change the two template patterns. Open the Slate Material Editor, and change the Front view template image to "knight_wireframe-frontview_04d." Change the side view template image to "knight_wireframe-sideview_04d."

Select the front polygons of the middle section, and clone them the same way we did with the first section. Hold the Shift key and drag the Select and Move tool forward. Rename the Clone to Mesh "foot_3_rt."

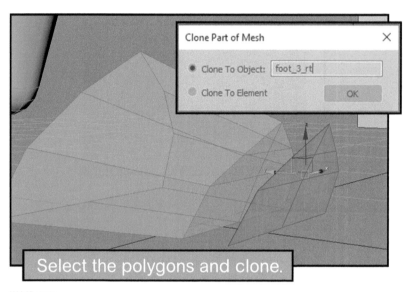

IMAGE 2.124

As we did with the previous mesh, open the Hierarchy panel and move the pivot point to the bottom of the new mesh, with the "Affect Pivot Only" button. Be sure to turn it off when finished.

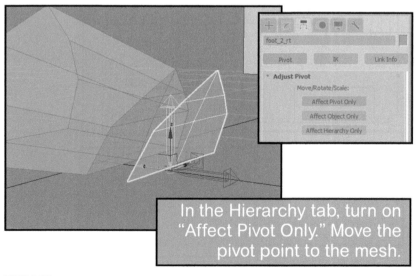

IMAGE 2.125

Extrude the polygons as we did with the previous section.

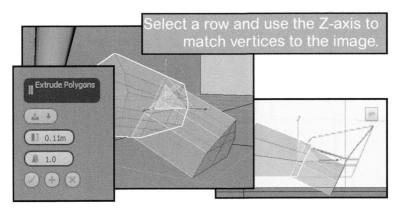

IMAGE 2.126

Switching to Vertex mode, move the vertices into position to match the Left Viewport template image. Note in Image 2.126 that the vertices are not moved to the end of the image mesh. Image 2.127 shows the center three vertices (from the bottom) are moved as a separate step to create a pointed edge on the toe of this section.

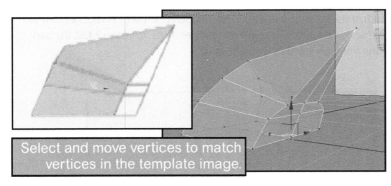

IMAGE 2.127

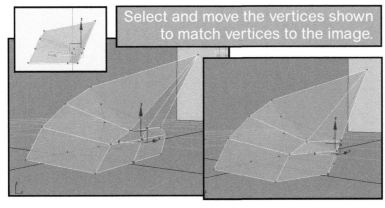

IMAGE 2.128

Position the Perspective Viewport, so you can see the open back of the mesh. Select the Border edges with the Border tool and then click on the Cap button to close the opening. With the Cut tool, make horizontal cuts across the polygon between the vertices to define the how the polygon is to be broken into three individual polygons.

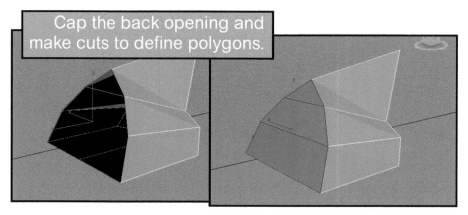

IMAGE 2.129

As before, it is to address the width of the mesh in the Front Viewport. Select a row of vertices as with the middle section, and use the Select and Scale gizmo to adjust the vertices. Note, in Image 2.128, the back row needs to be widened while the front row needs to be narrowed.

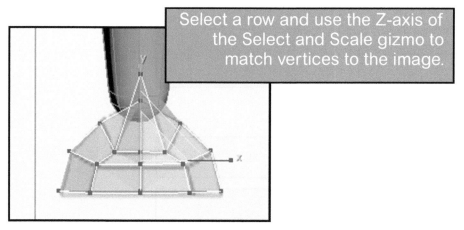

IMAGE 2.130

Lastly, make two cuts with the Cut tool on both sides of the mesh as shown in Image 2.131 to shape the pointed to.

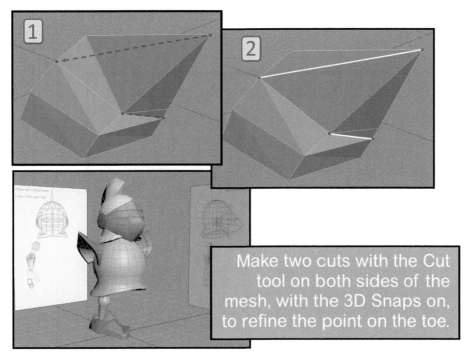

Make two cuts with the Cut tool on both sides of the mesh, with the 3D Snaps on, to refine the point on the toe.

IMAGE 2.131 (Max File Save 2.36)

That completes the three separate foot sections. Modeling it in the three sections will allow us to animate the character rising up on his toes or bending in a walk cycle.

Modeling the Upper Arm

The upper arm is going to be very easy to create. We are going to use a clone of the lower leg model, as it is, with no changes. Open the Slate Material Editor again and change the Front view template image to "knight_wireframe-frontview_05." Change the side view template image to "knight_wireframe-sideview_05."

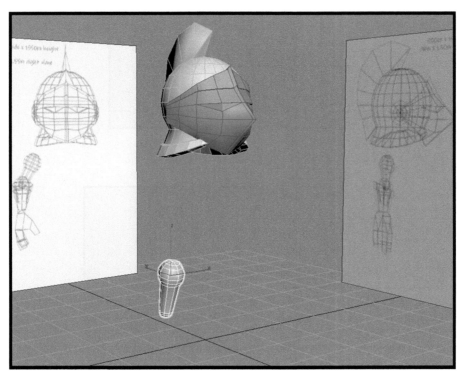

Turn off all the layers in the Scene Explorer except the helmet, visor and lower leg. Select the lower leg mesh. Make a clone of it by holding down the Shift key while clicking and dragging the Select and Move tool gizmo vertically in the Y-axis. In the Clone-type pop-up window, select "Copy." Rename the mesh "arm_upper_rt."

Use the Select and Move tool along with the Select and Rotate tool to position the upper arm mesh over the front and side template images in the Front and Left Viewports. The upper arm is complete.

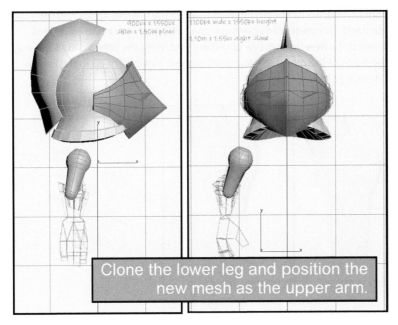

IMAGE 2.133 (Max File Save 2.37)

Modeling the Lower Arm

Start the lower arm by cloning the upper arm and position it over the template image of the lower arm. Rename the mesh "arm_lower_rt."

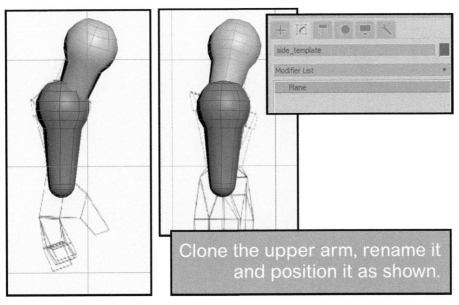

IMAGE 2.134 (Max File Save 2.38)

With the lower arm in a vertical orientation, we can begin modeling. Select the bottom vertex and the three vertex rows above it. Delete them. This creates an opening in the bottom we can make extrusions from as we shape the arm. Next, select the new bottom row of vertices and using the Select and Move tool, and raise the row by dragging the Y-axis of the gizmo to keep them aligned. Move them up to the line on the template image as shown in Image 2.135.

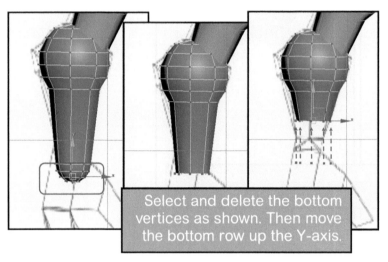

Select and delete the bottom vertices as shown. Then move the bottom row up the Y-axis.

IMAGE 2.135

Select the bottom edges using the Border mode. Do you remember the roof peaks we made for the Castle Keep in Volume I? The next step will be similar. We will be moving the polygons with a few moves that will not make sense until we are done. So, let's get to it. Hold down the Shift key, and drag the yellow area of the Select and Scale gizmo until it forms a flat plane as shown. To make this work, drag the gizmo until so the diameter of the new plane is larger than the diameter of the sphere. Look ahead at the next few images, and you will see where we are headed.

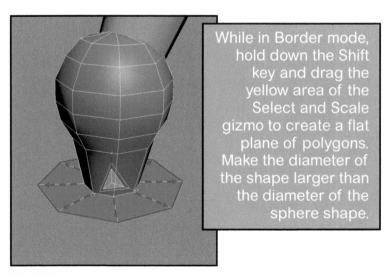

While in Border mode, hold down the Shift key and drag the yellow area of the Select and Scale gizmo to create a flat plane of polygons. Make the diameter of the shape larger than the diameter of the sphere shape.

IMAGE 2.136

84

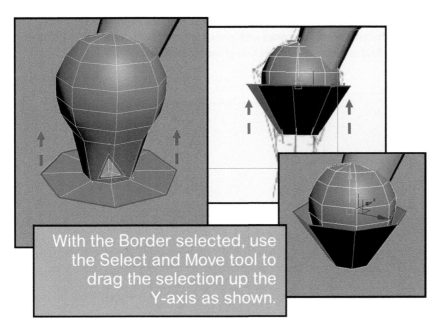

With the Border selected, use the Select and Move tool to drag the selection up the Y-axis as shown.

IMAGE 2.137

With the edges still selected in Border mode, use the Select and Move tool to raise the border up the Y-axis of the gismo. Moving it up will create a cone shape that will be the inside of the arm gauntlet that would protect the knight's forearm. If the diameter of the flat disk shape was too small, the top of the cone shape will be inside the elbow sphere. If it is, scale it larger to be outside the sphere. Next, hold the Shift key down again and drag the Border edges down the Y-axis of the gizmo to align with the image as shown. This will create a cylinder shape. Use the Select and Scale to reduce the diameter of the Border edges at the bottom of the mesh to create the wrist area.

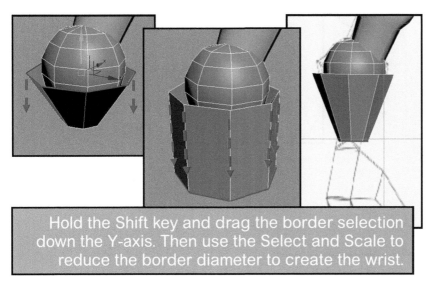

Hold the Shift key and drag the border selection down the Y-axis. Then use the Select and Scale to reduce the border diameter to create the wrist.

IMAGE 2.138

To give the gauntlet some visual interest, we will angle the elbow end. Select the vertices as shown in Image 2.138 by selecting two adjacent vertices (the ones with arrows pointing at them) and then go up to the Ribbon and select the Loop Tool in the Modifying Section of the Modeling tab.

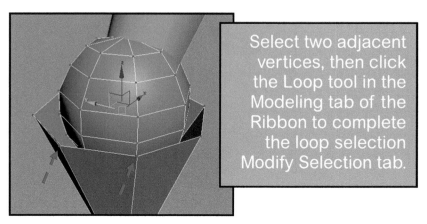

Select two adjacent vertices, then click the Loop tool in the Modeling tab of the Ribbon to complete the loop selection Modify Selection tab.

IMAGE 2.139

Selecting it will automatically select the other vertices in the row, making a complete row selection.

You could manually select each vertex while holding the CTRL key, this is just a faster, easier way to select them. With the vertices selected, use the Select and Rotate tool to rotate the row of vertices about 20 degrees clockwise.

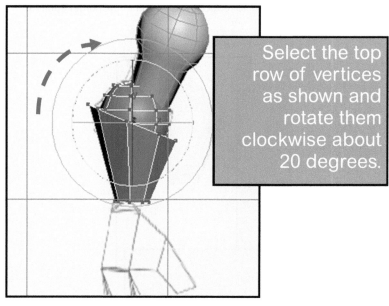

Select the top row of vertices as shown and rotate them clockwise about 20 degrees.

IMAGE 2.140

We will use the Ribbon tools for the next step too. The same end of the gauntlet will get a trim piece similar to the Body, helmet and pauldron meshes. In the Modeling Tab, find the Swift Loop tool in the Edit menu. We used this tool on the Castle Turrets in Volume I to add splines parallel to existing ones on our meshes. We will do the same thing here. After clicking on the Swift Loop tool, move your mouse over the gauntlet part of the mesh to create a spline as shown in Image 2.141. Click when positioned to create the spline, then turn off the Swift Loop tool.

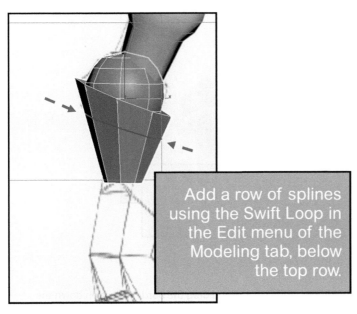

Add a row of splines using the Swift Loop in the Edit menu of the Modeling tab, below the top row.

IMAGE 2.141

Select the newly created polygons. Open the Extrude Caddy and extrude the polygons using the "by Local" setting.

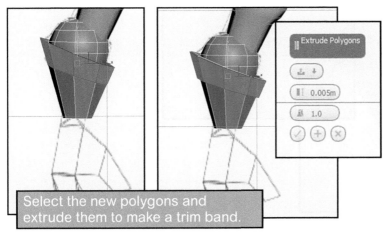

Extrude Polygons

0.005m

1.0

Select the new polygons and extrude them to make a trim band.

IMAGE 2.142 (Max File Save 2.39)

Rotate the Perspective Viewport to see the opening in the bottom of the mesh. We need to transition from the round forearm to the square wrist, just like your forearm does in real life. Select the two vertices shown in the next image and use the Select and Scale tool to bring them closer together so they come into alignment with the vertices adjacent to them. This will square the front and back sides of the wrist.

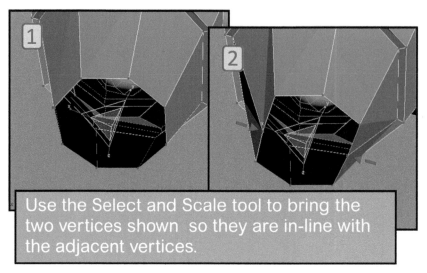

Use the Select and Scale tool to bring the two vertices shown so they are in-line with the adjacent vertices.

IMAGE 2.143

With the bottom edges still selected, hold down the Shift key and drag the Border selection down the Y-axis to the next line on the template image. This will be the wrist.

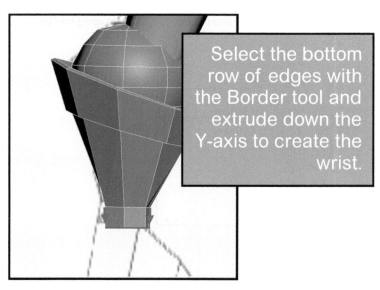

Select the bottom row of edges with the Border tool and extrude down the Y-axis to create the wrist.

IMAGE 2.144

Use the Select and Scale and the Select and Move tool to move the vertices horizontally, so they align with the template image in both the Front and Left Viewports.

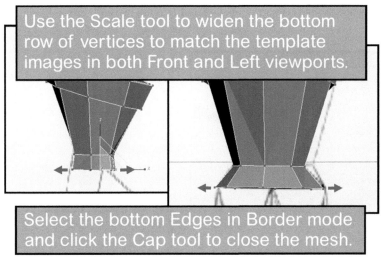

Use the Scale tool to widen the bottom row of vertices to match the template images in both Front and Left viewports.

Select the bottom Edges in Border mode and click the Cap tool to close the mesh.

IMAGE 2.145

Extrude the border again, use the Extrude Caddy to bring the polygons down to the next line on the template image. This will be the hand section of the mesh. After extruding, again use the Select and Scale and the Select and Move tool to move the vertices horizontally, so they align with the template image in both the Front and Left Viewports.

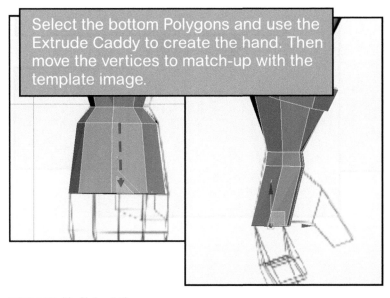

Select the bottom Polygons and use the Extrude Caddy to create the hand. Then move the vertices to match-up with the template image.

IMAGE 2.146 (Max File Save 2.40)

Rotate the Perspective Viewport again to view the bottom of the mesh. We want to be able to extrude four fingers from this area. To do that, we need to divide the single polygon into four separate ones. If we make cuts as it is now, there will be odd triangular fingers on the two ends. Turn on the 3d Snaps, so we can use the Cut tool accurately. The Midpoint and Endpoint selection set should still be set in the Grid and Snap Settings. Make cuts in the hand section as seen in Image 2.147. Be sure to cut the two ends too.

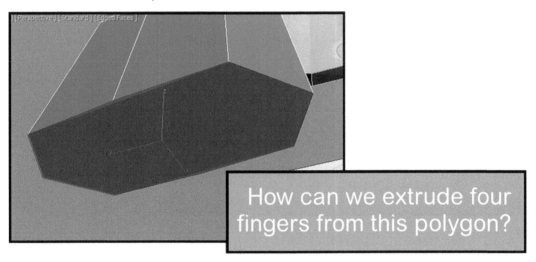

How can we extrude four fingers from this polygon?

IMAGE 2.147

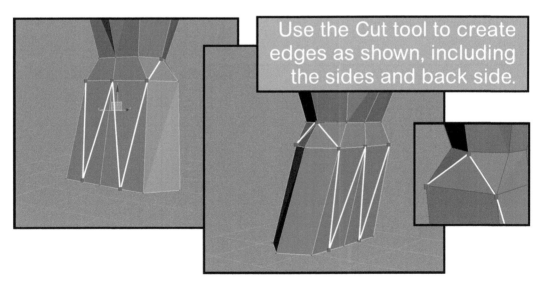

Use the Cut tool to create edges as shown, including the sides and back side.

IMAGE 2.148

On the ends, we need to eliminate the center vertical vertices. Use the Target Weld tool to weld the center vertices to one of the corner ones to create single polygons as shown.

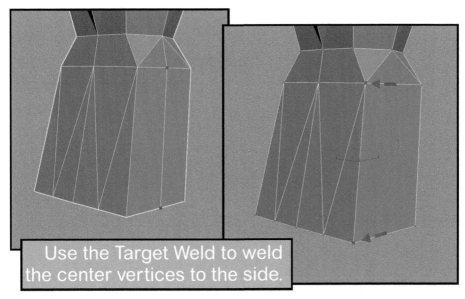

IMAGE 2.149

After making the cuts to the hand, rotate the Perspective Viewport to view the bottom. Use the Cut tool again to make three cuts creating segment edges between the vertices as shown in the next image.

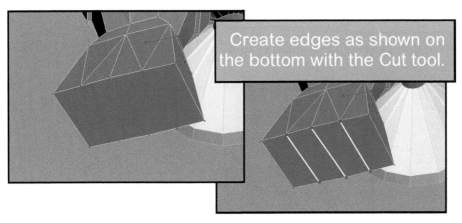

IMAGE **2.150** (Max File Save 2.41)

The vertices in the mesh most likely have shifted as a result of the last few modeling steps. Take a minute and reposition the vertices to closely match the template image again.

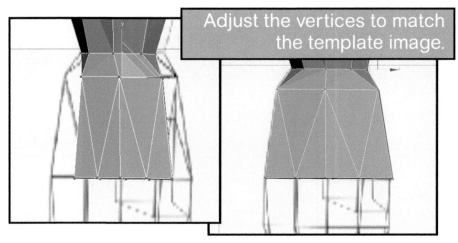

IMAGE 2.151

Now the bottom of the hand is ready to extrude four separate fingers. Rotate the Perspective Viewport to select the four bottom polygons. Open the Extrude Caddy and extrude the polygons as shown to reach the next line on the template image. Be sure to use the "by Polygon" setting. With this setting, the Caddy will extrude four separate shapes.

Once they are extruded, switch to the Select and Scale tool. Scale the end polygon slightly smaller to aid in creating separation between the fingers as shown in Image 2.152.

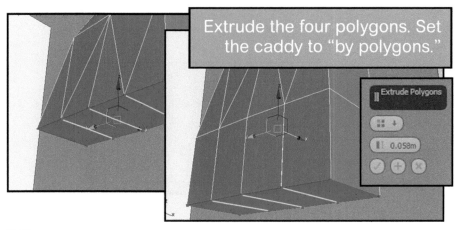

IMAGE 2.152

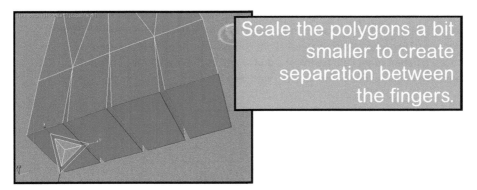

IMAGE 2.153

The character will only have two finger sections unlike a human having three sections. Use the Extrude Caddy again. Scale the end polygons slightly smaller to create a slight taper to the fingers.

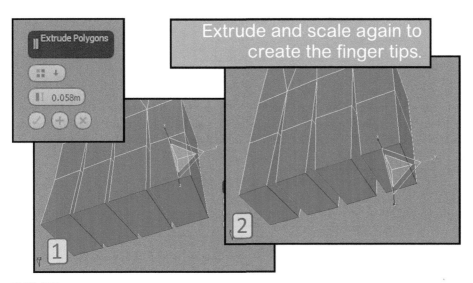

IMAGE 2.154

The next step will take a few minutes. First, adjust the finger lengths. Look at your own hand. The fingers are of different lengths. Make the mesh finger lengths similar to your finger lengths. Next, adjust the vertices of each individual finger to create a natural, slight curl to them. If you look at your relaxed hand, your fingers all have a different slight curl. Try to get a similar look to the mesh. Take your time, and think about how you want the finger to look before moving vertices.

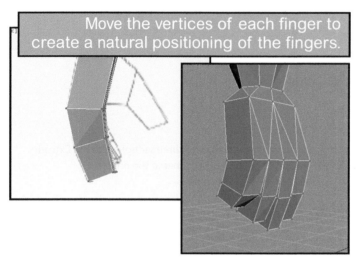

IMAGE 2.155

On the inside, palm side of the hand, we will create the thumb. Coming from this side, we will be recreating the opposable grip that humans have to grasp things. Our character will be able to "grasp" weapon handles, etc. Select the two polygons as shown in Image 2.156, and extrude them using the "by Group" setting.

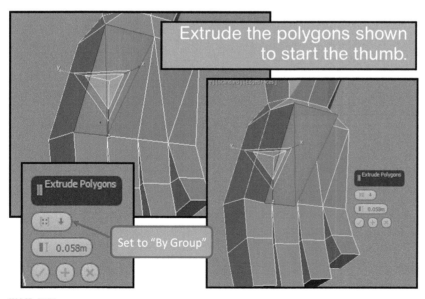

IMAGE 2.156

Adjust the vertices to match up with the template image. In the Front Viewport,

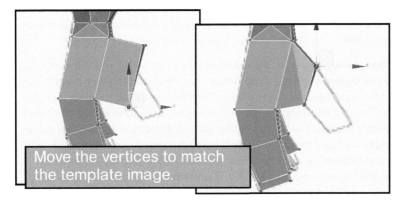

Move the vertices to match the template image.

IMAGE 2.157

Repeat the same steps: extrude and adjust the vertices.

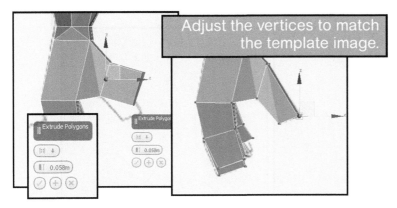

Adjust the vertices to match the template image.

IMAGE 2.158

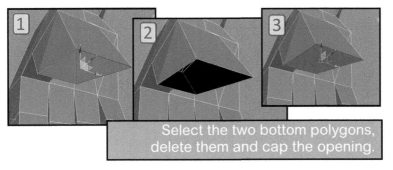

Select the two bottom polygons, delete them and cap the opening.

IMAGE 2.159

To finish the thumb, rotate the Perspective Viewport, so you can view the bottom polygon. It has a diagonal cut in it from the palm extrusion. Select the two polygons, then delete them. Use the Cap tool to close the opening with a single polygon.

That completes the modeling of the character. All that is left to do is to mirror some of the Body parts from the right side of the Body to the left side. In the Scene Explorer, turn on all the layers of the Knight.

Select the arm_upper_rt, arm_lower_rt, leg_upper_rt, leg_lower_rt, foot_1_rt, foot_2_rt and the foot_3_ rt. Select the two arm limbs, the two leg limbs and the three foot meshes. Hold shift and drag them to the right (the character's left). Select the Copy option in clone. Click on Modifier List and add a Mirror modifier. Do not use the Mirror Tool on the Top Tool Bar. Using the Mirror Tool will add a negative value to the mesh that will flip the faces when imported to Unity. The Mirror Modifier will not do this. Use the settings shown in the image. Position the meshes to the Body accordingly. Select each new cloned mesh individually, and right-click in the Modifier Panel and collapse the stack back to an Editable Poly (Collapse All). The new meshes all have names based on the original meshes. Take a few minutes to change the names, using "lt," for left, in place of the "rt," for right, on the original.

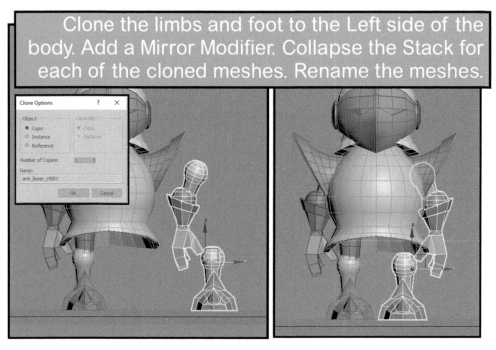

IMAGE 2.160 (Max File Save 2.42)

With that done, our modeling for the Knight is complete. Nice job!

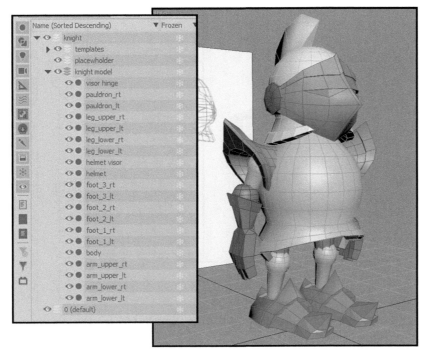

IMAGE 2.161 (Max File Save 2.43)

Unwrapping the Model

In Chapter 8 of Volume I, we covered unwrapping in great detail. Should you not be familiar with unwrapping, I suggest you go back to Volume I and follow the tutorials on unwrapping. Unwrapping is complicated and involved. Too much so to start from scratch again here. Understanding what the principles of unwrapping are is essential to doing it successfully. In Volume I, we did one of the simpler methods of unwrapping, using a planar approach. Our Knight model lends itself to using this approach again as there are no complicated textures that need to be fit to the mesh polygons. For the most part, we are using solid colors. Our model does not have a human face which simplifies things also.

We do need to unwrap our little guy, so we will go through it quickly, without the reasoning and explanations as we did in Volume I. In the Scene Explorer, you can turn off the template planes as we will not need them anymore. Select the helmet mesh and add an Unwrap UVW modifier from the Modifier Stack (Image 2.161). Remember to not be in sub-object mode when you apply the Unwrap UVW modifier, it will not work correctly if so.

In the Modifier Stack, expand the Unwrap UVW modifier to show the sub-object levels.

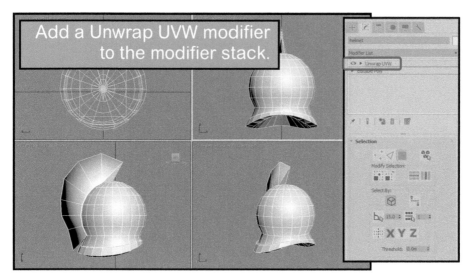

IMAGE 2.162 (Max File Save 2.44)

Select the Polygon level in the modifier (not the Editable Poly!). You can also select the level by using the icon buttons in the Selection section below the Stack.

For this mesh, we will be assigning all solid colors to it. So, we will select polygon groups according to how we want to break down the mesh into texture colors. Select polygon groups as shown and name them in the Create Selection Sets box on the Top Tool Bar as you did with the castle modules. The next few images show how I divided the mesh and named the polygon groups. The Helmet Comb and Trim will be a different color than the rest of the helmet.

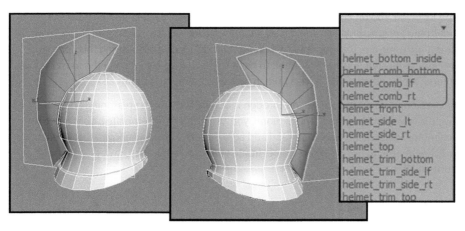

IMAGE 2.163

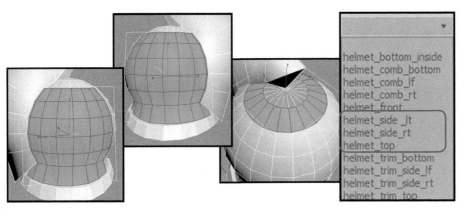

IMAGE 2.164

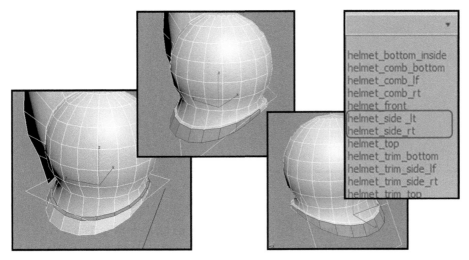

IMAGE 2.165

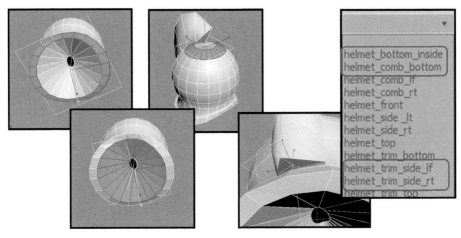

IMAGE 2.166 (Max File Save 2.45)

Open the Slate Editor and create a new texture by double-clicking on the Standard material in the Scanline section of the Materials list. Add the "knight texture 01" image to the Diffuse slot. Apply the material to the helmet mesh.

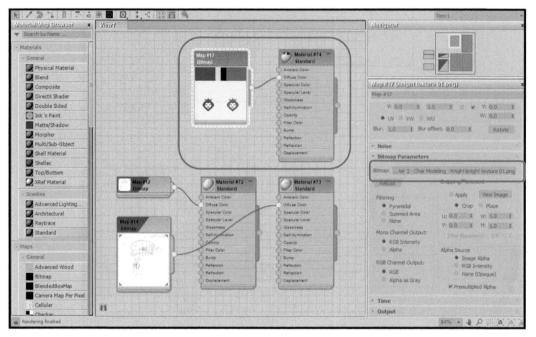

IMAGE 2.167

Open the Edit UVWs window from the Command Panel. On the right-hand top, select the "Pick Texture option from the drop-down menu. In the pop-up menu, select "Bitmap" and then navigate to where you saved the companion files for this chapter. In the Images folder, find the "knight texture 01.png" file and select it. The image will appear as a background image in the Edit UVWs window. As with the castle modules, your goal is to unwrap the polygon groups and locate them over the appropriate parts of the background image.

IMAGE 2.168

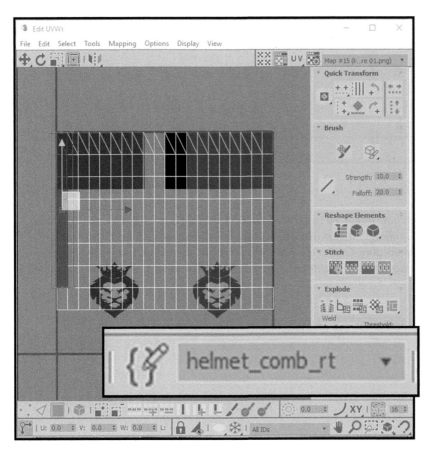

IMAGE 2.169

With the Polygon state of the Unwrap UVW modifier in the Modifier Stack, select the helmet_comb_rt or the equivalent of what you called it when naming it.

Next select Normal Mapping from the Mapping drop-down menu. In the Normal Mapping window that pops up, select Left/Right Mapping. This will unwrap the side of the comb at the best angle for mapping.

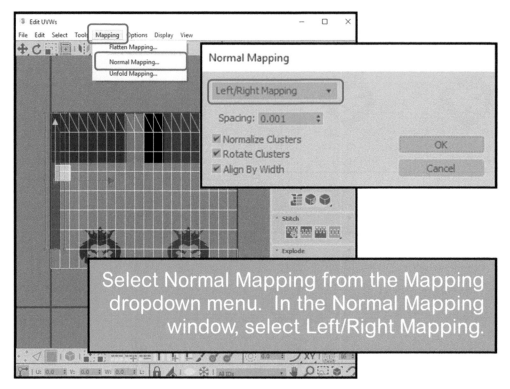

IMAGE 2.170

Drag the selected polygons from inside the Edit UVWs window to an area outside the window (the area bounded by the heavy, dark lines). Continue to the next polygon set in the drop-down list you created. Unwrap it using the same procedure. Choose the orientation of the mapping that best fits the polygon set shape. Move the new unwrapped polygon sets outside the Edit UVWs window as before. Take your time, work carefully.

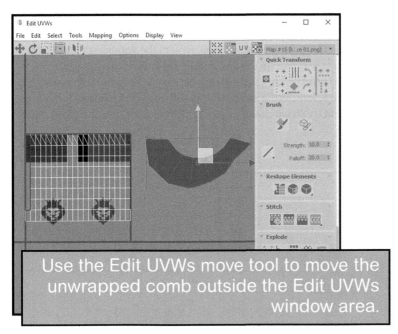

Use the Edit UVWs move tool to move the unwrapped comb outside the Edit UVWs window area.

IMAGE 2.171

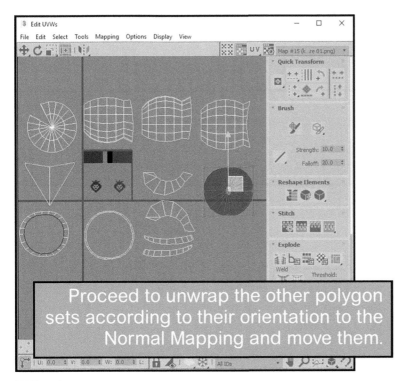

Proceed to unwrap the other polygon sets according to their orientation to the Normal Mapping and move them.

IMAGE 2.172

In Images 2.172 and 2.173, I have moved the remaining helmet polygon mesh sets or groups outside the Edit UVWs window, having mapped each mesh set. They are all scaled very large. The next step is to move the individual mesh sets back into the Edit UVWs window, so each aligns with the appropriate part of the texture image. In this case, the polygon sets or groups in the image below will all get the light gray color of the texture image. That area in the Edit UVWs window is below the blue/gold/black/red color band. The selected sets can go anywhere in this area as long as the entire set is scaled down to fit the inside the area. Use the Move and the scale tools in the Edit UVWs window Top Tool Bar to move the polygon groups to their respective areas as shown.

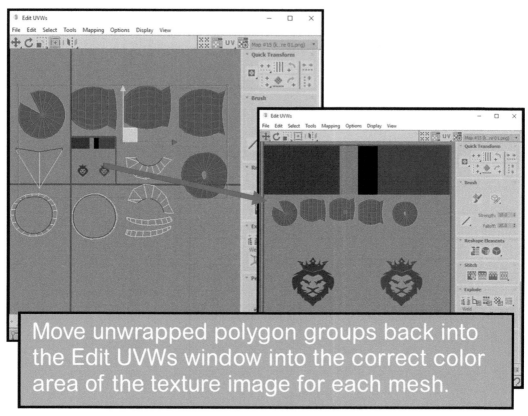

Move unwrapped polygon groups back into the Edit UVWs window into the correct color area of the texture image for each mesh.

IMAGE 2.173

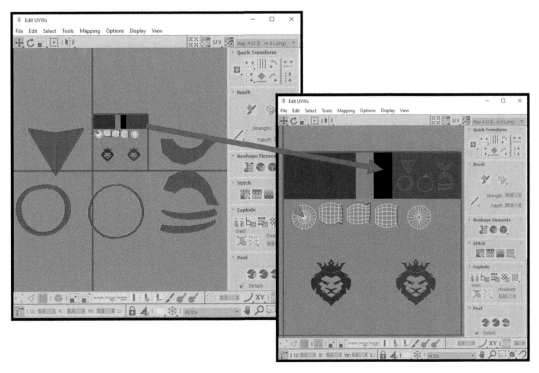

IMAGE 2.174 (Max File Save 2.46)

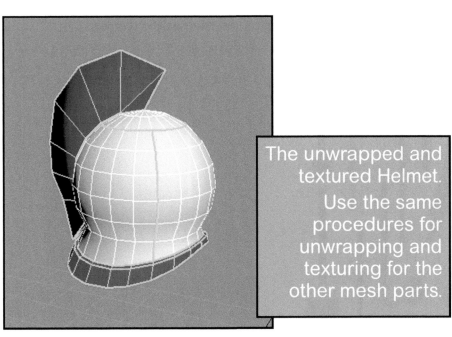

The unwrapped and textured Helmet. Use the same procedures for unwrapping and texturing for the other mesh parts.

IMAGE 2.175

When we started unwrapping the Helmet, we assigned the texture to it from the Slate Editor. With the unwrapping of the remaining mesh parts, the model will be finished. In the Companion Files (3dsMaxBasics.com), you will find the completed Knight model, with textures for reference.

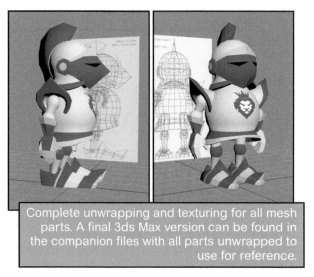

Complete unwrapping and texturing for all mesh parts. A final 3ds Max version can be found in the companion files with all parts unwrapped to use for reference.

IMAGE 2.176

Chapter 2 Exercise: The Knight Weapons

Model two medieval hand weapons for the knight that will fit in its hand. Research the design of the weapons and base your design off of authentic weapon imagery (not an artist interpretation). Unwrap and texture the weapons. Save the model files with a different name to access later if needed.

IMAGE 2.177 © Shutterstock. Used with Permission.

Rigging Basics

Topics in This Chapter

- Linking: Parent–Child Relationship
- Kinematics: FK and IK
- IK Solvers

Concepts/Skills/Tools Introduced in This Chapter

- Animating the Rig
- Rig Helpers: Controllers

Rigging a Basic Character

In this chapter, we will start learning the basics of rigging. We will be using our Knight character that we modeled in Chapter 2. He was purposely designed for this chapter.

Before we start working on our rig, we need to get an understanding of a few concepts first. The first is the concept of the Parent–Child relationship. In 3ds Max, create a new scene. Create and orient a box, a short cylinder and a small sphere, similar to the ones shown below or open the 3ds Max file "chapter 3 max file 01" in the companion files folder for this chapter.

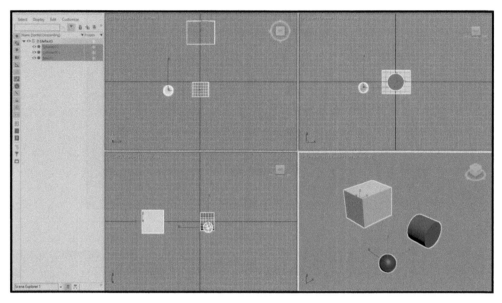

IMAGE 3.1 (Max File Save 3.01)

Linking: The Parent–Child Relationship

When we link one object to another object, we are creating a relationship between the two. In the modeling world, this is the "Parent–Child" relationship. When you link objects, you always link the Child object to the intended Parent object, not the Parent to the Child. This is an important concept to remember. We will start by linking the objects in the scene.

Do you remember linking the drawbridge to the drawbridge hinge when we modeled the Gate House in Volume I? We will use the same procedure here. The Select and Link icon button is in the upper left-hand corner of the Top Tool Bar.

Click on the Select and Link tool. Click on the cylinder and drag the mouse cursor to the box and release. When you release the mouse button, the selected object will briefly flash on the screen, indicating that the first object is linked to the target object. The two objects linked together form a chain.

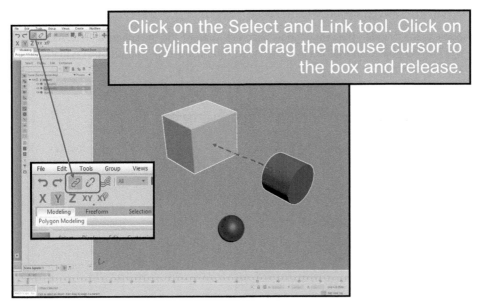

Click on the Select and Link tool. Click on the cylinder and drag the mouse cursor to the box and release.

IMAGE 3.2

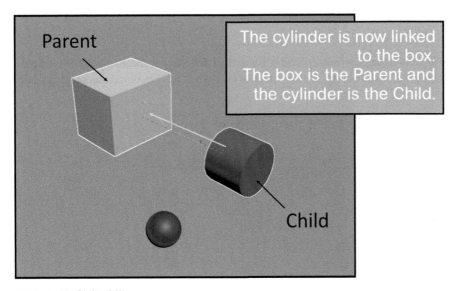

Parent

The cylinder is now linked to the box. The box is the Parent and the cylinder is the Child.

Child

IMAGE 3.3 (Max File Save 3.03)

A Parent object can have a Child object; in fact, it can have many Child objects linked to it. Linking sets up a unique property between two objects. Wherever the Parent object moves, the Child object will move relative to it, maintaining the same distance and orientation to the Parent. Select the Parent object in the scene, the box, and move it in a direction away from its current position.

The Child object should have moved too, keeping its orientation relative to the Parent object. Wherever the Parent object moves, the Child will move relative to it. Undo the move you just made to get the objects back to their original placement. Now, click on the Child and move it from its position. The Parent did not move. That is the difference. If you move the Parent after moving the Child, the Child will move again, from its new position, staying relatively positioned to the Parent.

Now, link the sphere to the cylinder. The cylinder now becomes a Parent and the sphere a Child. A Child and be a Parent to another object, and still act as a Child to its Parent. Move the various objects in the scene to see the relationships.

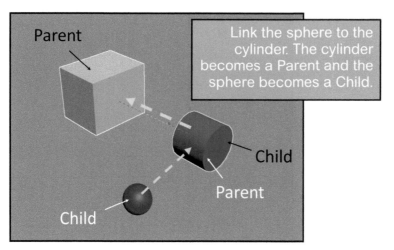

IMAGE 3.4

Once we create two or more chains, we have created a "Hierarchy Chain." In a scene, there can be multiple Hierarchy Chains. Remember, linked objects are not attached as one object. They remain separate objects.

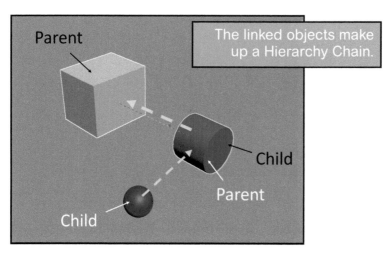

IMAGE 3.5

There are two more very important parts to remember. The first Parent in the Hierarchy Chain is called the "Root" of the chain. The last Child in the Hierarchy Chain is called the "End Effector."

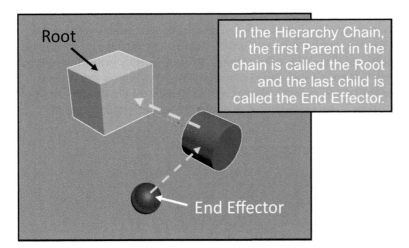

IMAGE 3.6

Another way to look at the Hierarchy Chain relationships is to open the Schematic View by clicking the Schematic View icon button on the Top Tool Bar.

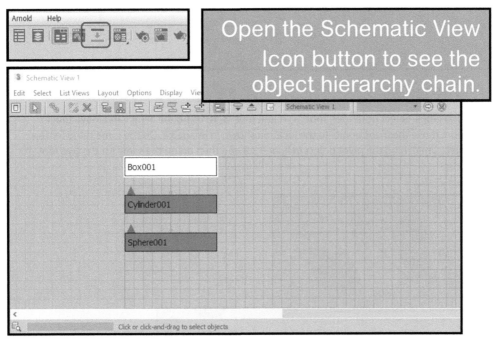

IMAGE 3.7

This is the simplest type of rigging: link objects together. As I mentioned at the start of this chapter, our Knight character was designed for this type of rigging. Open the last iteration of the completed Knight

3ds Max file. When it opens, re-save the file as "lastname_knight_linkrig_01." If you do not have access to it, use the companion file "culbertson_knight_47" from Chapter 2. When it opens, rename it as stated and turn off the template image planes in the Scene Explorer as we will not be needing them.

The Knight character is a collection of separate mesh parts. When we animate this character, none of the parts will have deformations or bending, and the parts maintain their shape. The first thing we must do is to correctly position the pivot points for all the Body parts, so they will rotate correctly. In the Hierarchy tab of the Command Panel, select the Pivot button, then click on the Affect Pivot Only button. The gizmo in the viewports changes its appearance to represent the pivot point. This is where the object will pivot when rotated. Most of the character parts have pivot points based on their origin when created or cloned.

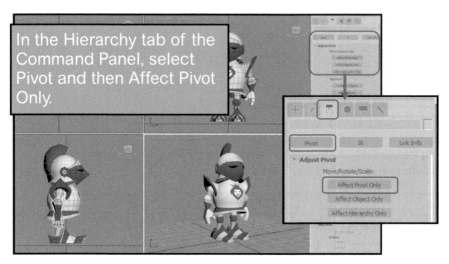

IMAGE 3.8 (Max File Save 3.04)

Let's start with the toes. Select both toes, foot_3_rt and foot_3_lt. Using the Select and Move tool in the Left Viewport, move the pivot points to the location shown in Image3.8. Do the same thing for the two foot_2 objects, matching the pivot points in Image 3.8 and then doing the same for the two foot_1 objects.

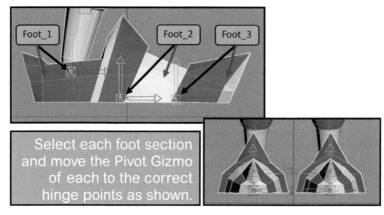

IMAGE 3.9

Continue by adjusting the position of the pivot point for the lower and upper leg objects as shown in the next two images.

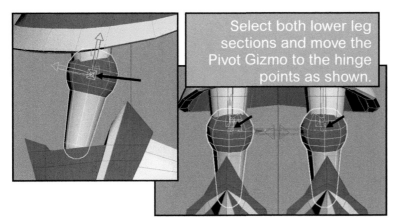

Select both lower leg sections and move the Pivot Gizmo to the hinge points as shown.

IMAGE 3.10

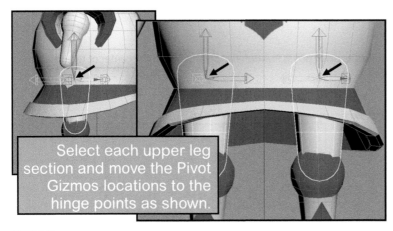

Select each upper leg section and move the Pivot Gizmos locations to the hinge points as shown.

IMAGE 3.11

The next part is the Body. The Body for our character is a little different than a typical biped or two-legged character. Our Knight has a single torso/pelvis rather than two separate pieces. If when being animated, he was to bend over, his entire torso/pelvis would rotate at the hip area. When you positioned the pivot point of the upper legs, you established the horizontal line where the hip pivot point is located. So, select the Body object and move the pivot point to the same horizontal height that the upper leg pivot points are.

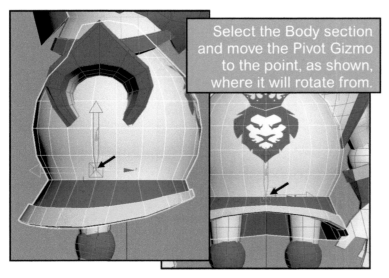

IMAGE 3.12

Move up to the Visor Hinge to adjust its pivot point. Position the pivot point to the center of the object in both the Left and Front Viewports.

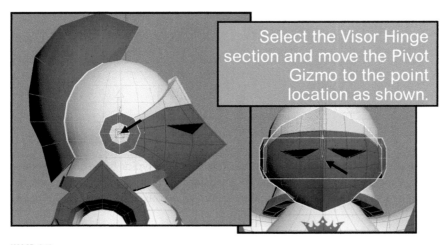

IMAGE 3.13

Use the Align Tool on the Top Tool Bar to align the Visor to the Visor Hinge. With the Visor selected, click on the Align Tool icon on the Top Tool Bar, then click on the Visor Hinge object. When the Alignment Selection window pops up, select the two Pivot Point radio buttons if not already selected and click the OK button to close the window.

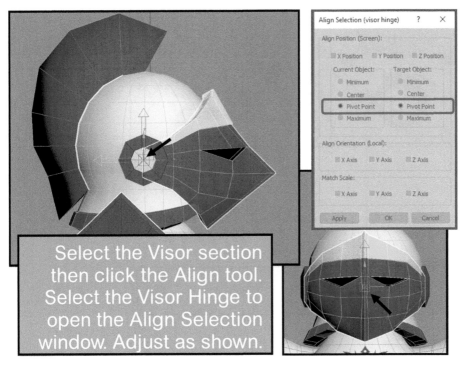

IMAGE 3.14

For the Helmet, move the pivot point to the location where the character's head would rotate on its neck if it were real as shown in Image 3.14.

IMAGE 3.15

Next, adjust the pivot points for the two Pauldron pieces. These likely will not be animated, but, in case there is a need to rotate them in an extreme arm movement or as secondary movement, we'll set the correct pivot points.

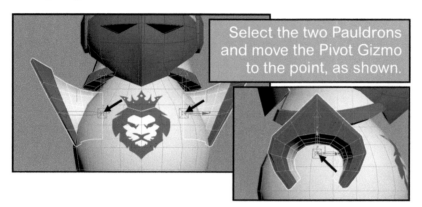

IMAGE 3.16

Adjust the two pivot points for the Upper Arms. We want them to rotate from the center of the spherical shape part of the objects.

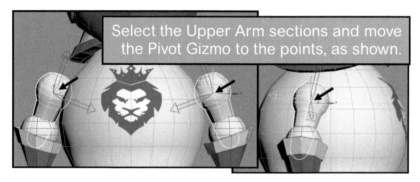

IMAGE 3.17

Lastly, adjust the pivot point of the lower arm objects. They will pivot at the elbow, the middle of the spherical part of the objects.

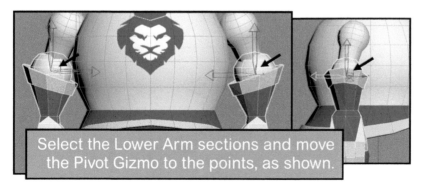

IMAGE 3.18

With the pivot points of all the character parts adjusted, we can turn our attention to the linking of the parts to form Hierarchy Chains. Click the Pivot button again to get out of Affect Pivot Only mode.

We will link all the parts of the Knight together, so he can be animated. How we link the various Body parts together is important to rigging the character successfully. When rigging a character using linking, the process is to start at an extremity and link toward the pelvis section of the character. The pelvis would be the Root of all the Hierarchy Chains. For example, start at, say, the toe and link toward the pelvis. Link the toe object to the foot object. The toe would become the end Effector, and the foot becomes a Parent. Then, link the foot object to the lower leg object which will become a Parent to the foot, its Child. Then, link the lower leg object to the upper leg object creating a similar Parent/Child relationship. Lastly, the upper leg object gets linked to the Pelvis, the Parent and Root of the Hierarchy Chain. We link in this manner as it is the equivalent to how you are "linked" together. As a forward kinematic creature, your limbs function the same way.

In the case of our Knight, as already mentioned, he has a single torso/pelvis, the Body. For the Knight, the Body will be the Root of our Hierarchy Chains we will be linking. Image 3.18 shows an exploded view of the Knight's 20 separate parts. (Note: you do not need to create an exploded version in 3ds Max, and these images are for illustration purposes.)

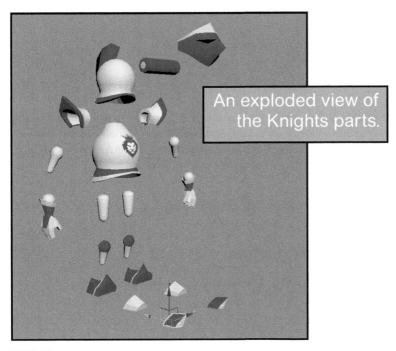

An exploded view of the Knights parts.

IMAGE 3.19

Starting at the ends of the extremities, we need to link the Body parts in ascending order from the End Effectors to the Root, the Body object. The next image shows the linking relationships for all the character parts. For example, the foot_3_rt is linked to the foot_2_rt. foot_2_rt is linked to foot_1_rt. Foot_1_rt is linked to leg_lower_rt, leg_lower_rt is linked to leg_upper_rt and, finally, leg_upper_rt is linked to the Body, the Root of this chain.

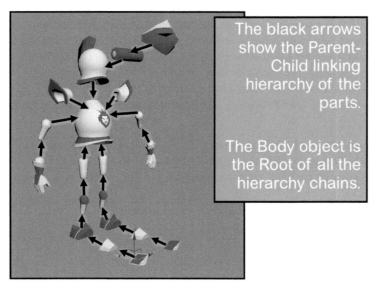

The black arrows show the Parent-Child linking hierarchy of the parts.

The Body object is the Root of all the hierarchy chains.

IMAGE 3.20

Start the linking process with the right leg. Click on the Select and Link tool on the left-hand side of the Top Tool Bar. Click on the foot_3_rt, drag the mouse cursor to foot_3_rt and release the mouse to link the two. When you release the mouse button, the Parent object, in this case, the foot_2_rt, will flash with a white outline in the viewport indicating that it is now the Parent of the Child you linked to it.

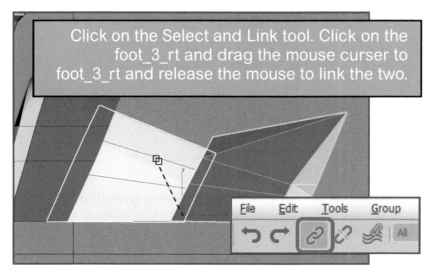

Click on the Select and Link tool. Click on the foot_3_rt and drag the mouse curser to foot_3_rt and release the mouse to link the two.

File   Edit   Tools   Group

IMAGE 3.21 (Max File Save 3.05)

Continue linking all the extremities, the arms, legs, pauldron objects and the helmet parts to the Root, the Body. There will be a total of seven Hierarchy Chains in total. When you are finished linking the character's objects, open the Schematic View by clicking the Schematic view icon on the Top Tool Bar. It should look like the one shown in Image 3.21 (there will also be the two template planes off to the side). Note that the Body is at the top of the Hierarchy Chains, it is the Root. The last object in each chain at the bottom is an End Effector.

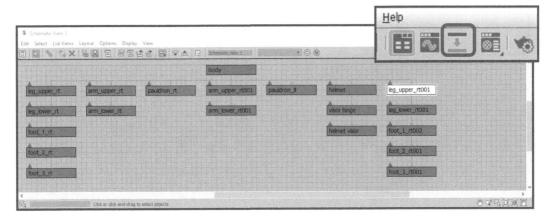

IMAGE 3.22 (Max File Save 3.06)

The Knight has been modeled, unwrapped, textured and now rigged. Granted it is a very simple rig, just linking. It is enough to animate the character.

Animating the Knight

Do you remember how we animated the Drawbridge and the Portcullis on the Gate House in Volume I? We will start the same way to animate the Knight. First, click on the Auto Key button on the Bottom Tool Bar. This will put 3ds Max in Animation mode. The Time Slider bar and the active viewport frame will turn red indicating it is in Animation mode. Remember almost anything you change while in Animation mode can be animated. Changing color, scaling, moving, etc., almost all animatable. If you do not want something animated, be sure to remember to turn off the Auto Key button. Select the arm_upper_rt. To create a keyframe at frame 0, click on the Set Keys button (the large "+" icon) to the left of the Auto Key button. Notice the new keyframe at frame 0.

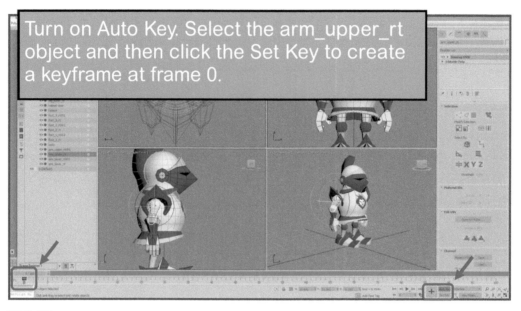

IMAGE 3.23

Move the Time slider forward in time to frame 10. With the Select and Rotate tool, rotate the arm_upper_rt counterclockwise as shown to about a 45-degree angle from its starting position.

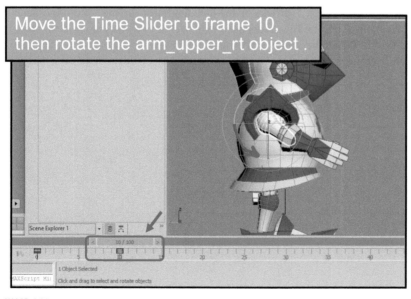

IMAGE 3.24

Hold down the Shift key on the keyboard, and select the keyframe we just created at frame 10. Drag the keyframe to frame 15, and release the mouse button then the Shift Key. The keyframe at frame 10 should have been copied to frame 15. This will create a pause in the animation. The arm will rotate from frame 0 to frame 10, then hold its position through frame 15.

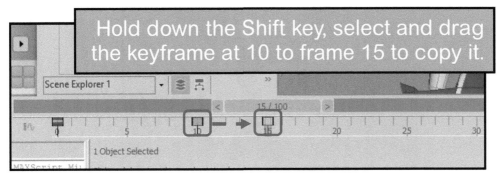

IMAGE 3.25

To complete this action, hold down the Shift Key on the keyboard and drag the keyframe at frame 0 to frame 20 to copy it. By doing this, the arm will return to its original position at frame 0.

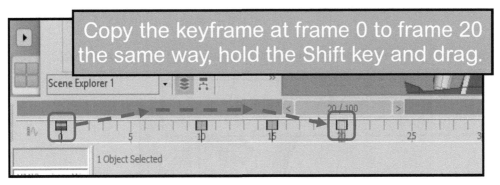

IMAGE 3.26

Let's add a second movement. Move the Time Slider to frame 5. Select the arm_lower_rt object and click on the Set Keys button on the Bottom Tool Bar to create a keyframe for this object at frame 5.

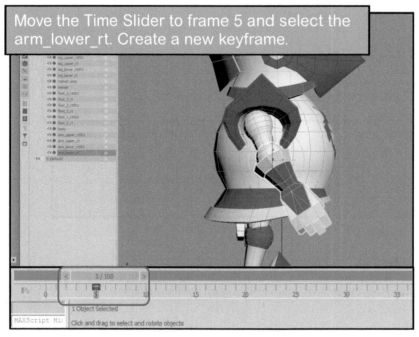

IMAGE 3.27

Move the Time Slider to frame 15, and rotate the object counterclockwise as shown in Image 3.27.

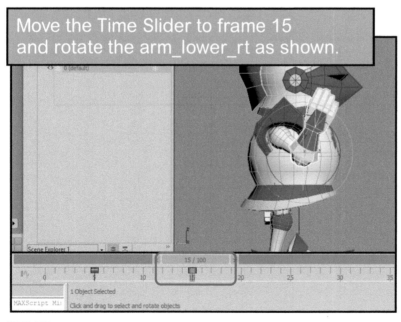

IMAGE 3.28

Lastly, hold down the Shift Key and copy the keyframe at frame 5 to frame 20. Scrub the Time slider to the left and right to see the movement action you just created. You can click the Play button to watch it also. Animation will only play in the active viewport.

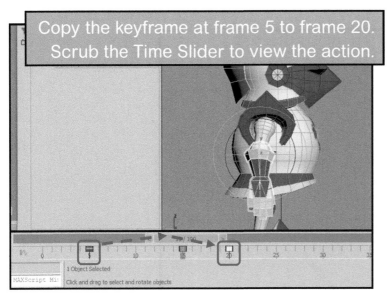

IMAGE 3.29 (Max File Save 3.07)

That was a little refresher on how to do basic animation in 3ds Max. Save this if you want to, then open the last version of the file you have from before the animating exercise we just did with the right arm. Everything should be linked. Rename the file lastname_exercise_1. Save another version of the file as lastname_exercise_2.

Bones Exercise

Using the lastname_exercise_1 file, create a 10-second animation of your Knight moving. Make the character take a step or two forward, move the arms, rotate the Body and bend a bit. We are looking to move all the Body parts in a single animation. Maybe it takes a step forward, turns its Body to the right and points to the sky: one continuous action for 10 seconds. It is important to make it take a step forward in this exercise.

You will need to change the length of the current animation time from 100 frames to 300 frames. Generally, in computer animation, 30 frames are used for each second of animation (30 frames×10 seconds=300 frames/second). On the Bottom Tool Bar, click on the Time Configuration icon button. In the Pop-up Time Configuration window, change the End Time from 100 to 300.

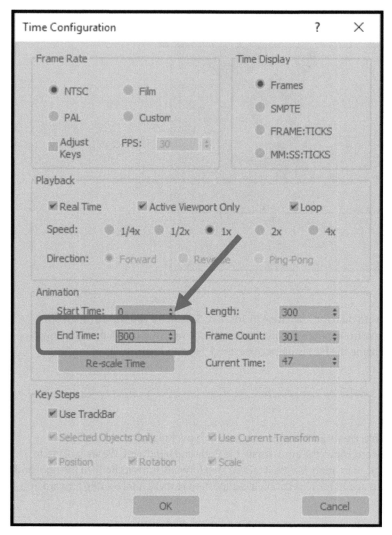

IMAGE 3.30

To render your animation when complete, open the Render Setup window by clicking the Top Tool Bar icon or the F10 key. To make an animation rendering, change from the "Single" setting in the Render Setup dialogue box to either Active Time Segment, Range or Frames.

In the Render Output, click the Save File button to open the Save dialogue window. Change the Type to an animation type (.AVI, .MOV, etc.) or render a still sequence (.JPEG, .TGA, etc.) if you are familiar with non-linear editor such as Adobe Premiere. For each type, also use the Setup box button to the left side of the window to adjust the options available for the file type.

This exercise, doing a 10-second animation should take at minimum an hour to complete. Work at making subtle moves and transitions. The walking sequence alone should take considerable time. It will be a challenge to make the walk/step forward smooth.

Bones

Bones are special objects in a 3d modeling program that allow you to animate other objects or Hierarchy Chains within a scene. A bone system is two or more bones that are linked, creating a rotatable joint between them. Bone objects can be rendered in a scene (visible in the rendering) or non-renderable (not visible in the rendered image). When you watch an animated 3d character in a scene, you do not see the bone system being used to create the animation because the bone objects have been set to non-renderable. They are there, and you just cannot see them.

To create a bone, click on the Bones button in the Systems icon tab of the Create menu of the Command Panel, the last one in the second row. There is a second way to create bones by using the Bones Tool. The Bones Tool is accessed by selecting the Bones Tool from the Animation tab drop-down list from the Top Tool Bar.

The Bones Tool window has lots of options for creating and manipulating bones that we can access when we are a bit more familiar with the bone basics.

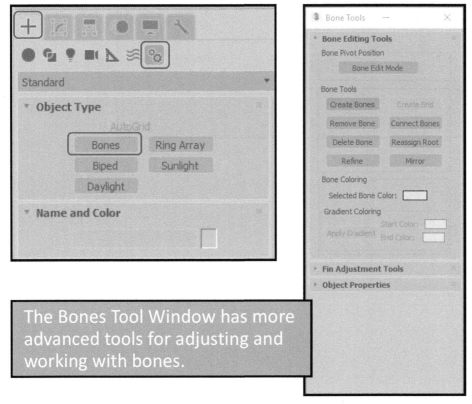

The Bones Tool Window has more advanced tools for adjusting and working with bones.

IMAGE 3.31

In the Front Viewport, create a two-bone system by left-clicking in the viewport to initiate the first bone. Move the mouse a distance away from the initial click, and left-click again to set the bone length. Move the mouse another distance away from the second click location, left-click to set the bone length and then right-click to end the bone chain. When you end the bone chain, a small tetrahedron shape object is automatically created. This is the node object. Delete the bones and create them again in the Front Viewport, arranging them as shown in Image 3.31.

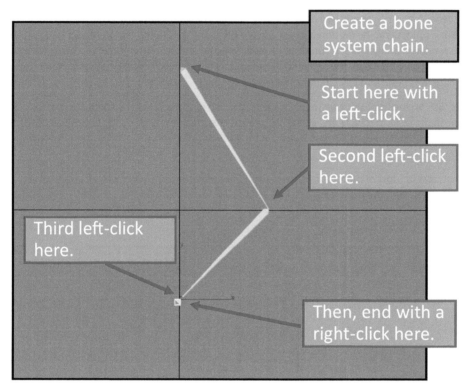

Create a bone system chain.

Start here with a left-click.

Second left-click here.

Third left-click here.

Then, end with a right-click here.

IMAGE 3.32 (Max File Save 3.08)

When I created my bones in Image 3.31, 3ds Max created very thin bones. The size of the bones can be adjusted in the Modify Panel as needed. If the bones you created are thin like the ones I created, make them larger by adjusting the Bone Object Width and Height as shown. Just adjust the first and second bones, not the node at the end of the bone chain.

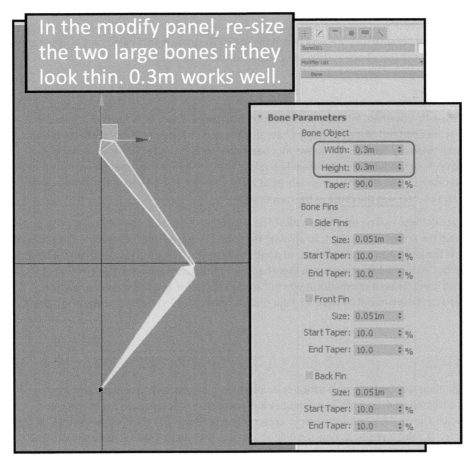

In the modify panel, re-size the two large bones if they look thin. 0.3m works well.

IMAGE 3.33

The next time you create a bone, 3ds Max should use the last parameters entered for the size.

There are other features to bones such as the fins that we will be using on later projects to assist in rigging. For now, know that the fins exist.

Kinematics

Another basic concept you need to understand for rigging is kinematics. When we talk about kinematics in 3d modeling, we are talking about the movement of a linked structure, such as a Hierarchy Chain of a bone system. There are two main types of kinematics we deal with: Forward Kinematics (FK) and Inverse Kinematics (IK).

Forward Kinematics

Let's start with FK. In an FK system, the movement of the chain is initiated with the root Parent of the chain. For example, when the root Parent bone is rotated, the Child bones that are linked to it follow, relative to the Parent. Your arms and legs are great examples of Forward Kinematics. To raise your hand up over your head, your brain does not signal your hand to rise up but it signals the muscles controlling your shoulder to contract accordingly to cause your upper arm to rotate up. The lower arm and hand follow the upper arm's movement. They have to because they are attached at the joints. The movement initiates at the upper arm shoulder, the "Root" of your arm's bone system. Your legs work the same way.

Inverse Kinematics

The opposite of FK, with movement initiated at the Root of the chain, the movement with IK is initiated at the End Effector at the Child end of the Hierarchy Chain. Image someone takes hold of your hand, the end effector of your arm hierarchy, and raises it above your head. Your forearm and upper arm followed your hand as it moved up. Your shoulder muscles played no role in completing the movement. Your forearm and upper arm appeared to move in the same manner as if you alone had raised your arm. This is Inverse Kinematics. The End Effector was the cause of the movement.

Why do we care about these two types of kinematics? The answer has to do with animation. Remember when you animated the Knight in Exercise 1. To animate the hand moving forward, you needed to position the upper arm and the lower arm countless times to position the hand correctly. You were using a Forward Kinematic Hierarchy Chain of linked objects. You likely had a very frustrating time animating the legs to take a step forward using forward kinematics. It was not an easy endeavor. Maybe you should be more impressed that you can walk without falling over. Your brain is pretty amazing at controlling things, don't you think?

IK Solvers

IK solvers are algorithms that create mathematical solutions to rotate and position the links or parts in a kinematic chain assigned to part of a hierarchy. In a kinematic chain, there is a start joint and end joint, or End Effector. The Goal is a cruciform helper object that is used to move the end joint of the kinematic chain. The IK solution controls how the links respond in the Parent/Child relationship through IK Controllers. There are many types of IK solvers, developed for specific uses. 3ds Max has four IK solvers, each designed or specialized for specific needs. The solvers calculate where in space the links (the objects in the Hierarchy Chain) need to move to follow the goal that the animator moves.

History-Independent IK Solver (HI)

The HI solver is the most commonly used solver in 3ds Max. It is the fastest solver because it only calculates the next position of the links based on their current location. Every calculation is done this way. The equations are relatively small. HI solver solutions are not the most accurate, but they are the quickest. As the animation solution progresses, the calculations for each frame are computed based on just the last position of the object in the previous frame. The solutions stay fairly small.

History-Dependent IK Solver (HD)

The HD solver is a more accurate solver than the HI solver, but it is much slower due to its process. When a HD solver calculates a solution, it starts with the objects in the chain at the first frame of the animation. It makes the second frame calculations based on where the objects are in the first frame. In the third frame, it calculates where the objects should be based on the first and second frames. In the fourth frame, it calculates where the objects should be based on the first, second and third frames. On it goes, always starting at the first frame of the movement. In a lengthy animation, it doesn't take long for the calculated solution to become very large and slow to solve. The HD solver has more advanced tools not found in the HI solver, such as damping, precedence and spring back. The accuracy of the solution is very, but the solution can take a very long time to compute.

IK Limb Solver

This is a solver that was designed specifically for animating the limbs of human characters. Only two bones are involved in the solution. It is a fast solver that displays accurately in the viewports.

Spline IK

This solver has the unique ability to handle the curvature of a Hierarchy Chain with a series of bones or liked objects. An example would be a snake character having 15 bones in a Hierarchy Chain to enable it to make serpentine movements. While other solvers would likely leave the chain in a curled up know, the Spline IL solver can compute the multiple link positions.

Adding IK to a Bone Chain

To use IK in 3ds Max, we assign an IK solver to the bone chain. The IK solver is a mathematical solution to the movement of the bones based on the movement of the IK Goal. If you move the IK Goal, the IK solver computes the movement of the bones up the Hierarchy Chain to the Root. In a while we will discuss the different types of IK solvers in the program. For now, let's apply one and see what happens. In our current 3ds Max scene that we have open, we have two bones and an End Node, the End Effector. Select the Root bone of the Hierarchy Chain, the top bone. It is important to always select the Root bone first when assigning most IK solvers in 3ds Max. Click on the Animation tab on the Top Tool Bar to open the drop-down menu. Move your mouse cursor down to select the IK solvers heading, then select the HI Solver. Your mouse cursor will change, and there will be an "ant-line" trailing it to the top of the Root bone.

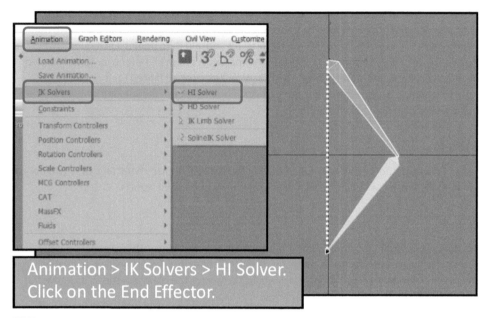

Animation > IK Solvers > HI Solver.
Click on the End Effector.

IMAGE 3.34

Click on the End Node, the End Effector of the Hierarchy Chain. A white line will connect the top of the Root bone and the End Effector. Additionally, there will be a blue or white, if selected, cruciform icon called the Goal and a familiar gizmo at the end of the kinematic chain at the End Effector. If the cruciform-shaped Goal is blue, select it (it will turn white). With the Select and Move tool, move your mouse cursor over yellow triangle part of the move gizmo to click and drag the Goal's gizmo in different directions. What happens?

The bones should follow the movement of the End Effector… Inverse Kinematics at work. If you move the cursor beyond the reach of the bones, they will go completely straight in a line, but remain intact.

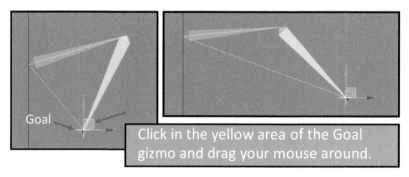

Goal

Click in the yellow area of the Goal
gizmo and drag your mouse around.

IMAGE 3.35 (Max File Save 3.09)

If your Knight had IK on the arms and legs, your exercise in animating it would have been much different.

130

Do undo's to get your bone chain back to the position it was in after you added the IK solver. Create two capsules (in the Extended Primitives menu of the Create panel). Adjust their size and position as shown in Image 3.35. One capsule should encapsulate the top bone and the other encapsulate the second bone.

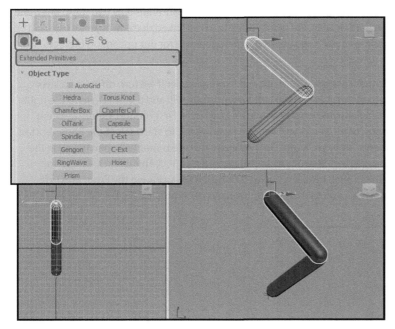

IMAGE 3.36

Next, link the top capsule to the top, Root bone, and link the lower capsule to the middle bone (not the End Node). Mouse over the bone, watching for it to highlight when looking for it. Once they are linked, select the cruciform at the end of the IK line. Move the Goal's gizmo around again. As you would expect, the capsules follow the movement of the bones.

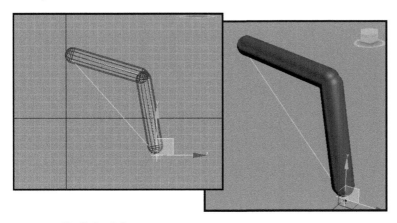

IMAGE 3.37 (Max File Save 3.10)

Next, we will add IK to a bone chain and then to your Knight character. Hopefully, you will see a big difference when you animate the character using IK and appreciate its addition to your toolbox of skills.

Exercise 2

Re-open your Knight model file named lastname_exercise_2. Everything should be linked to the model. We will upgrade this model by adding IK solutions to the arms and legs and some other controllers. We could add the IK solutions directly to the arm and leg links. However, the arms are only two mesh links, and the IK solutions we will use require three links. We would need to add a linked dummy object to the end of the lower arms for it to work. Adding bones and IK will be a good practice for our upcoming projects later in later chapters.

We will start with the legs. Once the file is open, it might make things easier if we turn off the arm layers and the Body layer in the Scene Explorer. Next, in the Left Viewport, we will add a bone chain to the right leg, just like the one we created earlier with two bones and an End Node. First though, before creating the leg bone chain, change the size of the bones in the Bone Parameters. To start, select the Bones button in the Systems tab of the Command Panel in Create. The properties for the bones will open below in the panel. Change the bone Width and Height to 0.075 m as shown in Image 3.37. This will scale them to a good working size relative to the model. Also, if not already in wireframe, change the Front and Left Viewports to Wireframe mode to allow you to view the bone placement more easily.

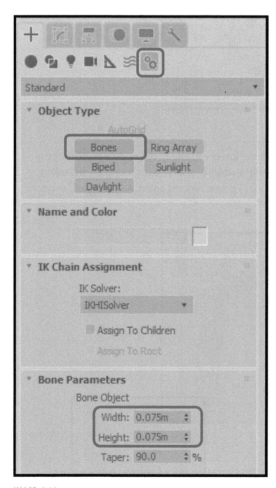

IMAGE 3.38

Notice that when we modeled the legs, we positioned them, so they had a slight bend at the knee. While it looks aesthetically pleasing with the slight bend, the real reason we did it was for rigging. By putting a slight pre-bend in the bone chain, we are telling 3ds Max which direction to bend the joint. If we create the bones without any bend, 3ds Max could determine the bend in the opposite direction. By pre-bending the bones, we take control of the decision-making.

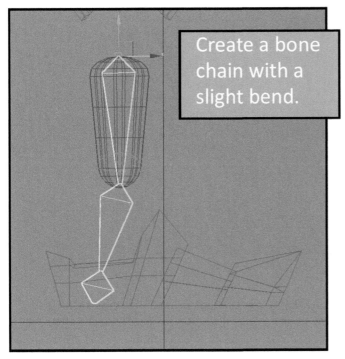

Create a bone chain with a slight bend.

IMAGE 3.39

Create a bone chain in the right leg as shown in Image 3.39, making sure to put a slight pre-bend in the knee. When you create the bones, they will be located on the X-Y axis. Select all three bones and move them to the right so they are centered in the right leg mesh parts, similarly to when you placed the capsules over the bones to encapsulate them.

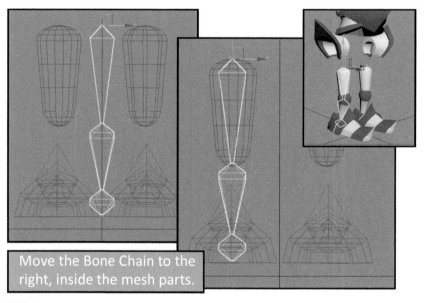

Move the Bone Chain to the right, inside the mesh parts.

IMAGE 3.40

Link the leg_upper_rt object to the Root bone, the top one. Link the leg_lower_rt to the middle bone (not the End Node). Select the Root bone, the top one. Add an IK Limb Solver to the bone chain from the Animation tab on the Top Tool Bar.

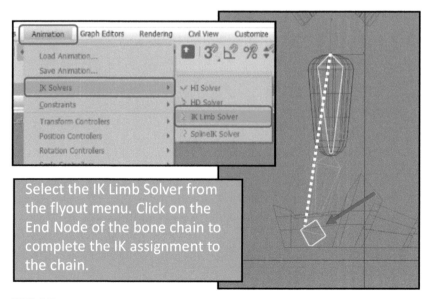

Select the IK Limb Solver from the flyout menu. Click on the End Node of the bone chain to complete the IK assignment to the chain.

IMAGE 3.41

134

Use the Select and Move tool in the Left Viewport to test the limb movement by moving the IK chain gizmo. You might notice the bone objects protruding through the Body part mesh objects. That is alright. When we animate the character, we will turn off the bone visibility. For now, it is not an issue.

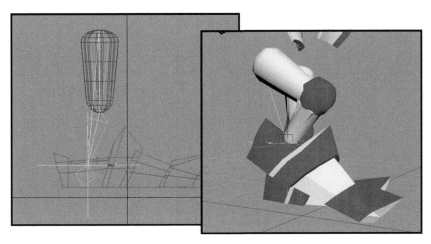

IMAGE 3.42

Undo any movements you just did to get back to the standing pose. Select the three bones (not the IK Chain). In the Front Viewport, hold down the Shift Key on the keyboard and drag the bones to the right to center them in the middle of the left leg. Release and choose the Copy option on the Clone Options window.

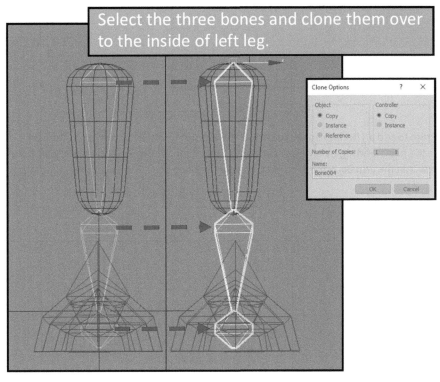

Select the three bones and clone them over to the inside of left leg.

IMAGE 3.43

Link the leg_upper_lrt to the new Root bone and the leg_lower_lt to the middle bone (not the End Node). We didn't clone the IK Chain along with the bones as sometimes this can cause unforeseen issues. It only takes a few seconds to assign it, so assign a new IK Limb Solver to the bone chain as you did with the right leg.

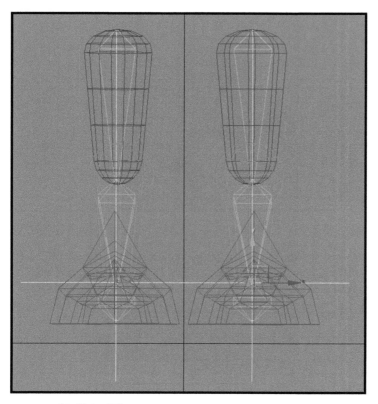

IMAGE 3.44 (Max File Save 3.11)

Use the same procedure to add an IK Limb Solver to each of the arms. Turn on the arm layers in the Scene Explorer. Turn off the IK Chains, and leg mesh layers for clarity. In the Front Viewport, add a three-part bone chain and position it within the arm Body mesh objects. Be sure the bone chain has a pre-bent angle at the elbow.

Note the bone chain will again be created on the X-Y axis. Select the three bones in the Left Viewport and move them to the left of the Root Bone and position correctly in the middle of the spherical part of the arm_upper_rt object as shown in Image 3.45.

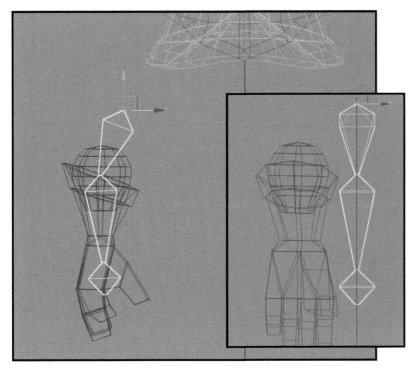

IMAGE 3.45

Notice that the bones do not follow the positions of the arm meshes. They align when viewed from the Front Viewport, but not from the Left Viewport.

We can adjust the bone positions by using the Bone Tools. Open the Bone Tools window from the Animation tab on the Top Tool Bar.

Click on the "Bone Edit Mode" button in the Popup Bone Tools window.

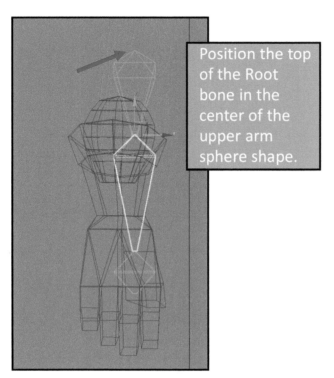

IMAGE 3.46

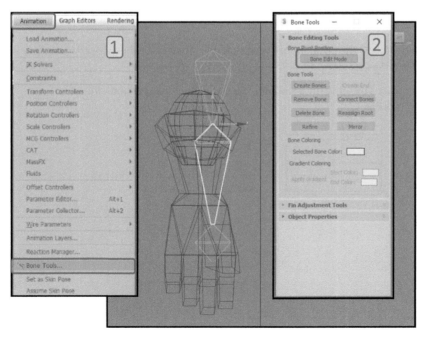

IMAGE 3.47

With the Bone Edit Mode turned on, the bones take on a new property. Using the Select and Move tool, you can move the bone links to adjust their placement. Select the middle bone in the bone chain. A move gizmo appears at the head or top of the bone. Use the Select and Move tool to slide the bone into position at the center of the spherical shape of the arm_lower_rt object as shown.

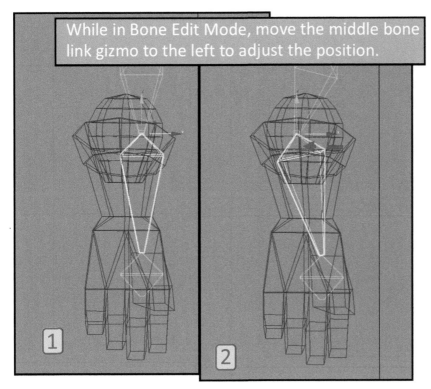

While in Bone Edit Mode, move the middle bone link gizmo to the left to adjust the position.

IMAGE 3.48

Adjust the End Node so it too is in the correct position as shown.

Next, link the arm_upper_rt to the Root bone of the bone chain and the arm_lower_rt object to the middle bone in the bone chain (not the End Node).

Finish this part of the arm rigging by adding an IK Limb Solver to the Hierarchy Chain. Select the Root bone first, then add the IK Limb Solver.

Test the movement of the arm by moving the IK gizmo around. Undo when finished to return the arm to the correct position.

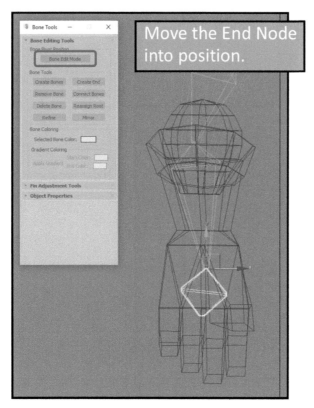

Move the End Node into position.

IMAGE 3.49

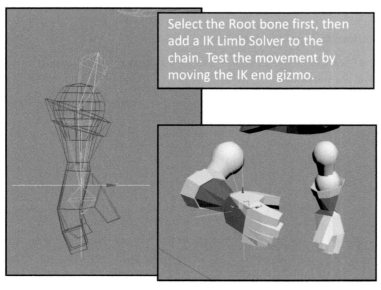

Select the Root bone first, then add a IK Limb Solver to the chain. Test the movement by moving the IK end gizmo.

IMAGE 3.50

We need to copy the bone chain over to the left arm. Clone the three bones in the bone chain as before using the Shift Key and the mouse. Move the new bone set to the open area between the arms. With all three selected, click on the Mirror Icon on the Top Tool Bar.

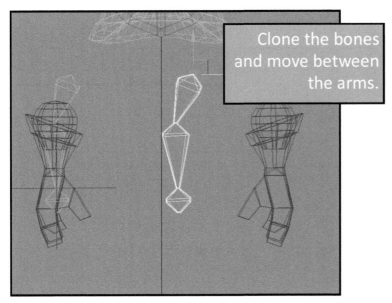

IMAGE 3.51

Select the proper axis to mirror and the "No Clone" option in the Mirror pop-up window to flip the bones horizontally so they are oriented correctly for the left arm objects.

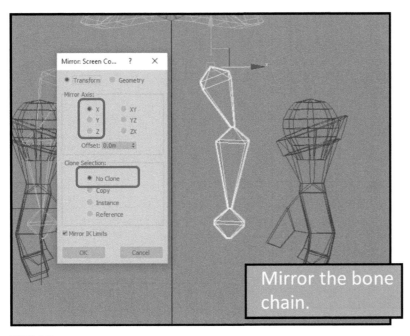

IMAGE 3.52

Move the bone chain into the proper position inside the left arm objects. Link the arm_upper_lt object to the Root bone, the top one in the chain. Then, link the arm_lower_lt object to the middle bone in the bone chain (not the End Node). Add an IK Links Solver to the Hierarchy Chain to finish the bone chain. Test the left arm movement. Return the arm to its start position with undo's. That completes the addition of IK Chains to the rig.

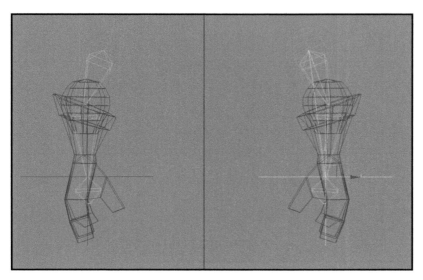

IMAGE 3.53

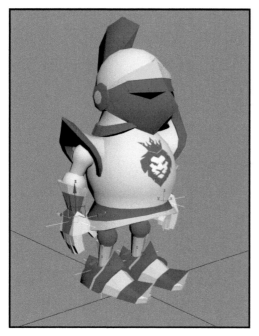

IMAGE 3.54

Rig Helpers: Controllers

One of the goals as a rigger is to create a rig where the animator does not have to touch the actual model. To do this, the rigger creates handles and controllers where possible to aid the animator. In our company, you and I are the modelers, riggers and the animators. We will still optimize our rigging by adding some controllers/helpers. Remember this is a fairly simple rig and we will not be adding complicated controllers and constraints at this point. We are gradually building up to the more complex rigs. For now, it is more important for you to understand how things work.

First, create a new layer in the Scene Explorer. Call it helpers. The first controller we will make for this layer will be a helper for the Body. In the Top Viewport, create a circle (a 2d spline shape) with a radius of 0.5 m.

Rename the circle "helper_body." To make it visible in the viewports, we need to go to the Rendering drop-down menu in the Modify tab of the Command Panel. Click on the Enable in Viewport tick box. Also, change the Thickness value to 0.01 m and the sides to 10.

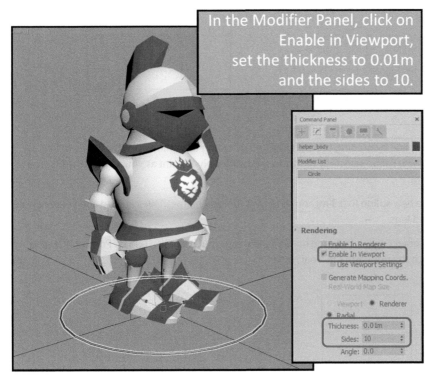

IMAGE 3.55

Next, align the new helper with the Body. Select the helper_body ring, and then click on the Align Tool icon on the Top Tool Bar. Then, click on the Body object. In the pop-up window for the Align Tool that appears, click on the X, Y and Z tick boxes in the Align Position section and check to see that both of the Pivot Point radio buttons are selected. Click OK.

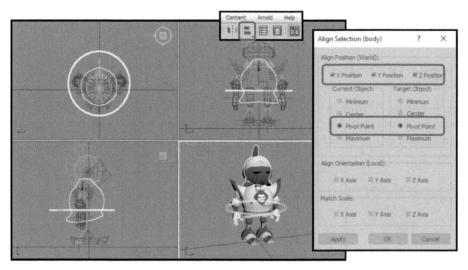

IMAGE 3.56 (Max File Save 3.12)

Clone the helper_body spline by holding the Shift Key and dragging the spline up in the Y-axis to the level of the helmet. With the new spline selected, align it to the helmet pivot point as you aligned the first spline with the Body pivot point.

Reduce the radius of the new spline to 0.3 m, and rename it "helper_helmet." We can also add some handle controls for the arms and legs.

Clone the helper_body object again, this time making the radius much smaller, 0.15 m. Position the new circle helper to align with the right arm's IK Goal.

Use the Align Tool as you did previously. Clone the new right arm circle, and align with the left lower arm.

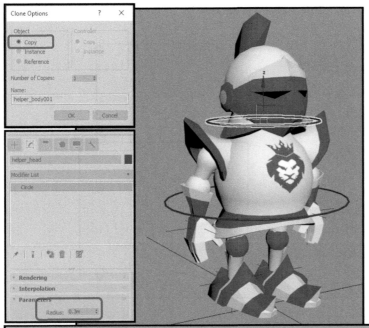

Clone the helper using the Shift Key and drag it up. Use the align tool to align with the helmet and reduce the Radius to 0.3m

IMAGE 3.57 (Max File Save 3.12)

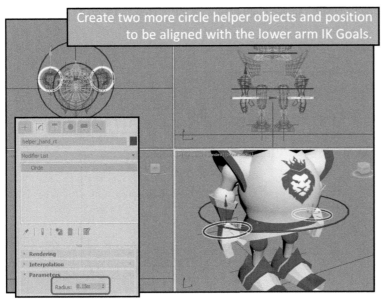

Create two more circle helper objects and position to be aligned with the lower arm IK Goals.

IMAGE 3.58 (Max File Save 3.13)

Let's add two foot helpers for the leg IK Goals. Typically, riggers use a rectangular shape around the foot with controllers for the heel, ball and toes of the foot. We are making a really simple rig here, so we will just create a handle for the animator to control the IK Chains in the legs.

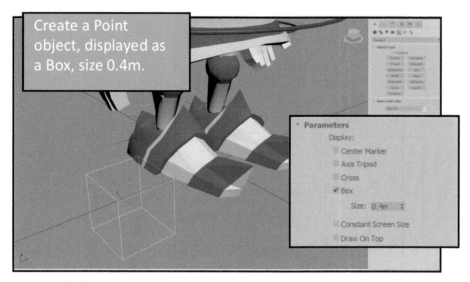

Create a Point object, displayed as a Box, size 0.4m.

IMAGE 3.59 (Max File Save 3.14)

In the Geometry section of the Command Panel, select Point in the Helpers tab. In the properties section, select Box and make the size 0.4 m. Next, click in the Perspective Viewport to create the Point Helper. Place it near the right foot.

Next, use the Align Tool to reposition the box with the IK Goal of the right leg. Select the point helper box and then the Align Tool on the Top Tool Bar. With the pivot points and X-, Y-, Z-axes selected, click on the IK Goal of the right leg. When complete, create a similar Point helper for the left leg and align it to the left leg IK Goal.

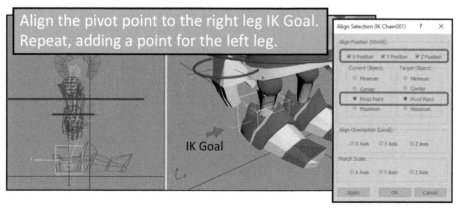

Align the pivot point to the right leg IK Goal. Repeat, adding a point for the left leg.

IK Goal

IMAGE 3.60

The last step for these helpers is to link the IK Goal of each leg to its respective Point Helper. By linking these, the animator can use the Point Helper to animate the leg action.

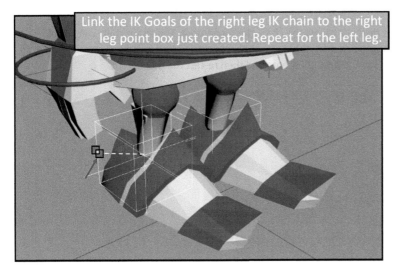

IMAGE 3.61 (Max File Save 3.16)

The last helper we will create will be the Master helper. Moving it will move the entire character as a single object. In the Top Viewport, create an NGon spline shape (found in the Splines tab of the Create panel). Set the Rendering and Parameters to the setting shown in Image 3.61. Locate it as shown below the character. Rename the NGon to "helper_master."

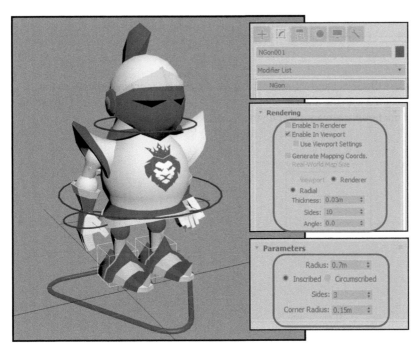

IMAGE 3.62 (Max File Save 3.18)

Re-link the helper_body to the new helper_master. Next, re-link the two helper_hands to the helper_master.

Lastly, re-link the helper_foot_lt and helper_foot_rt to the new helper_master.

Move the helper_master a short distance to test the character movement. The entire character should move as a unit with no parts lagging behind. If there are some stray object not following correctly, take a few minutes to re-link those parts to the proper Parents and then re-test the movement.

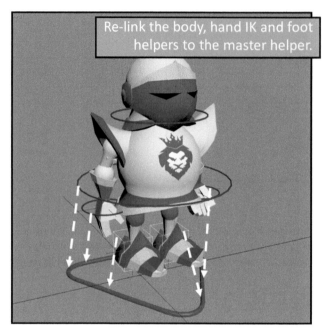

IMAGE 3.63 (Max File Save 3.18)

Select then helper_master. Use the Select and Move tool to move the character down vertically so the bottom of the two feet are aligned with the X-axis line of the X-, Y-, Z-axes. Our figure was raised up off the line because the bottom of our template images was on the X-axis.

Let's check the Scene Explorer and do some housekeeping. When we started working on the helpers, we created a new layer helper layer within the knight layer. If they are not there already, move all the helpers we created into this layer. If there are any other un-named objects in the Scene Explorer go ahead and name them correctly.

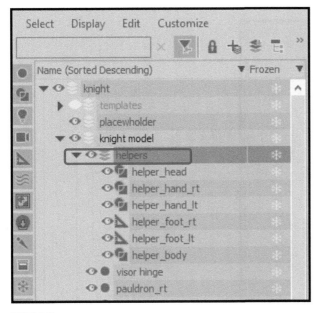

IMAGE 3.64

As indicated several times previously, this was a simple rig for our character. Most character rigs are more complicated with more helpers, and controllers to aid the animator.

Chapter 3 Exercise: Animating the Knight

Using the new rig helpers, animate the Knight character. This time, animate him in a walk cycle; only make him walk in place, not moving forward. This is how game characters are animated. They do their moves in one place. When the character is imported into the game engine, the game engine moves the character in the direction the player chooses with the control device (keyboard or hand-held device), calling on the requested animation cycle.

Make this animation 1 second long. You will need to change the length of the current animation time from 100 frames to 30 frames (30 frames per second, 30 frames×1seconds=30 frames/second). On the Bottom Tool Bar, click on the Time Configuration icon button. In the Pop-up Time Configuration window, change the End Time from 100 to 29. The frames start at 0 (0 to 29=30 frames, including 0s). Do not expect a great animation sequence the first time. It will take lots of practice and instruction to learn good animation techniques. We do not have that luxury here. Do the best you can for now. Try things, experiment and learn by doing. The important thing this time is to notice how much more control you have using the new helpers.

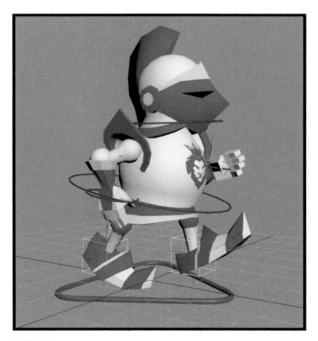

IMAGE 3.65

When you are animating with the helpers, you will soon get used to controlling them. When you render out the animation, you can turn off the helpers and splines in the scene. In the Control Panel, open the Display Icon tab. Click the tick boxes for Shapes, Helpers and Bones in the Hide by Category section to turn them off. They are still present, just not being rendered.

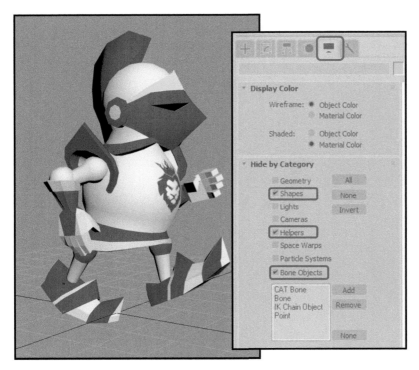

IMAGE 3.66 (Max File Save 3.19)

In the next chapter, you will model a knight on horseback. When we rig this character, we will use a rigging system called CAT Rig.

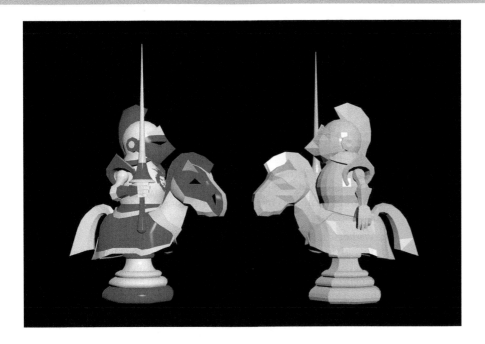

Character Modeling:
The Warhorse Knight

Topics in This Chapter

- Character Design
- Templates
- The Slate Editor

Concepts/Skills/Tools Introduced in This Chapter

- Polygon/Box Modeling
- Lathe, Extrude, Bridge

The Warhorse Knight

The next character we will model will be the Warhorse Knight. Just as with the knight and the castle modules, we will check with our Game Design Document and then find reference images.

Game Castle Keep, Blue vs. Red	
• Character	Warhorse Knight
• Who	In the game, the Warhorse Knight is a mobile character that will attack and defend an assigned position. The Warhorse Knight has the ability to attack other characters by trampling them or attacking with a jousting-type weapon. His movement is strong, skilled and confident
• What	The Warhorse Knight is a single-legged figure. The character has a cartoonish look. For his proportions, he stands, on horseback, four and one half "heads" high. He wears a stylized suit of armor (creating an air of confidence/tough guy). The knight is mounted on a horse that, instead of having four legs, has the "leg" of a chess player, a single post. The horse moves by hopping on the single post. The character has markings that can be used to assign the character to either the Blue or Red team (one character used for both teams with different skins)
• When	The character is middle to late medieval time period, refined armor and weapons, appropriate to the modeled environmental castle modules
• Where	The Warhorse Knight will fight at the ground or surface level (regular gravity) • Movement: WASD movement with jump, mouse turn 360 degrees. SHIFT for fast hopping • Animations: Idle, hop slow, hop fast, die
• Model	
	Poly limit: 6000 poly limit (low poly)
	Height limit: 2.5 m (scaled to castle environment: fits through doorways. climb stairs, etc.)
	Complexity: Can be simple, horse leg (post) deformable.

From the document, we can see our character has a unique manner of locomotion by hopping. This will be a nice animation. We can use our knight character model for the mounted figure and design an appropriate horse.

The next images are of medieval warhorses with armor. Note the armor pieces to protect the horse while allowing it to move freely through its normal range of motion. Our horse will not be moving normally, but it will still need to be based on real armor.

IMAGE 4.1 © Shutterstock. Used with Permission.

IMAGE 4.2 © Shutterstock. Used with Permission.

IMAGE 4.3 © Shutterstock. Used with Permission.

From these images and other reference, I started doing some rough concept sketches, incorporating our existing knight model and the chess piece base.

IMAGE 4.4

IMAGE 4.5

The GDD calls for the character to be 4.5 heads high. With the Knight character, we established how big a head height was. Remember he was three heads high. I used the same head height for the horse's body, making it two heads long and making the head one head height for the main mass. To counter the top of the character being too top heavy visually, I made the foot of the base wide enough to visually balance the top. It seems large enough to be a stable footing for the horse and knight.

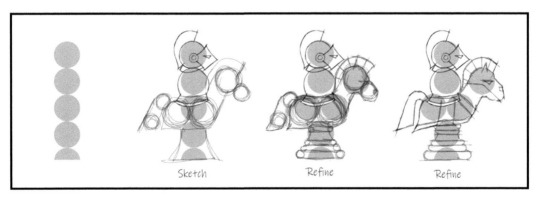

Sketch   Refine   Refine

IMAGE 4.6

To make the template images for the 3ds Max scene, again, the drawings for the front and side view need to have features that align horizontally. Image 4.7 shows the horizontal alignment of features. The two images after it are the front and left images I used as templates in 3ds Max to model the character.

IMAGE 4.7

IMAGE 4.8

As with the Knight model, I have created a series of template images for you to use to simplify the modeling process. The designs in the series of templates are slightly different than the images above as I made some design decisions during the modeling process for both aesthetic and functional reasons.

Setting up the Warhorse Knight Scene

Create a new scene in 3ds Max. Save the scene using the name "lastname_warhorse_01." The units should be set to meters in metric as that was the last setting used in the previous chapter. If you have changed them to something else, please change the settings back so the numbers used in your scent will correspond correctly with those in the book.

In the Scene Explorer, create a new layer named "templates." In the Front Viewport, create a Plane with parameters as shown in Image 4.9. This will be for the front view image template. Rename the plane object "warhorse_front_template." It should be in the templates layer of the Scene Explorer.

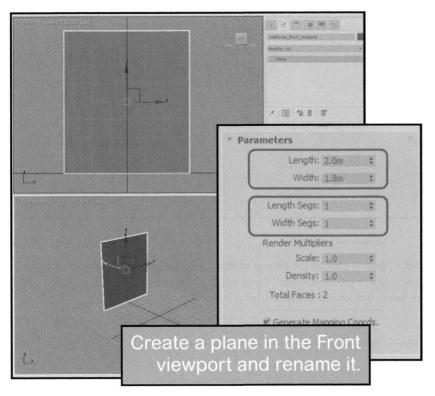

IMAGE 4.9

Open the Slate Material Editor. If there are materials from the last project still populating the window, click on the Edit tab on the top menu bar and select Clear View to delete them. Select a Standard material from the Material/Map Browser list on the left-hand side of the Editor to create a new material. Double-click on the new material to open the parameters column on the right-hand side.

Click on the Maps rollout as we did previously, and then, click on the Diffuse color's "No Map" button to open the Material/Map Browser window.

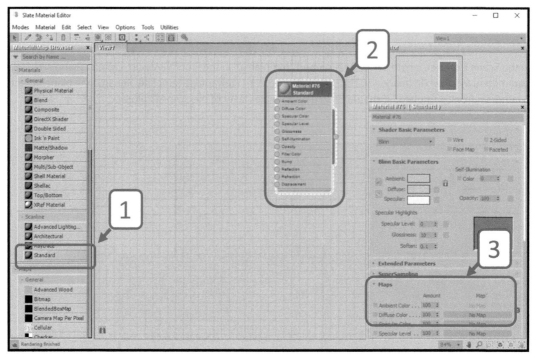

IMAGE 4.10

In the Material/Maps window, double-click on the Bitmap button. Then, navigate in the Select Bitmap Image File window to where you downloaded the template images on your computer (from www.3dsMaxBasics.com). Select the "warhorse_front_01.png" image file.

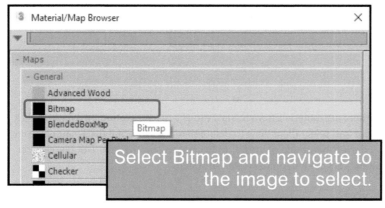

IMAGE 4.11

Assign the material to the plane by clicking the "Assign Material to Selection" button, then click the "Show Selected Material in Viewport" button. The material should be visible in the Perspective Viewport.

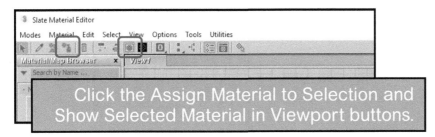

IMAGE 4.12

Next, Clone the Front template plane by holding down the Shift-key and dragging the object to the right. This plane will be for the Front view image. Rotate the new plane 90-degrees (type -90 in the Z-axis box in the Coordinate Display value box to rotate it. You might need a different value if the image is not facing you). Create another plane on the Y-axis with length and width values of 1.8 m. Position it as shown in Image 4.13. This will be for the Top view image.

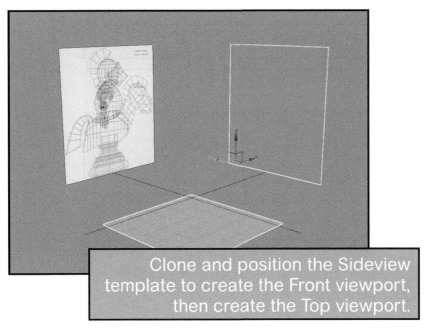

IMAGE 4.13

In the Slate Editor, create two new Standard materials as you did before. In the first, select the "warhorse_frontview_01.png" image for the Diffuse bitmap value, and in the second, select the "warhorse_topview_01.png" image for the Diffuse bitmap value.

Select the new cloned plane that has the side view image, then assign the Frontview image material to it. Assign the Topview image to the horizontal square plane. Make both visible in the viewport, and select the Show Shaded Material in Viewport icon button. Check the positioning of the planes to be sure they are not in the center modeling space where our model will be. Move the planes back away from the X-, Y-, Z-axis center. Lastly, rename the two new planes appropriately, and ensure they are properly located in the template layer of the Scene Explorer.

IMAGE 4.14

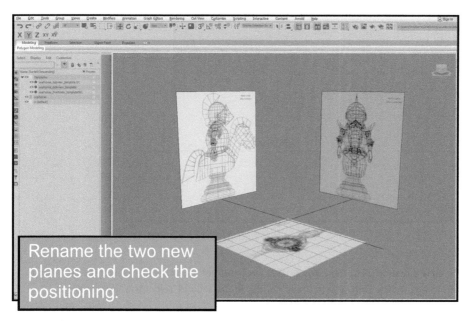

IMAGE 4.15 (3ds Max File Save 4.1)

Save the scene. We are ready to start modeling the placeholder.

162

Modeling the Placeholder

Again, we need to create a placeholder for the team to access the game development. As we did before, use Primitive shapes to create the horse. I used Capsules, cylinders, a box and a cone to create mine. Use your skill and model a quick placeholder. Link the parts with the base cone as the hierarchy root. Merge the Knight placeholder into the scene, without the legs. Position it on the horse's back and link the body to the horse body.

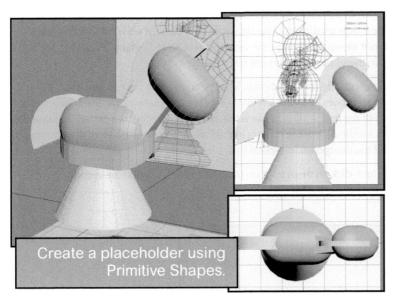

Create a placeholder using Primitive Shapes.

IMAGE 4.16

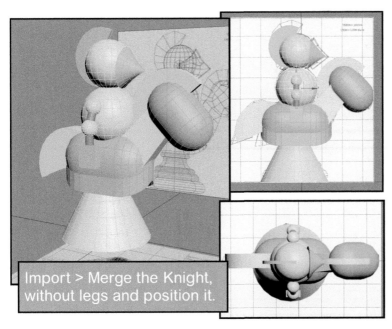

Import > Merge the Knight, without legs and position it.

IMAGE 4.17 (3ds Max File Save 4.2)

Modeling the Base Section

We will start the production model with the Base Section of the character, the part based on a chess piece. Since it is a round, cylindrical object, using a Line and the Lathe tool will be ideal to create it. We used the Lathe in Volume I to create the Corner Turret. If you remember, we created a 2D line and then adjusted the vertices to follow a pattern image. The Lathe tool then rotated the line around the center axis creating the 3D shape.

Select the Side view template plane. In the Slate Editor, change the Diffuse bitmap image to the "warhorse-base pattern_01.png" image. The image on the template shows the line pattern we want to follow while creating our line shape. In the Front Viewport, change the viewport setting to "Default Shading" and "High Quality" in the viewport setting in the upper left-hand corner of the viewport.

In the Command Panel, Select Shapes under the Create tab. Select the Line icon button. Maximize the Front Viewport if it is not already and zoom in on the line pattern of the template image. Start clicking to create the line at the bottom left of the image's line to place the first vertex. Follow the pattern to place the next seven vertices, ending with a right-click of the mouse. In the Parameters drop-down of the Command Panel, set the Steps parameter of the Interpolation section to 6.

Next, select all the vertices and right-click on them to open the Quad Menu. Change the vertices to the Bezier Corner type by selecting the type in the menu.

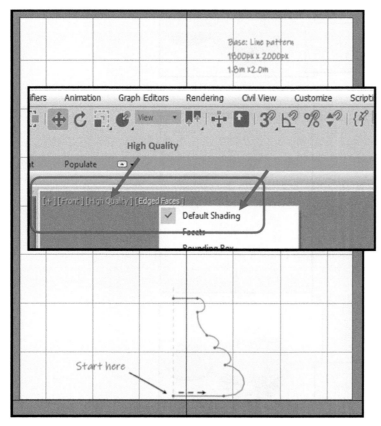

IMAGE 4.18 (3ds Max File Save 4.3)

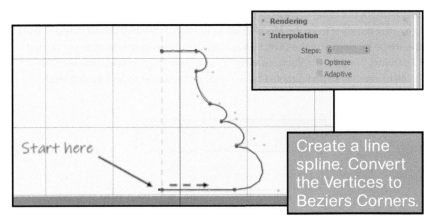

> Rendering

▾ Interpolation

Steps: 6

☐ Optimize

☐ Adaptive

Start here

Create a line spline. Convert the Vertices to Beziers Corners.

IMAGE 4.19

You might have noticed that the line pattern is not aligned with the grid line. When the character is complete, the base is not centered on the gridline. Select a vertex, the two Bezier handles will appear. Select one of the green handles, and move using the Select and Move tool. Adjust the handle, so the line starts moving in the direction of the curve. It will not move completely into position. Adjust the next vertex Bezier handle to get the curve closer. Repeat adjusting between the two until the curve closely approximates the pattern. While trying to move the handle, you might find the movement locked to either a horizontal or vertical direction. If this happens, right-click on a gray space on the Top Tool Bar. IN the pop-up menu, select Axis Constraints (if it is not already open on the Tool Bar). The Axis Constraint menu is a floating tool bar that can be anchored to the Top Tool Bar. To correct the locked vertex issue, click on the XY icon button in the Axis Constraints menu; the vertex will be able to move in both X and Y directions.

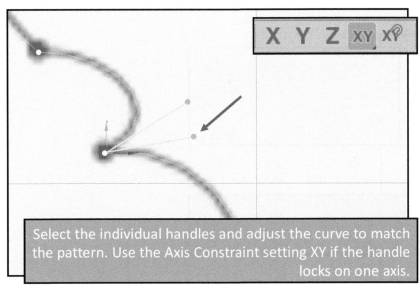

X Y Z XY XY

Select the individual handles and adjust the curve to match the pattern. Use the Axis Constraint setting XY if the handle locks on one axis.

IMAGE 4.20

Complete the vertex adjustment for the other vertices of the line, following the line pattern. When the line is adjusted correctly, add a Lathe modifier from the Modifier list to the line. The initial lathed shape is likely a bizarre shape. Adjust the shape by changing the Direction and Align buttons in the Parameters section on the Command Panel. For mine, the correct selections were "Y" and "Min." Right-click in the Modifier Stack, and select Collapse All to simplify to an Editable Poly. If the object reduced to an Editable Mesh, right-click and convert to an Editable Poly.

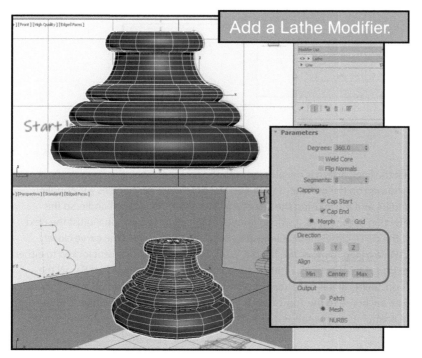

IMAGE 4.21 (3ds Max File Save 4.4)

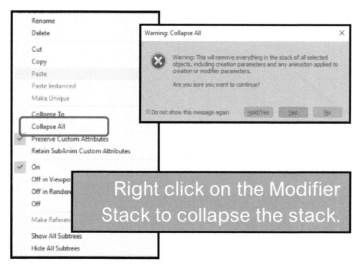

IMAGE 4.22

166

When the character is complete, we will be animating the horse body, possibly rotating it on an axis located at the top of the Base Section. We might create an unwanted visual gap between the two pieces. Extend the top with a single extrusion to minimize the added polygons. Select the top polygons and delete them. To select them quickly, drag a selection box across the top and sides of the object in the Front Viewport to select the polygons. Then, hold down the Alt-key and drag another selection box in the same viewport selecting all the side polygons, not the top ones. The subtraction will leave just the top ones, much faster and easier than individually selecting each polygon.

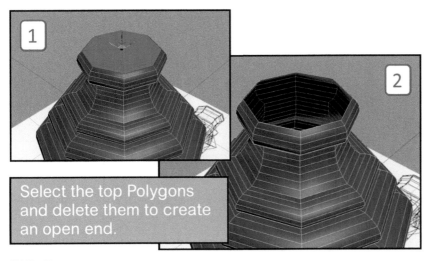

1

2

Select the top Polygons and delete them to create an open end.

IMAGE 4.23

Next, select the open-end edges using the Border selection tool. Hold the Shift-key and drag the border selection in the up direction of the Y-axis to raise new polygons. You only need to go a short distance; a quarter of the object's height will work. If it is too high, they will protrude through the horse body later. It is not a critical height. Rename the object "warhorse_base" in the Scene Explorer.

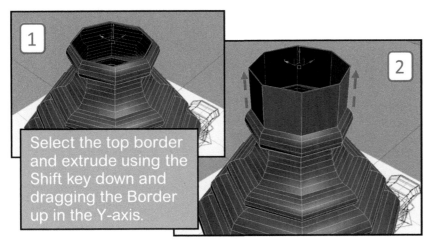

1

2

Select the top border and extrude using the Shift key down and dragging the Border up in the Y-axis.

IMAGE 4.24 (3ds Max File Save 4.5)

167

Modeling the Warhorse Body

The body of the warhorse will be a separate object from the base. Change the Front view template image to "warhorse_frontview_03.png" and the Sideview template image to "warhorse_sideview_03.png." Replace the Top view template image with "warhorse_topview_03.png." We will model the body, so it has a caparison, a medieval horse cloth covering with decorative trim.

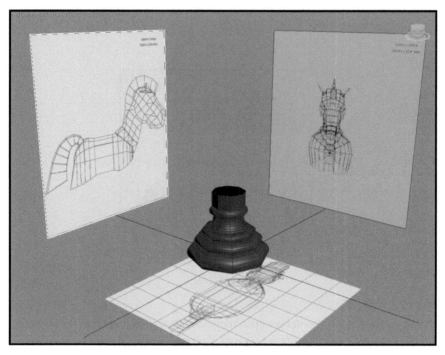

IMAGE 4.25 (3ds Max File Save 4.6)

Select one of the template planes by right-clicking on it, and select Object Properties from the menu. In the Object Properties window, uncheck the "Show Frozen in Gray" tick box. Repeat with the two remaining templates. Now, to make sure we do not accidentally select them when modeling, select the three template planes and right-click on them again, this time selecting "Freeze Selection." To make the images more accessible for viewing, turn off the warhorse_base layer in the Scene Explorer.

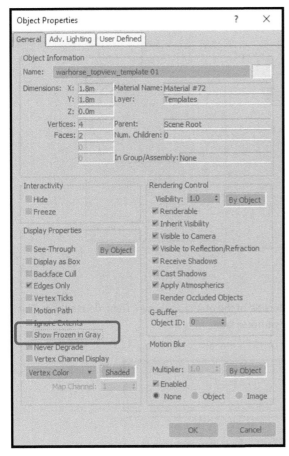

IMAGE 4.26

Start the body section by creating a Capsule in the Left Viewport. Change the Parameters to those shown in Image 4.27 and align the Capsule in Front and Left Viewport template images as shown. Rename the object "warhorse_body." Convert to an Editable Poly.

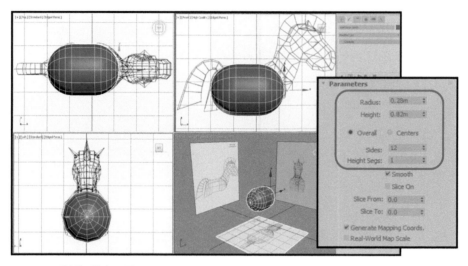

IMAGE 4.27 (3ds Max File Save 4.7)

In the Left Viewport, select the polygons on the underside of the object as shown. Then, delete them. This will allow us to model and shape the bottom of the warhorse later.

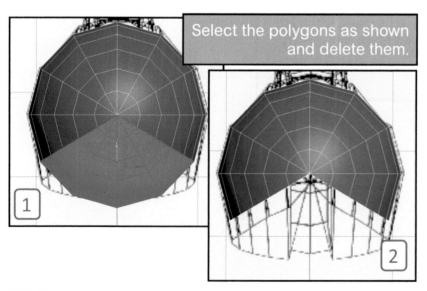

IMAGE 4.28

170

Rotate the Perspective Viewport to get a clear view of the front, head end of the object. Select the 18 polygons as shown in Image 4.29, then delete them to create an opening to extrude the collar and neck of the warhorse.

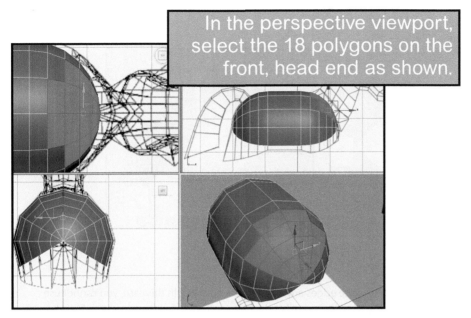

IMAGE 4.29

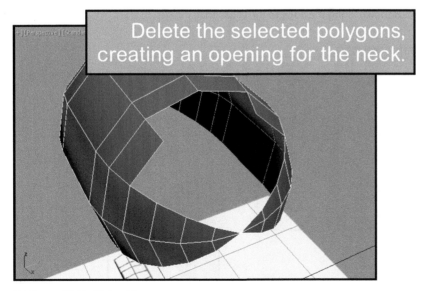

IMAGE 4.30 (3ds Max File Save 4.8)

In vertex mode, use the Target Weld tool to weld the two vertices indicated in the next image, welding them to the next vertex in the direction of the backend of the Warhorse Body as shown in Image 4.31.

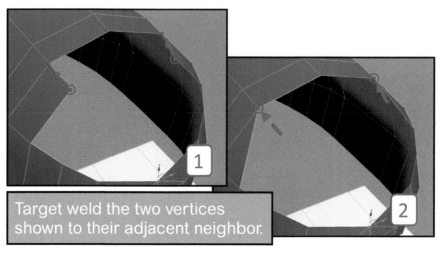

Target weld the two vertices shown to their adjacent neighbor.

IMAGE 4.31

Start to create the collar by selecting the edges around the new opening. In this case, you cannot use the convenient Border tool, you need to individually select them all while holding down the Shift-key. At the very front, there is a single vertex bridging the two halves of the mesh. If you use the border tool, the single vertex will allow the tool to select the edges on the underside of the mesh too.

Once selected, hold down the Shift-key and use the Select and Move tool to drag the edges as an extrusion toward the head as shown. Bring the edge to the collar edge image.

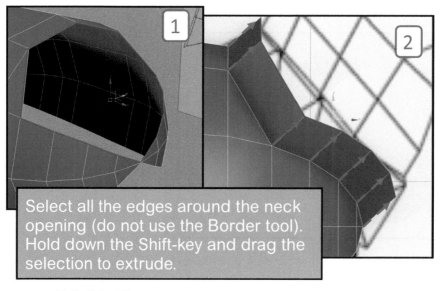

Select all the edges around the neck opening (do not use the Border tool). Hold down the Shift-key and drag the selection to extrude.

IMAGE 4.32 (3ds Max File Save 4.9)

We can save some time doing the next few steps if we delete half the object and only work on the remaining half. Select the polygons shown in Image 4.33 and delete them. This way we only have to work one side of the mesh.

Select the polygons as shown in the top viewport and delete.

IMAGE 4.33

Continuing to shape the horse collar, target weld the two vertices circled in Image 4.34 to their neighboring vertices as indicated.

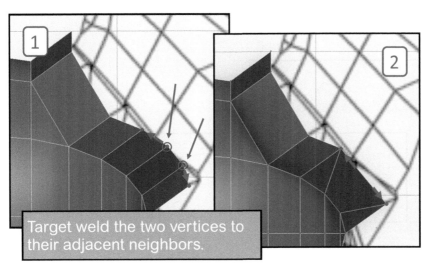

Target weld the two vertices to their adjacent neighbors.

IMAGE 4.34 (3ds Max File Save 4.10)

In the next step, we will be moving vertices to match the template image. Previously, we have right-clicked on the object and opened the Object Properties window to select the See-Through option. We can also use the Hot Keys to change the object to see-through by selecting the Alt-key +X-key. Use them to make the Warhorse Body see-through, and then, in the Front Viewport, start moving the individual vertices to their correct positions indicated by the template image. Begin moving the vertices along the top of the mesh.

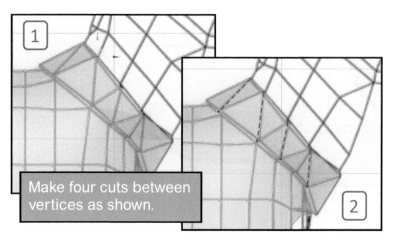

Make four cuts between vertices as shown.

IMAGE 4.35

Adjust the positions of the vertices in the collar area to match the template image. Note that there are missing edges between some of the vertices.

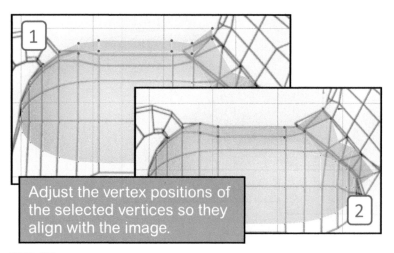

Adjust the vertex positions of the selected vertices so they align with the image.

IMAGE 4.36

Add the missing edges by making cuts with the Cut tool between the vertices shown in Image 4.37. Remember to turn on the 3d Snaps with Midpoint and Endpoint selected when using the Cut tool. When complete, turn off the 3d Snaps.

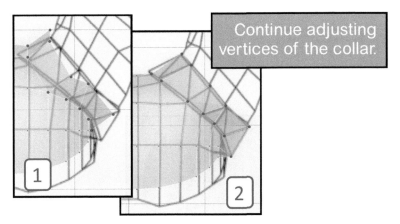

IMAGE 4.37 (3ds Max File Save 4.11)

Lastly, for this step, adjust the bottom row of vertices to match the template image. Adjust any other vertices that may be off the image marks before moving on to the next step.

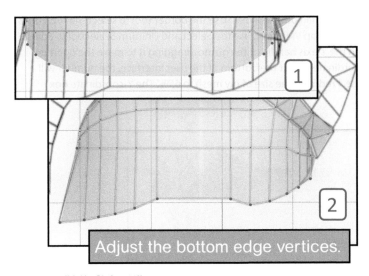

IMAGE 4.38 (3ds Max File Save 4.12)

Let's add back the other side of the mesh to adjust the collar. Select an Edge along the top of the mesh and then add a Symmetry Modifier. With the mesh back to whole, collapse the Modifier Stack in the Command Panel to an Editable Poly as we have done previously (Image 4.20). Click the Alt- and X-keys to undo the see-thorough property.

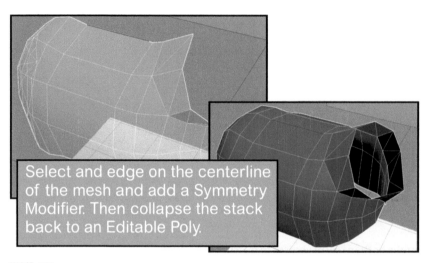

Select and edge on the centerline of the mesh and add a Symmetry Modifier. Then collapse the stack back to an Editable Poly.

IMAGE 4.39

A horse has narrower neck from side to side than our mesh has. Use the border tool to select the top edges along the neck opening on the mesh. In the Top Viewport, use the Select and Uniform Scale tool to adjust the width of the opening. Click only on the Y-axis handle of the gizmo, dragging it to make the opening width narrower. If you watch the Y-Coordinate box at the bottom of the user interface, the number will drop from 100% as you drag the mouse. I reduced the size of my mesh to 65%. The Y-coordinate box should be the only one changing.

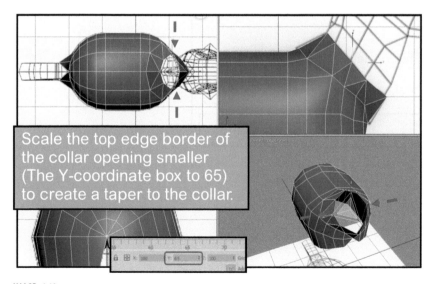

Scale the top edge border of the collar opening smaller (The Y-coordinate box to 65) to create a taper to the collar.

IMAGE 4.40

176

Complete the collar by adding some thickness to it. Select all the polygons around the collar area as shown and use the Extrude Caddy to add the thickness as shown in Image 4.41.

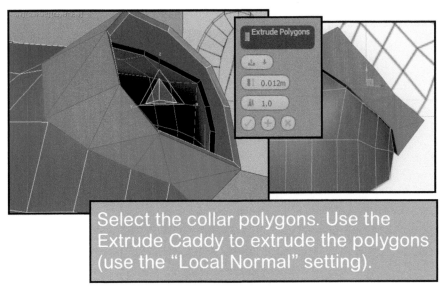

Select the collar polygons. Use the Extrude Caddy to extrude the polygons (use the "Local Normal" setting).

IMAGE 4.41

We will add a trim line along the bottom of the mesh like we did with parts of the Knight figure. Use the Swift Tool on the Ribbon menu in the Edit tab. Make the trim band approximately the width as shown in Image 4.42. This just adds a row of vertices on one side of the mesh.

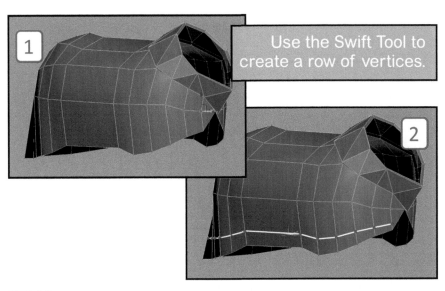

Use the Swift Tool to create a row of vertices.

IMAGE 4.42

Complete the trim band at the front end of the mesh below the collar opening. Make two cuts as shown in Image 4.43. Remember to turn on the 3d Snaps with Midpoint and Endpoint selected when using the Cut tool. When complete, turn off the 3d Snaps.

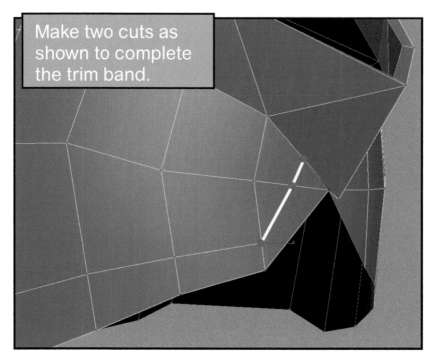

Make two cuts as shown to complete the trim band.

IMAGE 4.43

Delete the opposite side of the mesh, the side we did not add the cuts to.

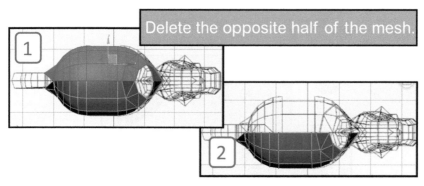

Delete the opposite half of the mesh.

IMAGE 4.44

Next, there is a vertex at the back end of the band that seems out of place. It is making the trim band uneven as it rounds the corner to go up toward where the tail will be. Carefully adjust the vertex to even up the trim band width as it wraps up the end. Be sure to adjust the position only in the Front and Left

Viewports, not in the Perspective Viewport. Moving the vertex in the Perspective Viewport can result in unwanted results.

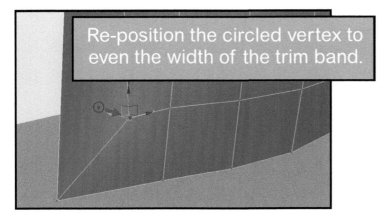

IMAGE 4.45

Select the bottom row of vertices, and extrude them as shown in Image 4.44.

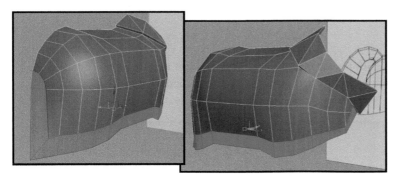

IMAGE 4.46

Use the Extrude Caddy to add the thickness to the trim band as shown.

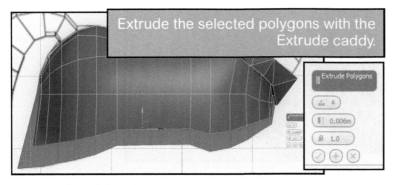

IMAGE 4.47 (3ds Max File Save 4.13)

Make the mesh whole again. Select a top edge, and apply the Symmetry Modifier. The changes we made to the trim band will now be on both sides of the mesh. Once again, Collapse the Modifier Stack to reduce the object to an Editable Poly.

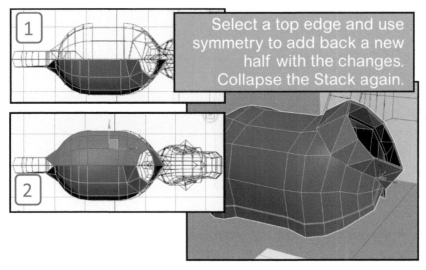

IMAGE 4.48

To complete the bottom of the mesh, we will close it using the bridge tool. First, select the inside border edge with the Border tool. Delete the border edge, removing the lip around the edge.

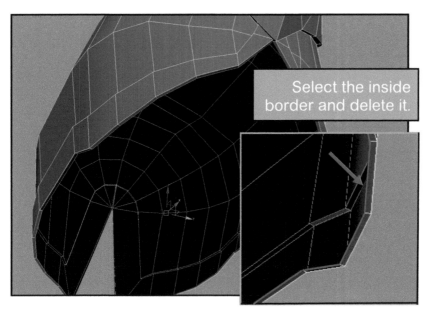

IMAGE 4.49

Click on two of the edges opposite each other, on each side of the mesh bottom. Open the Bridge Caddy. Change the settings to match the ones in Image 4.50. Continue to bridge the edges across the mesh opening to the tail end of the mesh.

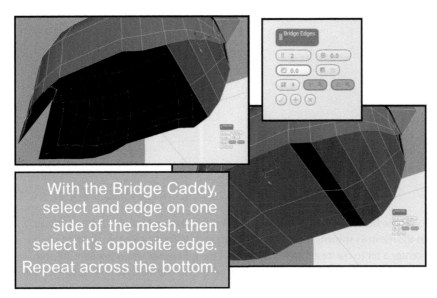

With the Bridge Caddy, select and edge on one side of the mesh, then select it's opposite edge. Repeat across the bottom.

IMAGE 4.50 (3ds Max File Save 4.15)

Close the front opening by selecting the triangle border edges and then clicking on the Cap icon button in the Command Panel.

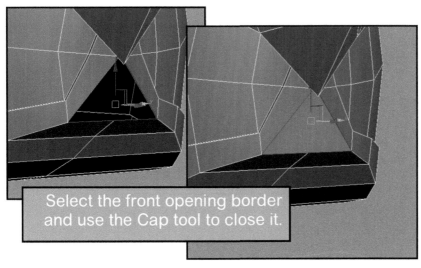

Select the front opening border and use the Cap tool to close it.

IMAGE 4.51

Repeat the same steps to close the opening at the tail end of the mesh.

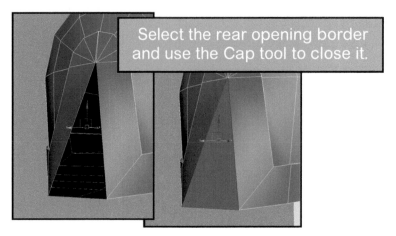

IMAGE 4.52

To break up the solid look of the bottom connecting to the mesh sides, use the Extrude Caddy to make a negative extrusion into the mesh as shown. Then, use the Select and Uniform Scale tool to bring the polygons in toward the center a bit to create a tapered lip around the perimeter. Using the extrude and scale tools instead of the Inset and scale tool maintains the look on the horizontal bottom and the vertical tail end piece.

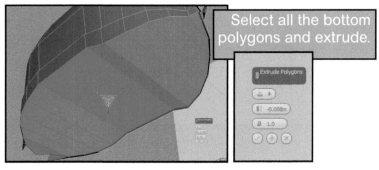

IMAGE 4.53

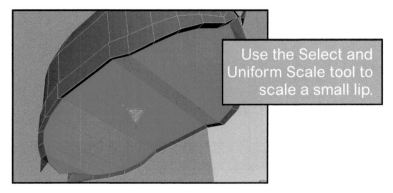

IMAGE 4.54 (3ds Max File Save 4.16)

The bottom of the mesh should flair outward a bit as is typical in the reference images gathered. Use the Select and Uniform Scale tool to widen the bottom two rows of the mesh using the Y-axis handle of the gizmo as shown. After widening the two rows, reselect just the ones on the bottom row and widen those a little more. This shaping helps to create a horse-like body shape with hips and shoulders. How much should you widen the vertices? You be the judge. Do what looks right to you.

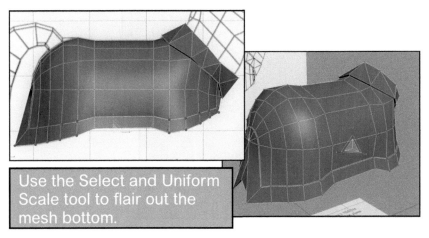

Use the Select and Uniform Scale tool to flair out the mesh bottom.

IMAGE 4.55 (3ds Max File Save 4.17)

Adding the Tail

The tail for the Warhorse will be extruded from the polygons on the rump area. Looking at the polygons, they really are not the right size – they are too big and wide. In the next image, you can see where I made some cuts to create a smaller base to extrude form. Make the same cuts, remember to turn on the 3d Snaps with Midpoint and Endpoint selected when using the Cut tool. When complete, turn off the 3d Snaps.

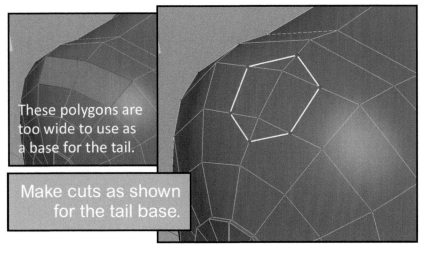

These polygons are too wide to use as a base for the tail.

Make cuts as shown for the tail base.

IMAGE 4.56 (3ds Max File Save 4.18)

Next, select the six polygons as shown in Image 4.57, and use the Inset tool to create an inner border of edges.

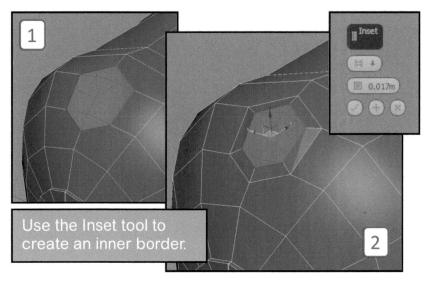

Use the Inset tool to create an inner border.

IMAGE 4.57

In the Front Viewport, move the polygons slightly toward the center of the mesh to recess them from the rest of the surface. This will help to make the tail not look like it is just growing directly out of the caparison covering. The template images will not reflect this step. This is a revision we are making as we model.

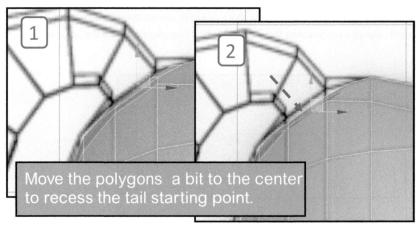

Move the polygons a bit to the center to recess the tail starting point.

IMAGE 4.58

While still in Polygon mode, use the Extrude Caddy to start extruding the tail from the body as in Image 4.59.

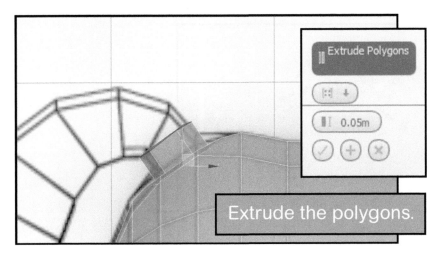

Extrude the polygons.

IMAGE 4.59 (3ds Max File Save 4.19)

Adjust the vertices to follow the pattern on the template image. Select the row of vertices, and use the rotate tool to rotate counterclockwise to match the angle of the next row of vertices in the template image. Then, move them into position with the Select and Move tool. They do not need to exactly match the template image.

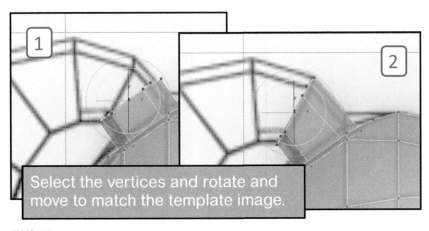

Select the vertices and rotate and move to match the template image.

IMAGE 4.60

Repeat the same steps to grow the tail along the template image. Extrude the polygons, rotate them to the next angle and then move into position. You might have noticed the width of the vertices increases with each new step. You might want to use the Select and Scale tool to assist with the widening. Again, the vertices do not need to exactly follow the template image, just be fairly close.

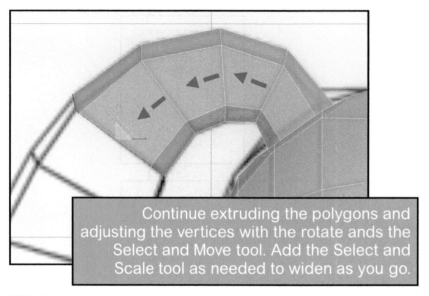

IMAGE 4.61

As you near the tip of the tail, you might need to do a bit more adjusting of the vertices to match the template image. This will complete the modeling of the Warhorse body and tail. All that is left is the head and neck.

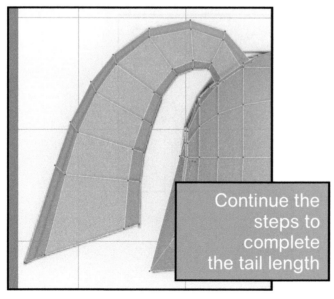

IMAGE 4.62

IMAGE 4.63 (3ds Max File Save 4.20)

Modeling the Warhorse Head

We will model the head as a separate object, and when finished, attach it to top the body with the neck, resulting in a single body mesh. To begin the head, create a box with parameters shown in Image 4.64.

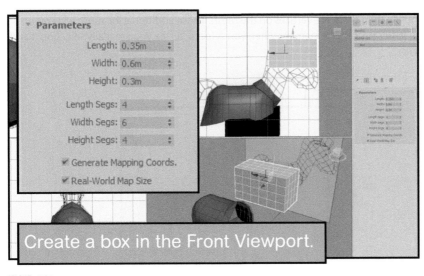

IMAGE 4.64

Use the Select and Rotate and Select and Move tools to position the new box over the head in the template image as shown in Image 4.65.

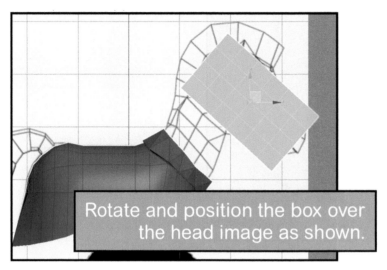

IMAGE 4.65

Turn off the warhorse_body layer in the Scene Explorer. Convert the box primitive to an Editable Poly. We will model the head mainly by repositioning the existing vertices. In the Front Viewport, move the vertices to match the locations on the template image as shown in Image 4.66. Notice there are more vertex intersections on the template than there are vertices on the mesh. Those additional locations will come into play in the next step in this process. Remember when you select a vertex you are really selecting it and the four aligned behind it.

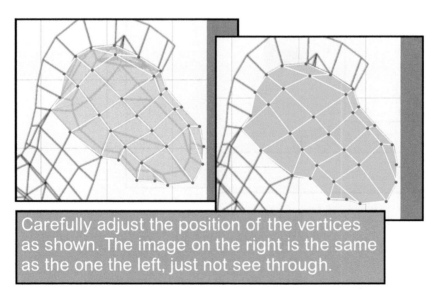

IMAGE 4.66

After carefully positioning the vertices, select the two outside rows of vertices on either side of the head as shown. In the Left Viewport, drag a selection box to select the first row of vertices, then hold down the Ctrl-key as you drag a second selection box over the other row of vertices to add the second row.

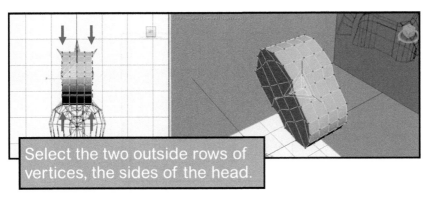

Select the two outside rows of vertices, the sides of the head.

IMAGE 4.67

Use the Select and Scale tool to scale the vertices inward toward the center of the head mesh. Watch the vertices as they move for when they align with the line intersections on the template image. I was also keeping an eye on the Coordinate Display boxes at the bottom of the UI window. My vertices appeared to align with the template at a reduction of 64-degrees in the Coordinate Display boxes. Concentrate on aligning the ring of vertices one row in from the outside edge.

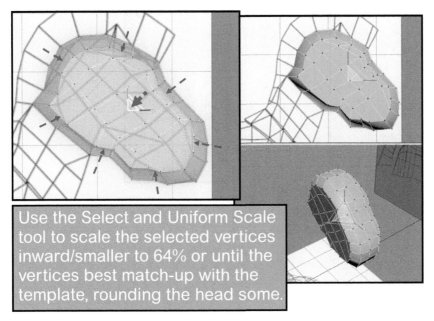

Use the Select and Uniform Scale tool to scale the selected vertices inward/smaller to 64% or until the vertices best match-up with the template, rounding the head some.

IMAGE 4.68 (3ds Max File Save 4.22)

The next few steps will be easier if we only have to make them on one side of the mesh. Go ahead and select the left half of the head in Polygon or Vertex mode and delete it.

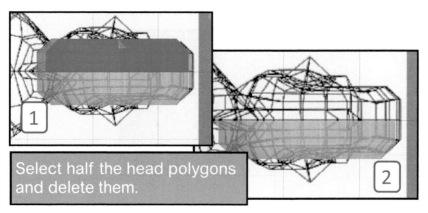

Select half the head polygons and delete them.

IMAGE 4.69

Scaling down the outside rows of vertices on the two outside faces of the mesh aligned the inner border of vertices, but it left most of the others off their targets on the template. Take a few minutes and carefully relocate those that are off-target back on to their proper locations. This will help with the next few steps.

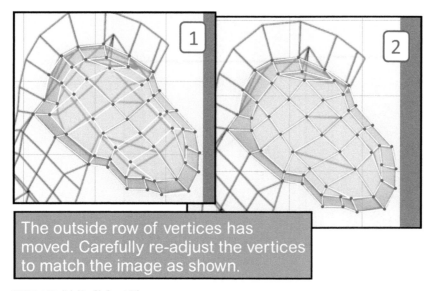

The outside row of vertices has moved. Carefully re-adjust the vertices to match the image as shown.

IMAGE 4.70 (3ds Max File Save 4.23)

The front of the warhorse head, the face, will have a piece of armor protection called a chamfron. We will create it by extruding polygons on the existing mesh. Before doing so, we need to make two cuts in the mesh. The first will create a triangular eye hole in the chamfron, and the second will define part of the shape along the bottom edge. Make the cuts as shown in Image 4.71. Remember to turn on the 3d Snaps with Midpoint and End Point active. When complete, turn off the 3d Snaps.

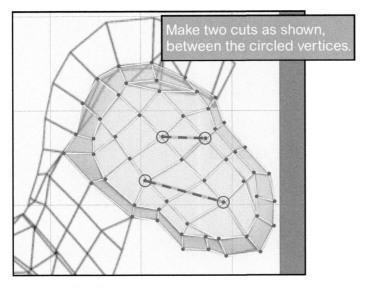

Make two cuts as shown, between the circled vertices.

IMAGE 4.71 (3ds Max File Save 4.24)

Next, select the polygons shown in Image 4.72. Be sure to select the polygons on the front and back of the mesh and to not select the polygons where the eyes, nose nostril and ear holes are.

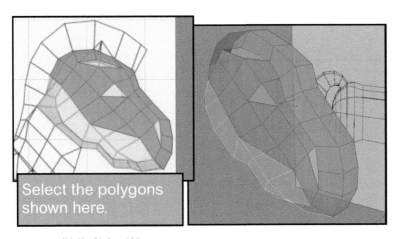

Select the polygons shown here.

IMAGE 4.72 (3ds Max File Save 4.26)

Extrude the polygons with the Extrude Caddy in the Local Normal setting using the parameters shown in Image 4.73. The extrusion will move the perimeter vertices beyond those in the template image. That is alright. Again, we do not need to exactly follow the template; just be close to get the general shapes correct.

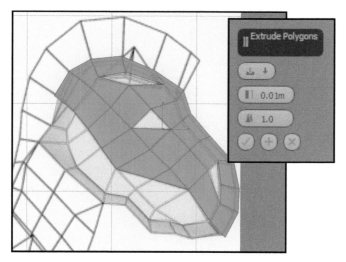

IMAGE 4.73 (3ds Max File Save 4.25)

The recess for the ear to protrude from needs some reshaping. Zoom into the area to see it better. Image 4.74 shows how the vertices are before moving them. The red arrows indicate the direction each group needs to move. Moving these vertices may take more than a few minutes. You might want to save the file before starting the repositioning of vertices, so you can have a place to restart if things get messed up beyond repair.

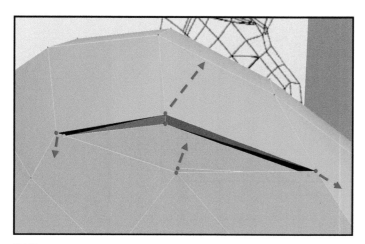

IMAGE 4.74

Image 4.75 shows where to move the vertices. Move the top two vertices first. They will help to align the others. Note the white dotted lines show the alignment relative to the surrounding vertices. The end vertices move to be in a straight-line alignment with the ones to either side and the top vertex. The resulting shape is an upside-down "V" shape, like a chevron.

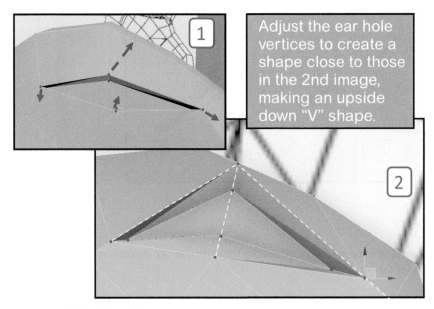

1

Adjust the ear hole vertices to create a shape close to those in the 2nd image, making an upside down "V" shape.

2

IMAGE 4.75 (3ds Max File Save 4.27)

Once the vertices are all in position, switch to Polygon mode and select the inner polygon. Extrude it with the Extrude Caddy. It will extrude out at a near horizontal angle.

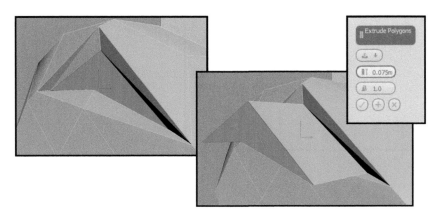

Extrude Polygons

0.075m

1.0

IMAGE 4.76 (3ds Max File Save 4.28)

Switch to Vertex mode and select the four vertices that were just extruded. Use the Weld Caddy to weld the four vertices into one vertex.

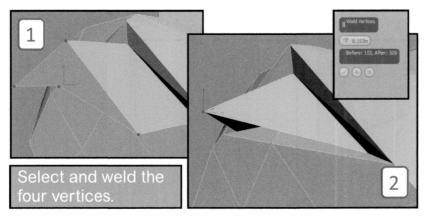

Select and weld the four vertices.

IMAGE 4.77

In the Front Viewport, use the Select and Move tool to move the vertex up into position as indicated by the template image for the tip of the ear.

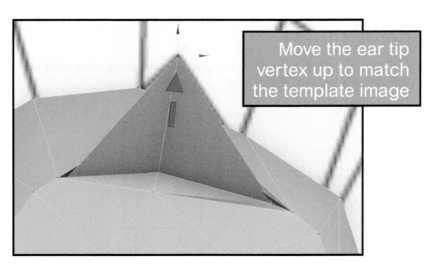

Move the ear tip vertex up to match the template image

IMAGE 4.78 (3ds Max File Save 4.29)

With the ear done, we can add the Symmetry Modifier to return the mesh to its whole. Select an edge along the midline and add the Symmetry Modifier. When it is whole again, collapse the Modifier Stack.

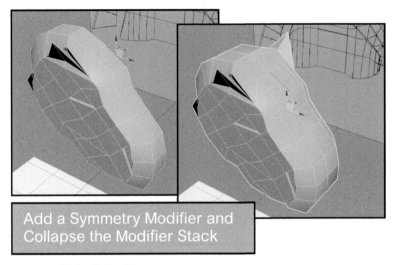

Add a Symmetry Modifier and Collapse the Modifier Stack

IMAGE 4.79 (3ds Max File Save 4.30)

Next, we will shape the head to be more horse-like. Select the vertices as shown in Image 4.80.

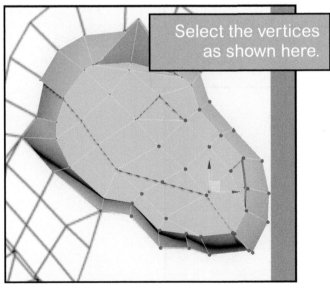

Select the vertices as shown here.

IMAGE 4.80

In the Top Viewport, use the Select and Uniform Scale tool to bring the selected vertices closer to the centerline, using the Y-axis handle. My scaling was 80% of the starting position and seen in the Coordinate Display. This will start to create the muzzle part of the head.

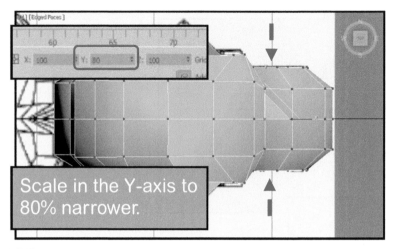

IMAGE 4.81

Next, select the five vertices shown in Image 4.82. We will widen the head here where the jaw and cranium part of the skull would be.

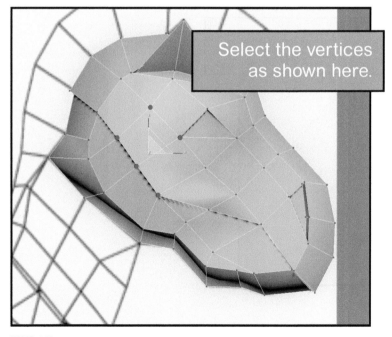

IMAGE 4.82

196

Again, in the Top Viewport, use the Select and Uniform Scale tool in the Y-axis to widen to 122% wider.

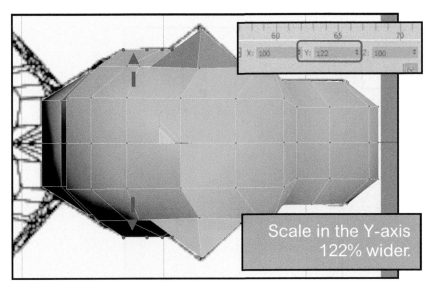

Scale in the Y-axis 122% wider.

IMAGE 4.83

The next area to shape is the top of the nose and face. Select the vertices shown in Image 4.84.

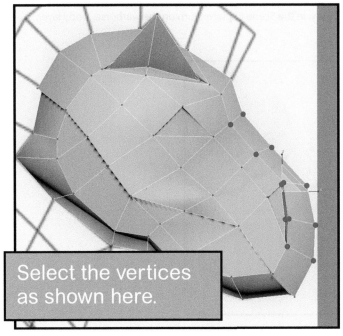

Select the vertices as shown here.

IMAGE 4.84

This time, in the Top Viewport, scale the vertices in the Y-axis to 85% of the starting positions. This will finish the shaping of the head. If you would like to tweak it some more, feel free to!

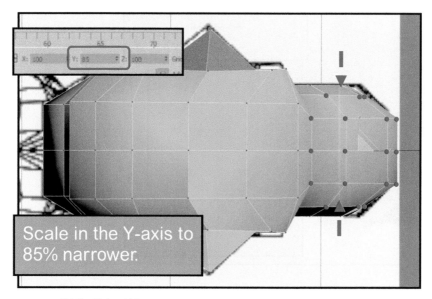

Scale in the Y-axis to 85% narrower.

IMAGE 4.85 (3ds Max File Save 4.31)

Connecting the Head to the Body

We are ready to attach the head to the body. In the Scene Explorer, turn on the warhorse_body layer.

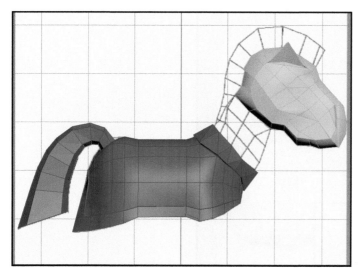

IMAGE 4.86 (3ds Max File Save 4.32)

Rotate the Perspective Viewport, so you can view the underside of the head object. Select the four polygons as shown in Image 4.87. These will be where the neck will connect to the head. Delete the four polygons. Note that the new opening has eight vertices, eight edges.

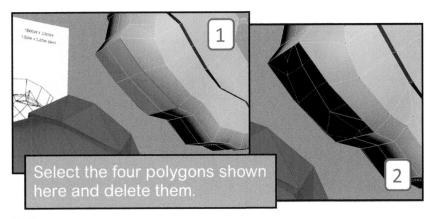

IMAGE 4.87

Next, select the four corner vertices of the opening. Use the Select and Uniform Scale tool to move the four vertices toward the center a bit, just enough to soften the square corners. This will result in a neck that is more oval than rectangular. I scaled my vertices to 80% of the starting size.

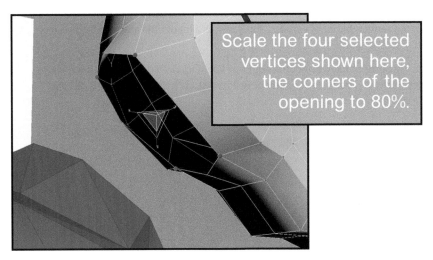

IMAGE 4.88 (3ds Max File Save 4.33)

Before we can connect the two meshes with a neck, we need to attach them to one mesh. Select the warhorse_body mesh, then click on the Attach button in the Command Panel. Click on the head mesh to complete the attachment. The two meshes are now one object, even though they appear to be separate objects. The color of the piece that is attached to the first piece becomes the color of the first piece, inheriting its properties.

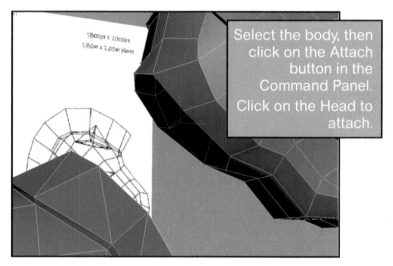

IMAGE 4.89

Connecting the two parts of the mesh is relatively simple. Because the head opening has eight vertices/eight sides and the warhorse_body has the same number of vertices/edges, the bridge tool can quickly connect the two. Knowing this was going to be part of the modeling construction, I planned ahead so the two sections would have the same number of vertices. This saves us a lot of time and aggravation trying to match up openings with different counts.

On the head section, use the Border tool to select the edges of opening. Hold down the Ctrl-key while selecting the edges of the warhorse_body neck opening. To connect, click on the Bridge Caddy and change the settings to match those in Image 4.90.

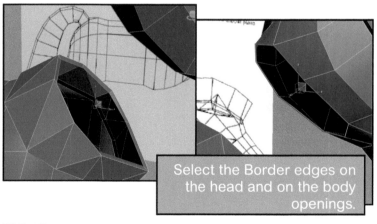

IMAGE 4.90

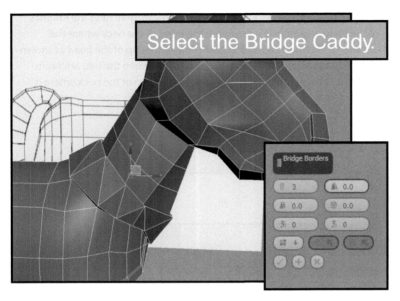

IMAGE 4.91

Use the Alt- and X-keys to switch the model to see-through. As we did previously, adjust the vertices to come close to matching the template image.

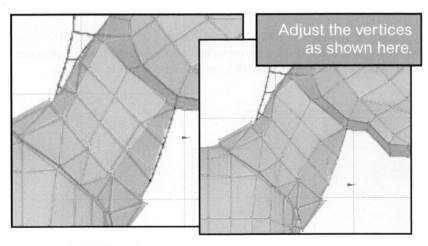

IMAGE 4.92 (3ds Max File Save 4.34)

Now that the head and body are connected with the neck, we can add the comb, matching the Knight's comb on the helmet, to the top of the head and extend it down the top edge of the neck where the horse's mane would be. In the Perspective Viewport, select the centerline of the top of the head as shown in Image 4.93 along with the centerline of the top of the neck edges. Select between the two arrows in the image. The comb will start at the top of the forehead and continue to the base of the neck where it connects to the body.

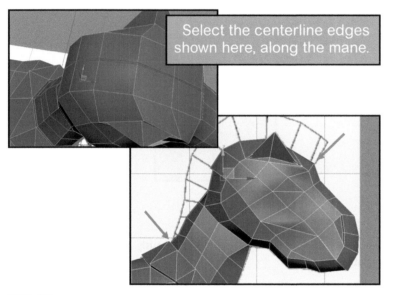

IMAGE 4.93

With the edges still selected, click on the Chamfer tool in the Command Panel. Use the settings as shown in Image 4.94 to create two parallel splines running along the centerline. It also creates a triangle of polygons at the ends of the centerline edge selection. Remember to click the green check mark to accept the chamfer.

IMAGE 4.94 (3ds Max File Save 4.35)

Zoom in on the front end of the new chamfered area. The tool created five polygons. To clean it up a little and simplify it, target weld the middle row of vertices to the one below it, leaving two triangles. The other end of the chamfer on the centerline has the same five triangle configuration. Perform the same operation on those to reduce them to two triangles too.

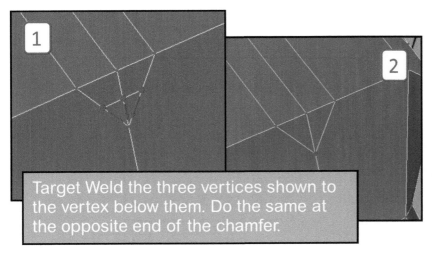

IMAGE **4.95** (3ds Max File Save 4.36)

Time to create the comb. Select the polygons along the two sides of the centerline that we chamfered. Select the two front triangles on the forehead too. Do not select the ones at the other end of the chamfer. They are not part of the comb.

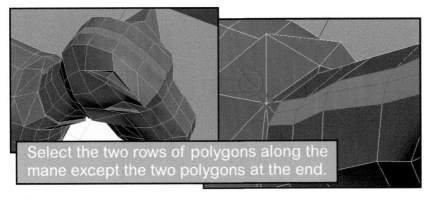

IMAGE 4.96

With the polygons selected, open the Extrude Caddy and extrude the polygons with a Local Normal setting. Change the settings to those in Image 4.97. They should bring the top edge of the comb close to the comb line on the template image.

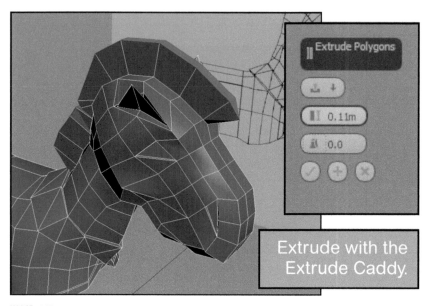

IMAGE 4.97

Use the Alt and X-key again to make the mesh see-through. You guessed it, in the Front Viewport, adjust the vertices to match the comb image on the template image.

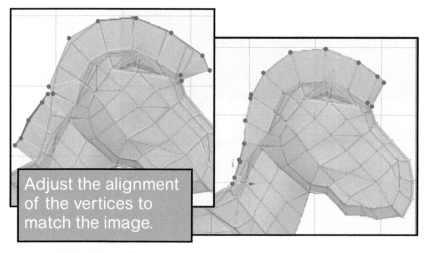

IMAGE 4.98 (3ds Max File Save 4.37)

The last step will be to weld the vertex groups along the comb top edge into single vertices. While still in the Front Viewport, use the Weld Caddy to weld the groups of three vertices into single vertices as shown in the next image. The comb will match the Knight's comb, echoing the shape – a good design feature.

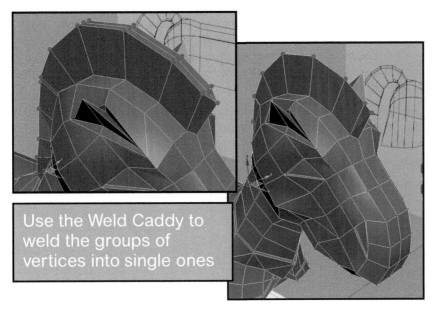

Use the Weld Caddy to weld the groups of vertices into single ones

IMAGE **4.99** (3ds Max File Save 4.38)

That completes the modeling of the Warhorse Body. We will need to unwrap and texture it, and mount the Knight on its back. Then, we can rig it for animation.

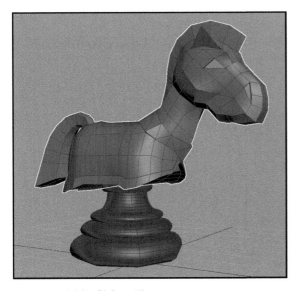

IMAGE **4.100** (3ds Max File Save 4.39)

Unwrap UVW: Quick Peel

There are several methods used to unwrap meshes for applying texture maps. For the Castle Modules in Volume I and the Knight, we used the basic Normal Mapping method. That method works well when unwrapping Hard modeled meshes having geometric shapes. For organic shapes with more complex rounded and concave surfaces, other methods often are more efficient to create the desired UVWs. Two of these other unwrapping techniques are the Pelt and Peel methods. We will use the Peel method for the Warhorse Base section. It is a simple shape to unwrap that will allow you to see and understand the basic process of using the Quick Peel approach. You might find the method easier and quicker. Remember, there are different methods for different needs.

In the Scene Explorer, turn off the Templates and warhorse_body layer. Turn on the warhorse_base layer. Select the mesh and add an Unwrap UVW modifier. Select Vertex Mode in the Unwrap UVW modifier (not in the Editable Poly layer of the Modifier Stack).

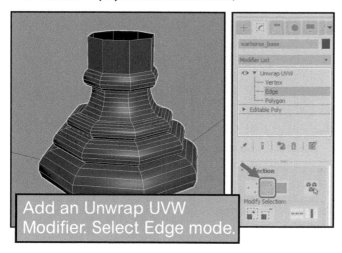

IMAGE 4.101 (3ds Max File Save 4.40)

Select one edge segment along the front, vertical spline as shown in Image4.102, then click on the Loop tool icon button in the Selection section of the Modifier panel.

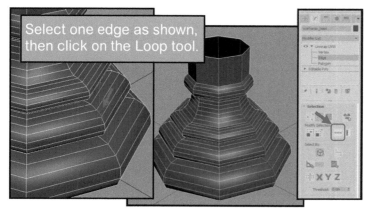

IMAGE 4.102

206

The red line indicates the selection you just made. It represents where we want to create a seam to unwrap the mesh. The red highlight extends down the mesh and continues under to the center vertex on the bottom of the mesh. Rotate the Perspective Viewport to view the bottom of the mesh. Hold down the Alt-key and select the red segments highlighted in Image 4.103 which will remove them from the selection. The bottom will be a separately mapped section, so our selection needs to stop at the bottom edge as shown.

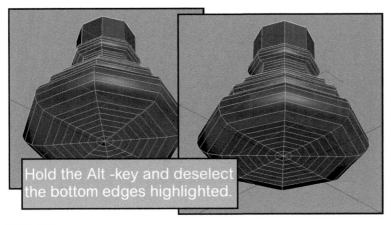

Hold the Alt -key and deselect the bottom edges highlighted.

IMAGE 4.103

While our line segments are still selected, convert them to a single seam by clicking on the Convert Edge Selection to Seams icon button in the Peel section of the Unwrap UVW Modifier column. The red line segments will turn blue, indicating they are now a seam.

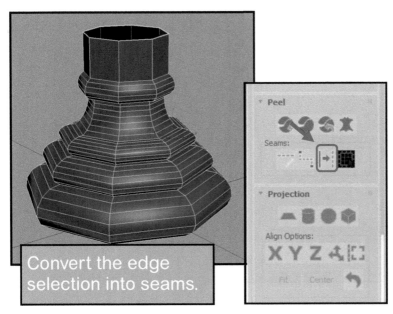

Convert the edge selection into seams.

IMAGE 4.104

Next, create a seam for the bottom of the mesh. Using the same process as we just did, start by selecting an edge segment as shown in Image 4.105. Click on the Loop tool to complete the selection. Convert the selection to a seam using the Convert Edge Selection to Seams icon button.

IMAGE 4.105

Create one more seam at the top of the bottom rounded shape. By doing this, we can make the bottom section a separate color from the rest of the mesh. Use the same steps above to create the new seam. The areas defined by the seams create mesh clusters that we will edit in the Edit UVW window.

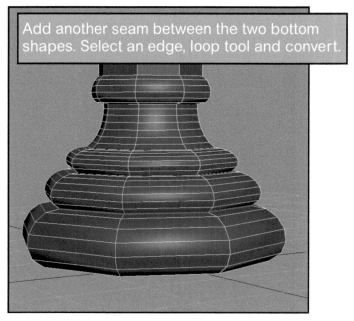

IMAGE 4.106

Create seams between the next two rings using the same steps and shown in Image 4.107.

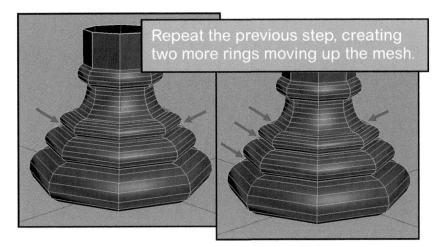

IMAGE 4.107

Add one more seam to the bottom of the top ring making the top ring and the polygons above it all one cluster.

IMAGE 4.108

The mesh is now unwrapped with seams we defined. The next step will take us to a familiar place, the Edit UVW window. However, we will be using it differently. Switch to Polygon mode in the Unwrap UVW modifier Selection section. Click the Ignore Backfacing icon button off. Select the entire mesh.

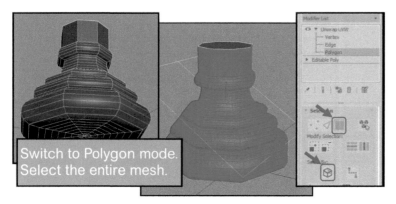

IMAGE 4.109 (3ds Max File Save 4.41)

Open the Edit UVWs window as we have done before, clicking on the button in the modifier column. The mesh clusters for the object will appear. Although there is no indication, all the clusters are all connected at the seams. To separate the clusters, click the Break icon button. Nothing will appear to have happened, but it did, the clusters are now all separate units.

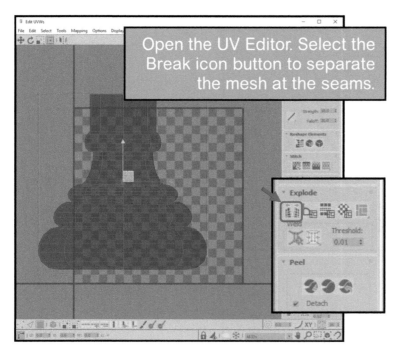

IMAGE 4.110

Next, select the Quick Peel icon button further down the Edit UVWs right side column. This will separate the mesh clusters across the window stage area.

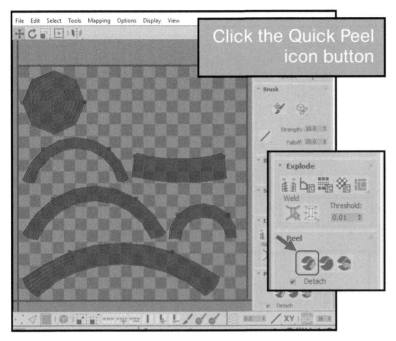

IMAGE 4.111

We are ready to arrange the clusters, so they are mapped with the appropriate textures. In the upper right-hand corner of the Edit UVWs window, select the Pick Texture option from the drop-down menu. In the pop-up window, select Bitmap by double-clicking on it. When the Select Image window opens, navigate to the knight_texture_01.png image we used in Chapter 2 to texture the knight and select it.

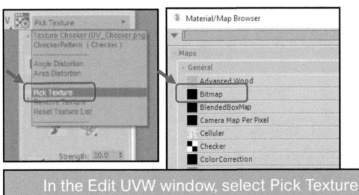

IMAGE 4.112

Move and scale the clusters to the appropriate color areas of the texture map. The round base and the narrow band of the base shape both go in the red area while the remaining cluster will be white, so it gets moved and scaled to fit into the white area.

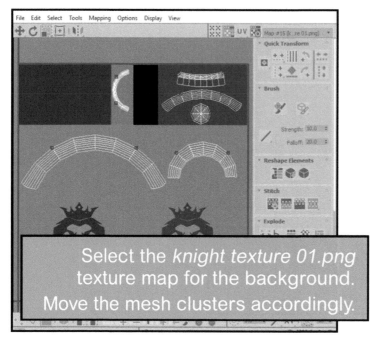

IMAGE 4.113

Click on the M-key of the keyboard to open the Material Editor (or select the icon button on the Top Tool Bar). Create a new material using the knight texture 01.png image. Assign the new material to the mesh.

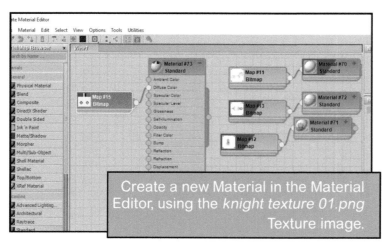

IMAGE 4.114

212

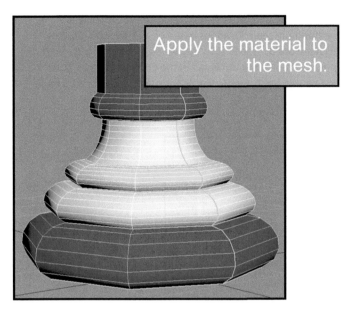

That completes the unwrapping and texturing of the Base. We used the Quick Peel technique to unwrap the object. This was a simple shape to use the technique on. It was chosen, so you could easily understand the process. Quick Peel is typically used the unwrap characters with complex organic shapes. Although we did not, you can still name the mesh clusters to facilitate selection on complicated models.

Next, we will unwrap the Warhorse Body. In the Scene Explorer, turn off the warhorse_base layer and turn on the warhorse_body layer. Add an Unwrap UVW modifier to the mesh.

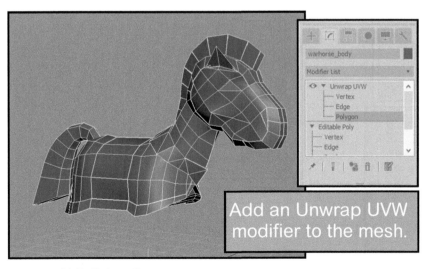

IMAGE 4.116 (3ds Max File Save 4.43)

Notice the green seam lines on the mesh. 3ds Max created these seams based on the original Primitive Capsule we used and by trying to select the optimum seam locations based on the polygon normals. There are not in the best locations. We will create our own seams. So that we are not fighting the existing seams, we can delete the existing ones by using a tool in the Utility tab of the Command Panel. The tool, the UVW Remove tool, will only work on an Editable Mesh. Right-click on the mesh, and convert it to an Editable Mesh.

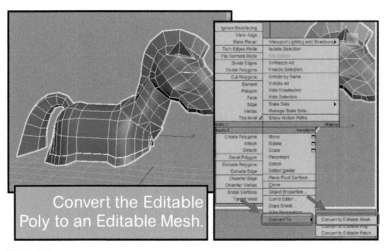

IMAGE 4.117

Back in the Modify Panel, select the Utility tab and select the "More…" button. In the Utilities pop-up window, select the UVW Remove tool. A new Parameters section will open at the bottom of the Utilities column. Select the UVW button. If the green lines were not removed, click on the mesh again and try the UVW button again.

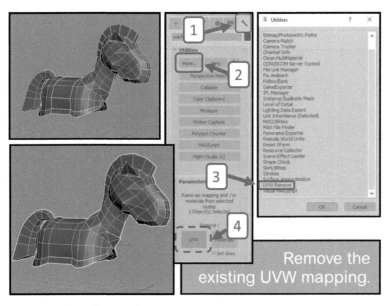

IMAGE 4.118 (3ds Max File Save 4.44)

214

As you did with the Castle modules and the Knight, create polygon selection sets and name them in the Create Selection Sets dialog box on the Top Tool Bar. Remember to hit the Enter-key to set the selection after typing in a name or it will not be there when you return to use it. In Image 4.119, you can see the list of sets I created doing my unwrapping. They are pretty straight forward. If you have a question of what should be included in a set, you can look forward to see images of the completed model (Images 4.121– 4.128) or download the corresponding 3ds Max file from the companion website (3dsMaxBasics.com). Take your time to carefully create the polygon sets.

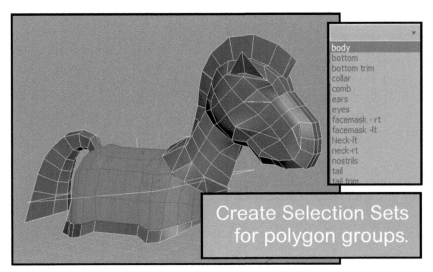

IMAGE 4.119

Once you have selected and named your polygon sets, you now have a choice for unwrapping. You can use the Normal Mapping that we previously used for the Castle Modules and the Knight, or you can use the Quick Peel technique. You can use a mix of the two. I used Quick Peel for the majority of the selection sets. Because all the clusters will be on solid colors on the texture map, we will not worry about texture detail fitting precisely as we did with the Castle modules. Map all the clusters, and move them outside the edit stage area.

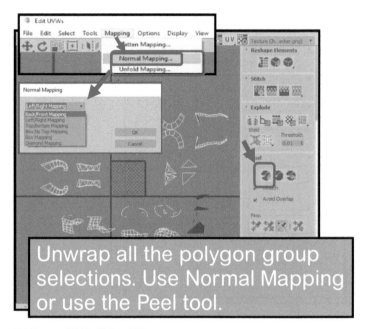

Unwrap all the polygon group selections. Use Normal Mapping or use the Peel tool.

IMAGE 4.120 (3ds Max File Save 4.45)

Remember to select the knight texture image 01 for the background image in the Edit UVW window as you did earlier if it is not already there and visible. When all the clusters have been mapped, move and scale them to their appropriate colors on the background texture image. Assign the material you created for the Base mesh to the warhorse_body. Take your time to work carefully.

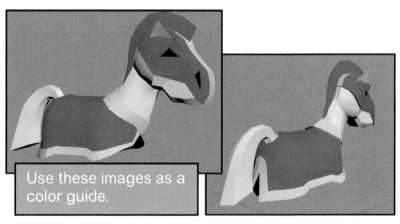

Use these images as a color guide.

IMAGE 4.121

216

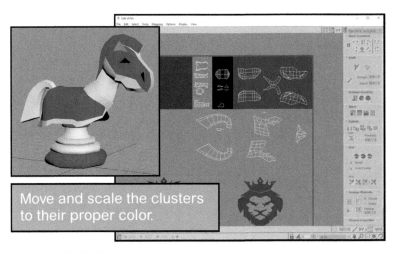

Move and scale the clusters to their proper color.

IMAGE 4.122 (3ds Max File Save 4.46)

If you used the Quick Peel button to create the cluster maps, you should have realized you did not crest the seams as you did when we used Quick Peel on the Base. After you created the selection sets of polygons that would have been the time to do the seams. However, as I said in the last paragraph, we do not have texture detail to be concerned with. We just needed the polygons to be mapped as groups or sets to be overlaid on solid colors. When the polygon clusters have all been scaled and moved to their proper positions, the warhorse_body is complete. In the Scene Explorer, turn the warhorse_base layer on to see the body and base together. To complete the model, we need to add the Knight model to our scene. Rather than model a whole new Knight character, we will use the one we already modeled. In the File tab of the Top Tool Bar, select Import>Merge.

Navigate to the final 3ds Max version of the Knight model and select it. In the Merge pop-up window, select all the Knight model parts except the legs, arms and template planes. Click OK to merge into your scene. Remember, you Merge a .max file into a 3ds Max scene, you Import a .3ds, .FBX or other formats into a 3ds Max scene.

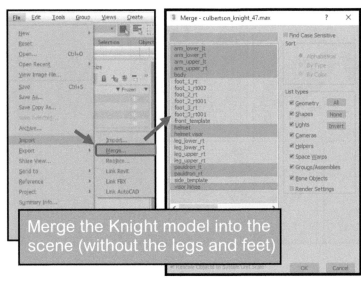

Merge the Knight model into the scene (without the legs and feet)

IMAGE 4.123

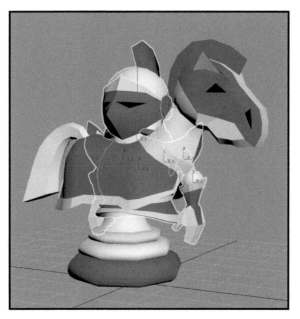

IMAGE 4.124

The Knight might appear in the wrong orientation to the Warhorse. Rotate and align properly, so it sits on the top of the horse back.

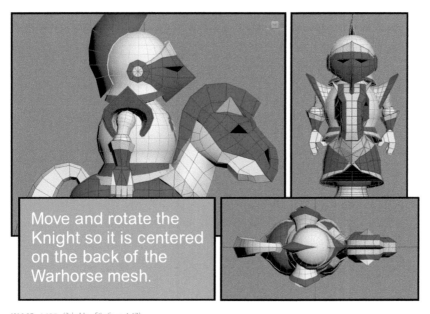

Move and rotate the Knight so it is centered on the back of the Warhorse mesh.

IMAGE **4.125** (3ds Max File Save 4.47)

The bottom edge of the Knight is probably penetrating the hip area of the Warhorse mesh. Make the warhorse see-through by pressing the Alt and X-keys together. Select the Knight's Body section. In the Modify Panel, go to the Editable Poly Vertex mode. Select each of the vertices sown in the next image and move them as shown so they rise in the Y-axis direction, gradually rising above the Warhorse's mesh. Switch back to the non-see-through state of the Warhorse to check the progress. I rotated the lower right arm of the Knight to get a better view as I worked. When complete the gold trim on the Knight's body should follow the curve of the Warhorse's back.

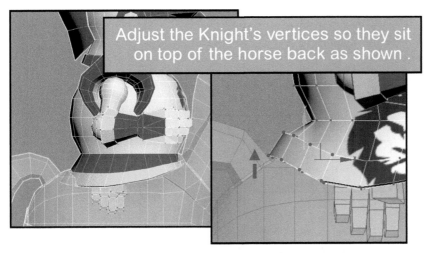

IMAGE 4.126

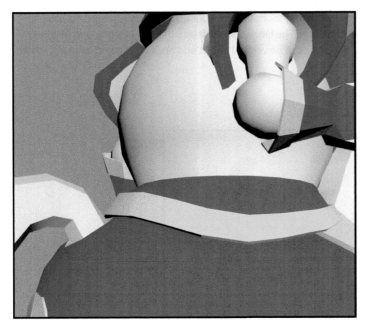

IMAGE **4.127** (3ds Max File Save 4.48)

That completes the modeling and texturing of the Warhorse Knight character. In the next chapter, we will rig the model for animation.

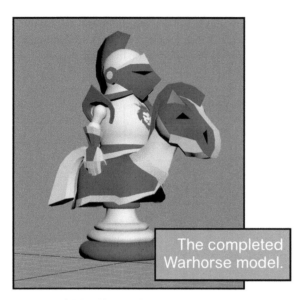

IMAGE 4.128 (3ds Max File Save 4.49)

Chapter 4 Exercise: The Warhorse Weapons

The Warhorse Knight can be equipped with different weapons. One weapon, the lance was a common weapon. Lances were used in battle and in jousting tournaments. Your assignment is to model a lance for our Warhorse Knight in the style of our character. The lance should fit into the knight's grip and be able to be positioned, so by rotating the arm, the lance can be vertical at rest and horizontal when in attack mode.

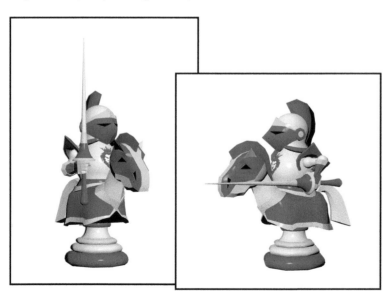

IMAGE 4.129

Character Rigging: Skin and the CAT Rig

Topics in This Chapter

- 3ds Max Biped
- CAT: Character animation Toolkit.

Concepts/Skills/Tools Introduced in This Chapter

- Creating and assigning materials with the Slate Editor
- Review of using the basic tools from Volume I

Character Rigging

We will continue with rigging characters, picking up where we left off with the Knight. We rigged him for animation using simple linking of objects and adding IK solvers for the limbs. As a project, you hand-animated the character by creating keyframes and adjusting the object positions. It was a very laborious task to complete. Perhaps the hardest thing to control when animating was the feet. As the character walked, his feet were likely sliding like it was walking on slippery ice. The feet did not anchor to the ground. The only way of fixing that movement with this rig is to keyframe almost every frame. Not fun at all.

For video games, we animate characters in cycles, short animated movements that the program code will repeat to create continuous, smooth movement. There is a better way of rigging characters that will have animated walk cycles than the basic linked rig. 3ds Max comes with two rigging system tools, Biped and CAT. Both are bone systems that create procedural figure rigs that can be used to rig characters including ones that require mesh deformation. These are characters where the mesh deforms or bends, for instance at a joint, like the elbow as it bends. This is accomplished by adding one of the 3ds Max two skeletal deformation tools, Skin or Physique to the mesh. The tool associates the mesh vertices to the bones in the rig. When a bone in the rig is rotated or moved, the vertices associated with that bone move with it, relative to the assigned weighting that has been assigned to it. It sounds complicated when explained that way. We will break it down into small digestible steps so you will understand what is happening and how you can control the results.

First, we will get an understanding of how the skeletal deformation tool Skin works. As stated above, 3ds Max comes with two skeletal deformation tool tools, Skin and Physique. When 3ds Max first came out, it was called 3ds Studio. At the time, it had the plugin Character Studio and had the tool Physique. Character Studio used a skeletal rig called Biped and used Physique to control the mesh deformations. It is a system that works but has limited controls. Later, the modifier Skin was added to the 3ds Max toolbox. It is a skin deformation tool with more controls than the earlier Physique tool. In recent years, Skin has become the more popular tool to use because of its abilities. Physique actually does a few things better than Skin, but Skin overall is the preferred tool. Because of that, and our limited space in the textbook, we will only be using the Skin Modifier in this book. Once you understand how Skin works, you might want to go take a look at Physique to see how it differs.

The Skin Modifier

To start the learning process for Skin, open 3ds Max to a new scene. Create a Capsule in the Left Viewport with the parameters shown in Image 5.1. The Capsule creation tool can be found in the Extended Primitives in the Create tab of the Command Panel. **Be sure to change the Height Segs parameter to 40 or more**.

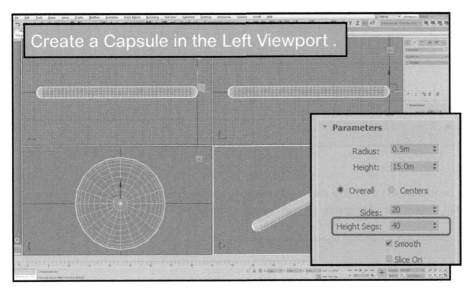

IMAGE 5.1

We are going to rig this capsule with bones. Create a two-bone chain along the length of the capsule as shown in Image 5.2, making a joint approximately halfway along the length. Remember, bones are in the Systems tab of the Creation tool bar in the Command Panel. We created a similar bone chain in Chapter 3 when we created the IK Chain. Select the Bones button to turn on bone creation. Click at the left end of the capsule in the Right Viewport to start the Hierarchy Chain. Then, click halfway along the length to create the first bone. Move the mouse cursor to the right end of the capsule, and click to create the second bone. End the chain by right-clicking the mouse, which will create the third bone, the node or End-Effector.

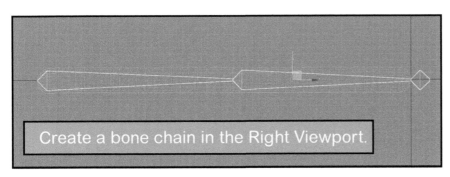

IMAGE 5.2 (3ds Max File Save 5.2)

Check the other viewports to make sure the bone chain is within the capsule. Move it if necessary. It is OK for the bones to project through the capsule. The rule for sizing the bones is to size the bones, so they fill approximately 70% of the mesh volume. If the bones are too small for the mesh, 3ds max will not assign the mesh vertices properly, causing problems.

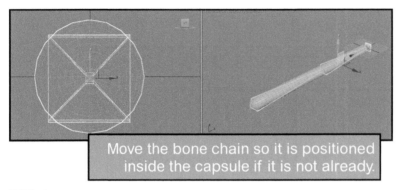

Move the bone chain so it is positioned inside the capsule if it is not already.

IMAGE 5.3

If the bones you created are too small, like the ones in the image below, adjust the size by selecting the bone and adjusting the width and height settings in the bone parameters in the Modify Panel.

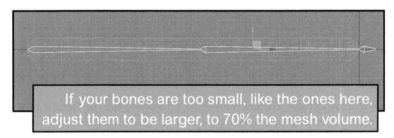

If your bones are too small, like the ones here, adjust them to be larger, to 70% the mesh volume.

IMAGE 5.4

Next, we will add the Skin Modifier to the capsule mesh (not to the bones!). Select the capsule mesh and add a Skin Modifier from the Modifier List in the Modifier Panel.

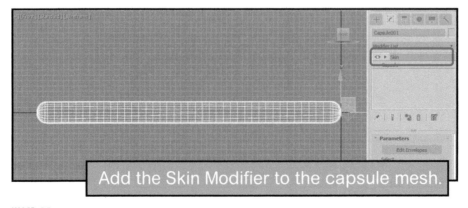

Add the Skin Modifier to the capsule mesh.

IMAGE 5.5

Adding Bones

So, now the capsule has a Skin Modifier attached to it. We will now associate the bones with the Skin Modifier. While still in the Skin Modifier panel, scroll down to the Bones section and select the "Add" button. A pop-up window called "Select Bones" will open on the screen.

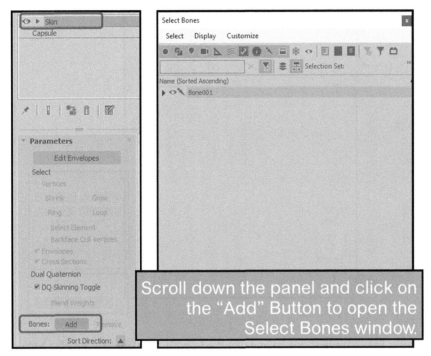

IMAGE 5.6

Notice there is only the first bone in the chain listed. The list is collapsed by default. In the top navigation bar, click on the "Display" tab to open a drop-down menu. In the drop-down menu, select "Expand All" to expand the list, so it shows all the bones in the scene.

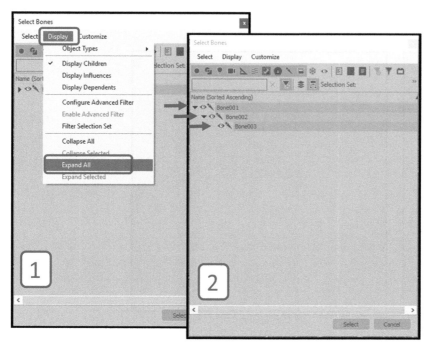

IMAGE 5.7

Select all three of the bones in the expanded bone list and click the Select button. The Skin Modifier has now associated all the mesh vertices with the bones you selected. It made an educated guess, based on the proximity of the bone location relative to each vertex to decide which bone each vertex is assigned to.

A vertex can be assigned to more than one bone at the same time. Skin does this by splitting the amount of "weight" or influence a bone has over a vertex. If two bones are assigned to a vertex, their combined "weight" will be 100% or 1.0.

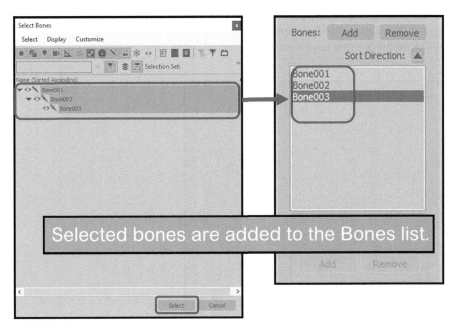

IMAGE 5.8

To see what the Skin Modifier does, rotate the second bone in our capsule's bone chain. Select the second bone, and rotate it up in the Y-axis. If you rigged everything correctly, the capsule should bend with the bone, creating an angled curve at the joint of the first and second bone.

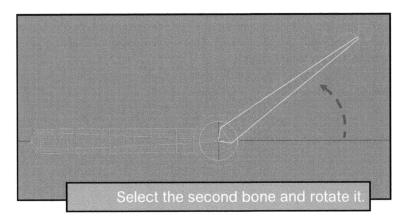

IMAGE 5.9 (3ds Max File Save 5.2)

If your capsule did not bend, most likely, you did not create height segments along the length of the capsule (Image 5.1). Without them, the capsule cannot bend. There are no vertices to associate with and follow the bones. The more height segments the capsule has, the smoother the curve will be.

If we look at the curved mesh at the bone joint, you can see that the vertices are stretched (moved apart) along the outside edge of the curve. On the inside of the curve, they have been moved closer together. This is the same thing that happens to your skin when you bend your elbow. Your skin has the property of elasticity that allows it to stretch over your elbow bone on the outside of the angle and to compress on the inside of the angle. That is what essentially is happening to our capsule. The skin on your forearm follows the path that your bone makes when your elbow bends. Your muscles are what make the elbow bend, pulling on the bones. Our model does not have muscles, and we just rotate the bone directly.

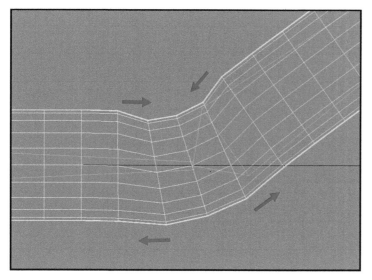

IMAGE 5.10

Envelopes

To see how this is happening, select the capsule mesh and go to the Modify Panel if it is not already open. In the Skin Modifier parameters, click the "Edit Envelopes" button. When you turn this button on, the active bone in the scene will show an Envelope around the bone, indicating the range of influence the bone has on vertices that have been assigned to it by the Skin Modifier.

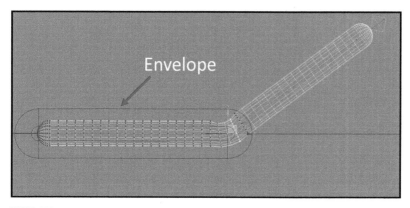

IMAGE 5.11

There are several parts to the Envelopes. The Outer Envelope encompasses the entire bone and assigned vertices. There is an Inner Envelope that is sometimes difficult to see. There is a very thin black line at the center of the Envelope that runs along the length. It represents the bone that is selected. If you select a different bone, either by selecting one of the thin black lines as just described or by choosing in the Bone list in the Modify Panel, the Envelope will switch to the new bone. You can select only one bone at a time, only one Envelope will be displayed.

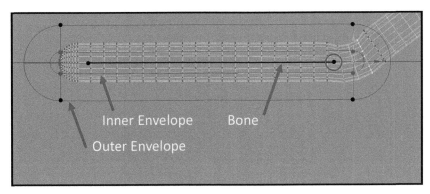

Inner Envelope   Bone

Outer Envelope

IMAGE 5.12

The Envelopes display the intensity the bone has over the vertices assigned to it through a gradation of colors. Using the bones in the image above (Bone 1 is on the left, Bone 2 is angled up on the right), look at the vertex coloration and what it means. If a vertex is displayed with a red dot, that means the vertex is "listening" to the bone with 100% or 1.0 of its ability, like it has tunnel vision focus on the bone, no distractions, or outside influences. It is "weighted" 100% to the selected bone. Wherever the bone moves, that red vertex will follow the bone, keeping its relative position.

As the vertices become red-orange, that means the vertex is mostly listening to the selected bone, but it is also partially listening to one or more other bones, dividing its attention. It might be listening to the selected bone, Bone 1, with 90% or .90 of its ability and listening to another bone, Bone 2, with 10% or .20 of the remaining ability. The weighting of that vertex is .70 (70%) on Bone 1 and .30 (30%) on Bone 2. The combined weighting of each vertex must always add up to a total of 1.0 (100%). When Bone 1 moves, the vertex will follow the bone 70% of the distance it would have had the weight been 1.0 (100%). In this case, 30% of the vertex's movement will be influenced by Bone 2's location.

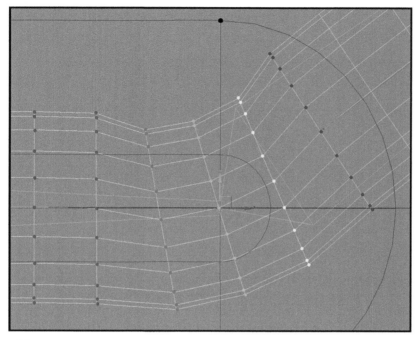

IMAGE 5.13

As the vertex color shifts to orange, the vertex weighting is likely .50 (50%) on each vertex. The movement of an orange vertex following Bone 1's movement will be half as than if it was weighted at 1.0 (100%). Half will be influenced by the position of Bone 2.

Shifting to yellow vertices, the trend continues. Only .30 (30%) will be listening to Bone 1, and .70 (70%) will listen to Bone 2. A blue vertex indicated the opposite of the red-orange vertex. Maybe only .10 (10%) of the vertex is influenced by Bone 1 and .90 (90%) is listening to Bone 2. If a vertex is not highlighted at all, that means it is not influenced by the selected bone at all. It must be listening to one or more other bones.

So, red at one end of the range of colors means listening 1.0 (100%) to the selected bone. Blue at the opposite end of the color range means the vertex is barely listening to the selected bone. The majority of a blue vertex's influence is coming from one or more other bones that are not selected at the time. Every vertex is being influenced to a total of 1.0 (100%) by one or more bones. This gradation of influence is what makes the mesh deformation possible. Understanding what is happening is to the individual vertices is fundamental to adjusting the mesh to the bone rig successfully. Looking at the next image, you can see the gradation of colors in the vertices. The red ones are totally influenced, 1.0 (100%), by Bone 1. The blue vertices are being influenced by Bone 1 only very slightly, .10 (10%). They are listening to Bone 2 at .90 (90%). So, as Bone 2 was rotated, the blue vertices followed Bone 2, moving .90 (90%) of the distance they would have traveled if they had been influenced by 1.0 (100%). Bone 1 still has .10 (10%) influence, so the vertex did move a little toward Bone 1. Apply that frame of logic to the other color vertices, and you begin to understand what is happening.

Select the thin black line of Bone 2, and you'll see the vertices that Bone 2 is influencing. They are the opposite degrees of influence that Bone 1 had on the same vertices. If a vertex is blue for Bone 1, it will be red-orange for Bone 2.

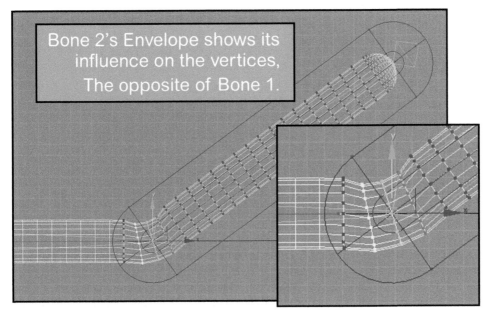

Bone 2's Envelope shows its influence on the vertices, The opposite of Bone 1.

IMAGE 5.14

Another way to visualize what is happening would be as follows: On the Envelope lines are small handles, as seen in Image 5.15. These handles are not the best design for users.

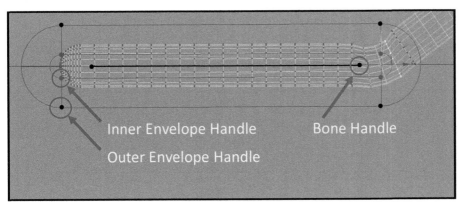

Inner Envelope Handle   Bone Handle

Outer Envelope Handle

IMAGE 5.15

Occasionally, they can behave unexpectedly, acting as a rotation pivot point for the Envelope. If that happens, selecting the opposite handle usually resolves the issue. Bottom line, they are not user-friendly.

For this example, we are interested in the Outer Envelope handles on the right side near the angled mesh. Select and drag the Outer Envelope handle in the up direction, away from the bone centerline.

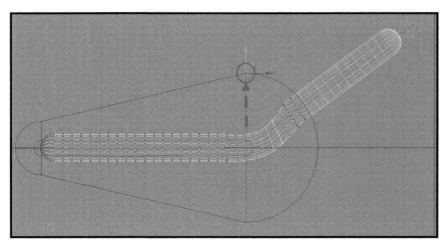

IMAGE 5.16

As you move the Envelope Handle, notice the Envelope becomes bigger. The area of its influence over vertices is increasing. As it expands, it assigns vertices that were previously not assigned to the selected bone to the bone. The wider the Envelope, the greater the influence on vertices closer to the bone centerline. Vertices that were previously only partially listening to the selected bone might become totally influenced, as indicated by the vertex becoming red. As you move the Envelope Handle up and down not only are the vertices changing color, they are changing position, changing the curve shape. You can see how the vertex weights change; the vertex position changes.

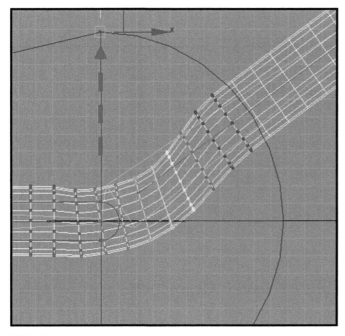

IMAGE 5.17

As the Envelope's influence increases, vertex weights are reassigned to be influenced by the selected bone to varying degree.

Remember, a single vertex's weighting must always add up to a combined weight of 1.0 (100%) regardless of how many bones are influencing the vertex.

The reason I am writing the weights as decimal numbers with the percentage in parentheses is in 3ds Max when working with vertex weights, the decimal numbers are used exclusively. Seeing the percentage, I thought, would help you to visualize the weight more easily. Image 5.17 shows how increasing the Envelope diameter changes the vertex assignments.

Remember this is all possible because of the Skin Modifier we added to the Capsule. The Skin Modifier was added to the mesh, not the bones. If you select Bone 002 from the Bone List in the Skin Modifier in the Modifier Panel and then click the Remove button above it, the bone will be removed from the calculations, vertex weighting and bone influence. As a result, the vertices snap back to their pre-Skin Modifier original position.

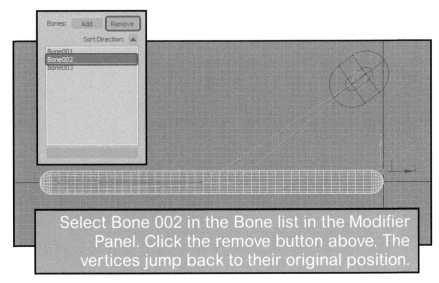

Select Bone 002 in the Bone list in the Modifier Panel. Click the remove button above. The vertices jump back to their original position.

IMAGE 5.18

Adjusting the bone influence on vertices is called "weighting the vertices." It is a tedious process that requires an investment of time to do successfully. We just did some simple weighting by adjusting the Envelope Handle position to increase or decrease the Envelope's area of influence. Typically, when weighting the vertices, you would begin by adjusting the Envelopes of each bone. By doing this, you are getting the vertices "in the ballpark" of what the weight values need to be. It is not accurate and by no means precise enough to yield finished weighting results. After getting the vertices roughly adjusted with the Envelopes, you would move on to the several additional tools meant for more precise positioning and weighting of vertices. Those tools include the Skin Weight Table, the Weight Tool and the Paint Weights tool. We will become familiar with and use these tools later when adjusting the vertex weights on our characters.

You can reset 3ds Max to a new start, and we do not need to save the capsule exercise.

Character Studio

The original 1988 version in of 3ds Max was called 3d Studio, written for DOS. It went through four versions until 1994 when it was rewritten for Windows NT and renamed 3ds Max. Character Studio was a $900.USD plugin for 3ds Max that included Biped and Physique for rigging characters for animation. When 3ds Max 4 was released in 2000 for Win 95/Win 2000, Character Studio was included in the package. From that time on, the name Character Studio has been dropped, the program simply having Biped as standard tool and Physique as a modifier. Very few improvements of note have been made to either of Biped or Physique over the years.

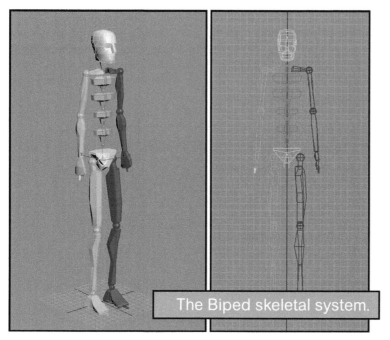

The Biped skeletal system.

IMAGE 5.19

The great feature that Biped has is the Footsteps. Footsteps are auto-generated walk/run/jump animations with parametric values to adjust the stride length, height, etc. The complete Biped bone rig can be created in just a click and drag mouse move. The individual bones can be adjusted to match a unique character's dimensions. The number of bones in some chains, spine, neck, ponytail and tail can be adjusted allowing a variety of characters from a long-necked giraffe or a long-tailed alligator. Another great feature, motion capture files can be applied to the rig, regardless of its proportions if the bones match up. The debut

234

of this feature was in 1988 with actress Calista Flockhart, as Ally McBeal, dancing with "Baby Cha-Cha." The dancing baby was "viral" hit for the time period. The big disadvantage to Biped is… it really is only effective with bipedal figures. It can be modified to be a quadruped with much effort, but the results are not that great, and the rig will have limited functionality.

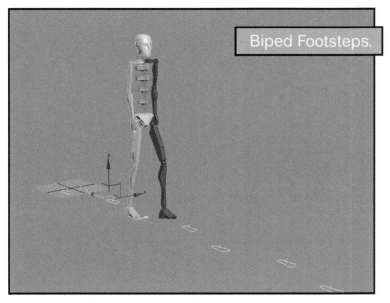

Biped Footsteps.

IMAGE 5.20

Biped also has a few quirky things that happen when you hand-animate that are irritating at best and make using it at times very frustrating. Luckily, there is a great alternative to Biped right inside 3ds max.

Character Animation Toolkit (CAT)

Beginning with the 2010 version of 3ds max, the former, very expensive, plugin for 3ds Max was incorporated into the program and included in the purchase. It basically was rarely used, partially because the documentation for using CAT was sorely lacking. It was almost a forgotten feature. For many animators, Maya is the preferred program for character animation. Few of them know about the CAT rigging system. If they did, they might re-look at 3ds Max for their projects. The Character Animation Toolkit is a very powerful, easy, and intuitive rigging system that is extremely adaptable. It includes custom rigging capabilities with unlimited appendages: multiple arms, legs, wings, etc. It accepts motion capture files. But most importantly, it imports very smoothly into game engines like Unity. For that reason, CAT has experienced a resurgence in popularity among video game developers. For that reason, we will be using the CAT rig for our characters in this textbook. Please feel free to try Biped if you like to explore its capabilities. I have used both for years. CAT definitely tips the scale for Video Game characters rigging and development. Third-party developers, including Miximo, that sell mocap files have files optimized for the CAT rig.

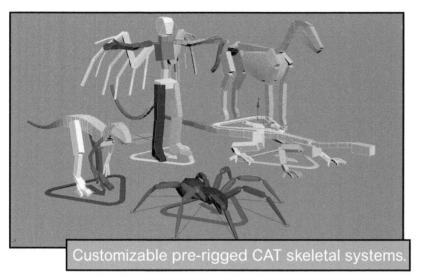

Customizable pre-rigged CAT skeletal systems.

IMAGE 5.21

Using the CAT Rig

Let's create a CAT rig. In the Create Panel of the Command Panel, select the Helpers icon tab. The drop-down menu directly under the Helpers icon tab is set to "Standard" by default. Select the drop-down menu and change the selection to "CAT Objects." There are three tool buttons in the Object Type section. Select the "CatParent" button.

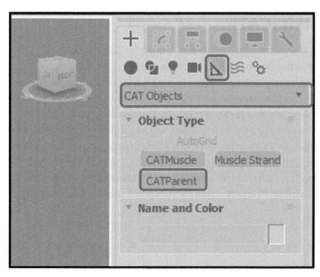

IMAGE 5.22

IMAGE 5.23

Scroll down the Modify Panel to the "CATRig Load and Save section." Select the Base Human from the list of rigs. In the Top Viewport, click and drag your mouse to create the rig.

The triangular spline with an arrow shape at the base of the rig is the CATParent. Remember when we learned about Hierarchy Chains? The root was the first bone in the chain. All other bones responded relative to the root of the chain. When we linked the Knight, the body section was the root of all the extremity chains. With CAT, the CATParent is the root of the rig. Wherever the CATParent moves, the rest of the rig will move with it. In a lot of character rigs, the pelvis object is the root of the rig. That can cause issues sometimes when needing to select it in a scene. With the CATParent, selection is easily achieved as it is away from the rig and mesh objects.

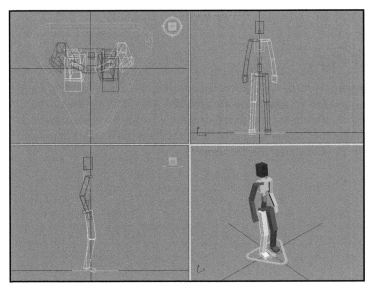

IMAGE 5.24

Looking at the Base Human rig, you can see the bones for arms, legs, spine and everything needed to animate a human character. The bones in this prebuilt rig are all customizable in terms of length, width and height. The basic building blocks of the rig are shown next.

Click the CATMuscle tool button to get out of the CATParent mode. Select the CATParent button again, and add a different type of character rig to the scene. Try adding quadrupeds, the spider and the centipede with multiple legs.

All the rigs are ready for animation. Look more closely at the rigs, and you will see there are some common base elements that create the rig. They all have a CATParent, hubs, appendages and spine segments.

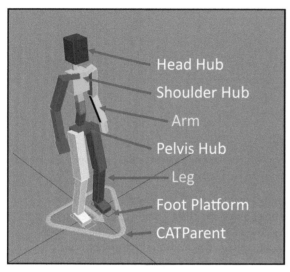

IMAGE 5.25

Using a pre-made rig, it may not fit your character. However, the size of the rig bones can be modified and adjusted to fit the mesh. A pre-made rig can save time when working to rig a character.

Creating Custom CAT Rig

When we modeled the Knight character, we made the legs straight, knowing we were going to be using linking to rig the mesh objects for animation. For using a skin deformation system, the rig needs to be modified with slightly pre-bent knees and arms. To make the process easier, I made these adjustments to the Knight and saved the 3ds Max file to the Companion site, www.3dsMaxBasics.com. Please download the new file **Vol2_Save 5-03** (Volume 2 > Companion Files > Chapter 5).

We will rig the Knight again, this time using a custom CAT rig. We could use the Base Human rig with some modifications, but by making a custom rig, you will gain a greater understanding of the CAT rig and how to do customization.

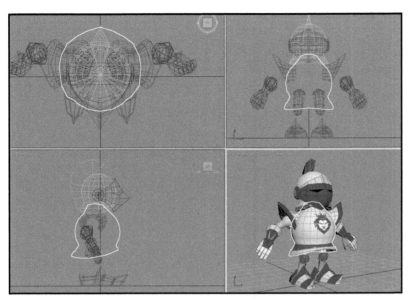

IMAGE 5.26 (3ds Max File Save 5.3)

When the file opens, rename it "lastname_KnightCATrig_01." If the texture is missing, open the Material Editor, reassign the image map file to the texture and then put the texture on the objects.

The Knight should be standing on the X-, Y-, Z-axis at 0, 0, 0. In the Scene Explorer, turn off the template objects, so they will not interfere with our work. The first thing we want to do is to freeze the Knight mesh parts, so they will not be selected by mistake while working on the rig. Select all the Knight mesh parts. Right-click on the selection to open the Quad Menu. In the left side of the Object Properties pop-up window, select "Freeze" and make sure "Show Frozen in Gray" is selected too. I also have "See-Through" active. In the text images, Freeze will be off for better visibility (you should keep the meshes frozen).

If it is not already open, open the CATParent button in the Helpers tab of the Create Panel. Scroll down again to the "CATRig Load and Save" section.

Select the top item in the list, "(None)." In the Top Viewport, click and drag the mouse to create a CATParent icon as shown in Image 5.27. Position it at 0, 0, 0 in the X, Y, Z-axes. If you made it too large or too small, delete it and recreate it.

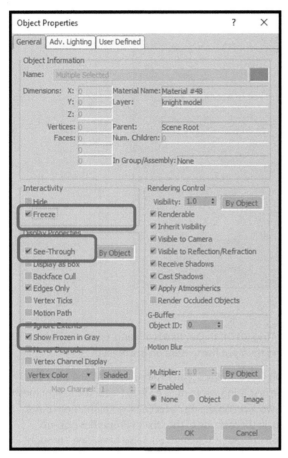

IMAGE 5.27

In the command Panel, change the Name and Color box from Character001 to Knight, and in the CATRig Parameters, change the name to KnightRig. All the rig's components will have this base name.

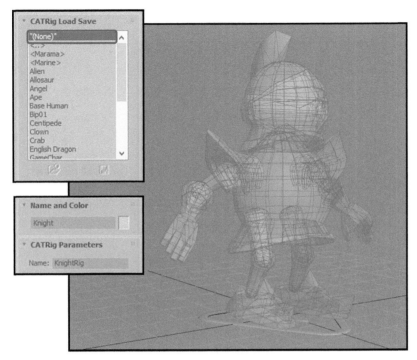

IMAGE 5.28 (3ds Max File Save 5.4)

This will be a custom rig that we are building. Our character is not like a normal biped figure. His hips and chest are one piece; he does not flex at the waist. Because of this, we do not need a spine that would allow bending. With the CATParent still selected, there is a button called "Create Pelvis" below the list of CAT rigs.

Click to create a pelvis bone. This is not just a bone; it is a hub. CAT uses hubs to make Hierarchy Chains possible. The pelvis hub is a Child of the CATParent. If the Create button is not active, in the Command Panel, switch to the Modify Panel and select the CATParent object.

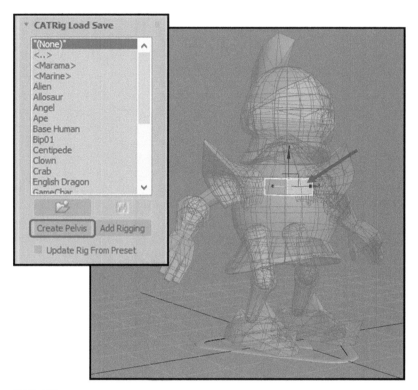

IMAGE 5.29

Next, resize and position the new Pelvis hub. Select the Pelvis hub. In the Modifier Panel, change the dimensions to those as seen in Image 5.30. Then, move the object, so it is positioned as in the image, between the top pivot points of the legs and toward the back some.

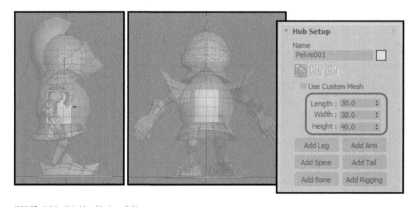

IMAGE 5.30 (3ds Max File Save 5.5)

242

Once the pelvis hub is sized and placed properly, we can add a leg. Hubs are unique in that they can be Parents to new Hierarchy Chains. CAT allows you to add several different types of hierarchy bone chains to a pelvis hub. Select the Add Leg Button in the Hub Setup section of the Modify Panel.

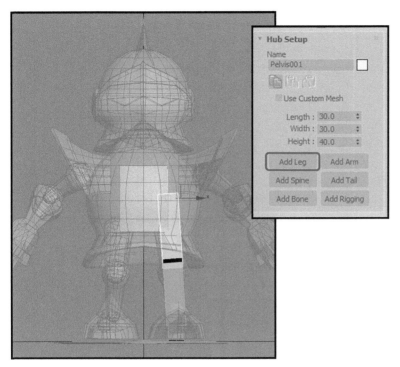

IMAGE 5.31 (3ds Max File Save 5.6)

CAT created a leg with the Hierarchy Chain starting at the top, from the Pelvis hub. The leg is a three-bone chain ending at the ankle. I have turned off the arms, the body and right leg in the Scene Explorer for clarity.

The chain includes an IK Solver with a fourth element under the ankle bone, the LegPlatform. Selecting and moving the LegPlatform allows inverse kinematic motion control.

When CAT creates a new arm or leg, it locates it relative to the center of the hub mass. The root bone of the limb hierarchy is a floating bone, which means you can move and adjust it to where you need it to originate from on the hub. Its functionality will remain in working order. That said, a left leg will function as though it were on the left side of the Hub and should be positioned there.

When positioning the leg bones, it is best to start with the ankle bone. Select the ankle bone with the Select and Move tool. Move it along the X-axis to align with the toe mesh object as shown in the next image.

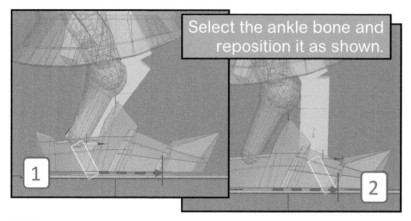

IMAGE 5.32

Next, change the Length value for the Ankle Bone in the Modifier Panel to 38.

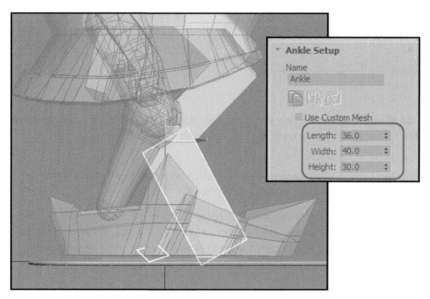

IMAGE 5.33

Using the Select and Rotate tool, rotate the Ankle Bone counterclockwise until the end of the ankle Bone aligns with the end of the Lower Leg bone mesh as shown. If your bone does not align to the center of the lower leg bone mesh, just adjust the length and rotation until it does.

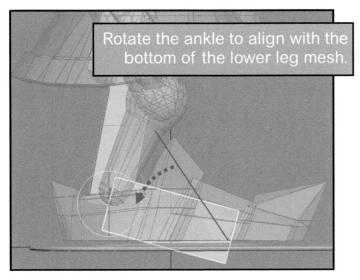

IMAGE **5.34** (3ds Max File Save 5.7)

Next select the upper leg bone, KnightRigLLeg1, and move the gizmo to align the top of the bone to the top of the Upper Leg Mesh. This will set the pivot point for the leg rotation at the hip. On some characters you might need to move the pivot to be in a different location relative to the end of the mesh. Each character you rig will likely be unique. Hide the arm meshes in the Scene Explorer if they are blocking your view for placement.

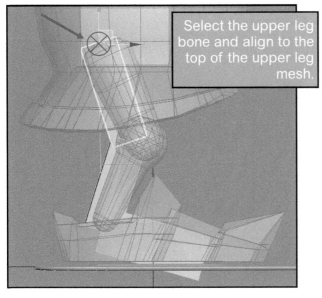

IMAGE **5.35**

Now select the lower leg bone, KnightRigLLeg2. Move the gizmo with the Select and Move tool so that it aligns with the center of where the "knee" joint would be on the leg meshes as shown. Notice that the length of the upper and lower bones automatically adjusts as you move the gismo.

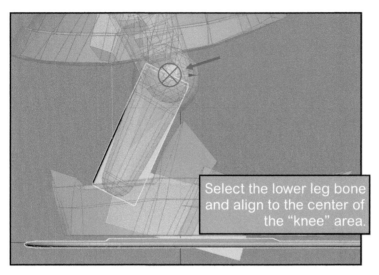

Select the lower leg bone and align to the center of the "knee" area.

IMAGE 5.36

Before proceeding, check the bone placement in the Front Viewport. Remember, it is 3D. Re-check the Left Viewport after adjusting see if more are needed.

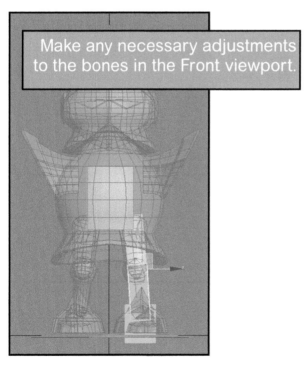

Make any necessary adjustments to the bones in the Front viewport.

IMAGE 5.37 (3ds Max File Save 5.8)

You probably noticed; the leg ends at the ankle. If the character we were rigging were a hoofed animal, we would not need feet. The ankle bone would suffice. This is a humanoid character, so we will need feet. Reselect the ankle bone. In the Modify Panel, change the value of the "Digits" from 0 to 1. This will add the toe bone. Also, change the width as shown. This will create a single two-segment toe bone. Since our character is wearing shoes, we do not need five separate toes, we just need just one. It will do the job of five toes.

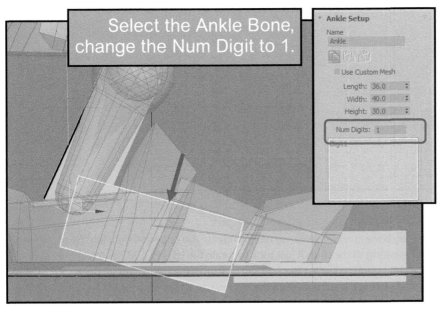

IMAGE 5.38

Next, select the first of the two toe bones, CATRigLLegDigit11. Change the Bones value to 1. Our toe bone will be in the toe mesh; it will not be bending along the toe, so we only need a single bone.

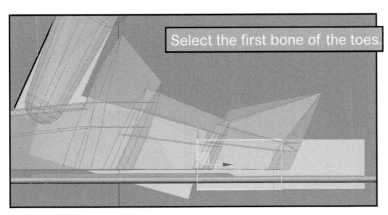

IMAGE 5.39

Change the Length in the Bone Setup area to a value of 25. When placing bones in fingers and toes, it is good practice to have the end bones extend beyond the ends of the meshes a bit to ensure better vertex weighting assignments by 3ds Max. Remember, when animated, the bones will be hidden, not rendering, so they will not be seen.

IMAGE 5.40 (3ds Max File Save 5.9)

That completes the left leg bone creation. Next, we need to create the opposite, right leg. We could hand position all the bones, repeating all the steps it just took to create the left leg. CAT has a real-time saving feature. Select the Pelvis hub, and then select the Add Leg button in the Hub Setup section in the Modify Panel. CAT will create the right leg exactly mirroring the left leg size and positioning.

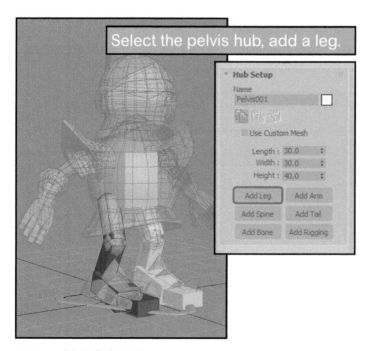

IMAGE 5.41 (3ds Max File Save 5.10)

If you make changes later to one of the legs and need to replicate the change on the opposite leg, simply delete the non-altered leg and create a new one. Cat will incorporate the changes. The same is true for arms when we create them next.

Now we can move on to creating the arms. Since our character does not have a torso that will require any bending, it is ridged, and we do not need to add a spine. The arms can originate from the pelvis hub. Select the Pelvis Hub, and click on the Add Arm button. Both legs will be complete.

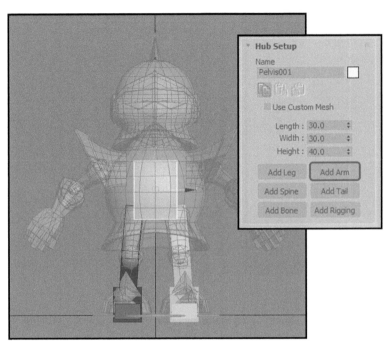

IMAGE 5.42

The CAT will create an arm on the left side of the Pelvis hub, and, like the leg, it will be out of position for our character, being created at the center of mass of the Pelvis.

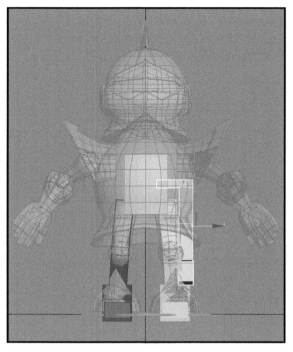

IMAGE 5.43

Just as you did with the leg, select the four arm bones in the Hierarchy Chain in the Front Viewport and reposition them for our rig. Position the collar bone, KnightRigLArmCollarbone, first. It should be level with the center of the shoulder part of the upper arm mesh. Check the Left or Right Viewport, the side view, to make sure aligned with the center of the upper arm mesh's "shoulder." Then, position the top of the upper arm bone, positioning the pivot point properly in the rotation part of the upper arm as shown.

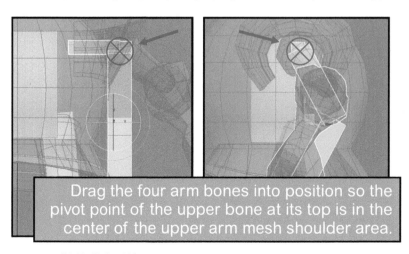

Drag the four arm bones into position so the pivot point of the upper bone at its top is in the center of the upper arm mesh shoulder area.

IMAGE 5.44 (3ds Max File Save 5.11)

Just as we did with the legs, we want to position the two end bones of the IK chain. The shoulder is set, and next, set the Palm. In the Front Viewport, drag the KnightRigLArmPalm bone into position so the pivot point is located at the wrist. Rotate the wrist, so the Palm orients correctly with the hand part of the lower arm mesh. Remember, I have prepositioned the Knight rig so the bones will easily fit the mesh configuration, so it should be close to fitting. Remember to adjust the position in both front and side views.

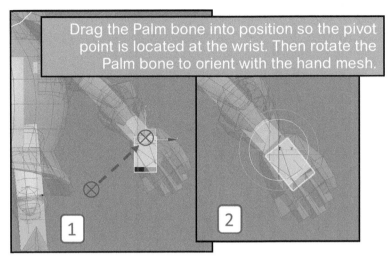

IMAGE 5.45

Select the lower arm bone, Knight RigLArm2. Use the Select and Move tool to position the top of the bone where the elbow would be on the figure. This will take some careful adjusting to get it centered in the mesh joint. Be sure to check the different viewports. Rotating the Perspective Viewport in different angles will help to check in all directions.

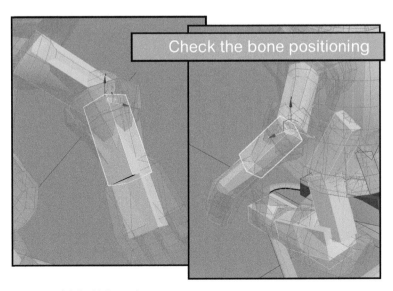

IMAGE 5.46 (3ds Max File Save 5.12)

We added foot bones to the ankle to complete the legs; now we will add finger bones to the Palm bone.

When we animate our Knight, all four fingers will move in unison, like a fingerless mitten. Because of this, we only need one finger bone chain to control all the fingers.

Select the Palm bone, and change the Num Digits setting to 2.

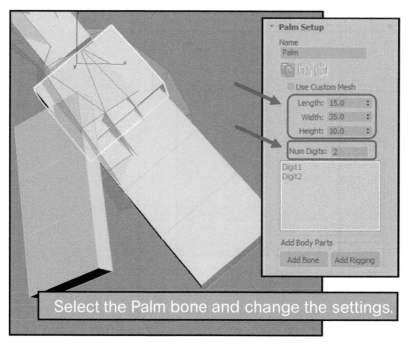

Select the Palm bone and change the settings.

IMAGE 5.47

This will add an opposable thumb and a broad single finger bone, both with three bones by default. Change the width value as indicated.

Next, select the first digit bone, KnightRigLArmDigit21. In the Modify Panel, change Bones value to 2 and the Length value to 7.0.

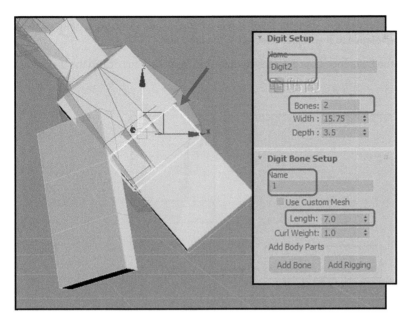

IMAGE 5.48

Select the end digit, KnightRigLArmDigit22. Change the Length in the Modify Panel to 8.0, leaving the bone slightly longer than the mesh fingers. This is done on purpose. Typically, when rigging fingers and toes, the bones should extend a short distance beyond the tip of the finger or toe. This helps in weighting the vertices, making sure that the vertices of the finger or toe are correctly assigned to the proper bone.

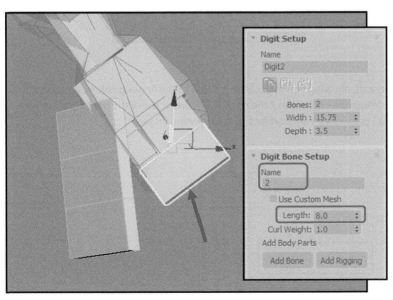

IMAGE 5.49

Look closely at the hand part on the lower Arm mesh. The fingers are in a natural curled position on this model. They also are slightly rotated. Our digit bones should follow this rotation. However, if we use the Select and Rotate tool to rotate them slightly, they will not rotate in the direction we want them to. This is because the rotational axis is set to View. They are rotating relative to the entire viewport. We need to change the rotation axis to be relative to the object selected or the local axis.

On the Top Tool Bar, change the Reference Coordinate System setting from View to Local in the drop-down menu.

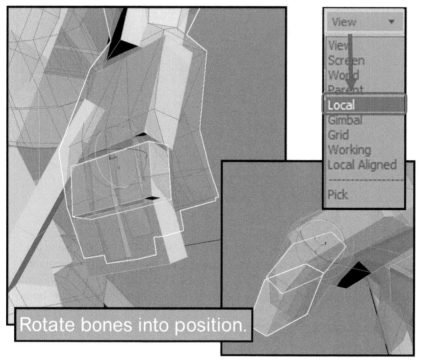

Rotate bones into position.

IMAGE 5.50

Now the digit will rotate on its axis, allowing you to position it closer to the finger position. Position both the first and second digits to follow the curvature of the fingers. Be sure to check the positioning in several viewports and by rotating the Perspective Viewport for the best viewing angle.

Next, the thumb bones need resizing and positioning. Again, select the first bone, Knight RigLArmDigit11, and in the Modify Panel, change the Bones value to 2. Change the Length value to 8.0.

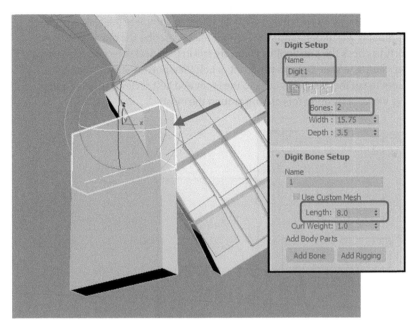

IMAGE 5.51

Moving on the second bone, Knight RigLArmDigit12, change the Length and Width parameters as shown to narrow and shorten the thumb bones.

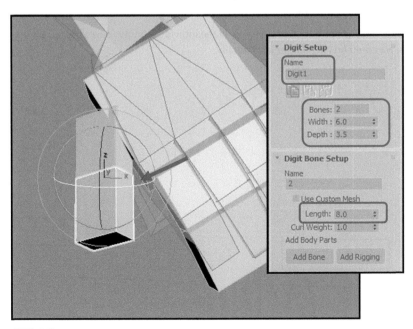

IMAGE 5.52

With the thumb bones resized, now comes the challenging part: position the thumb bones within the mesh properly. Select both bones together while getting them in the approximate position. The Select and Move and Select and Rotate tools should be your primary tools for this step. Have patience, think about where you want to position the bone and then use the best tool to complete the task. As you are positioning the bone, you probably will understand why I cannot really describe the moves to you in the text. Use all the viewports to check the positioning. If you are still in the Local Reference Coordinate System, that will help. If you rotate the View Cube in the Front or Left Viewports, they will change to Orthographic settings. Be sure to set the viewports back to the Front and Left settings to keep things squared-up. The Perspective Viewport is good for rotating around the mesh.

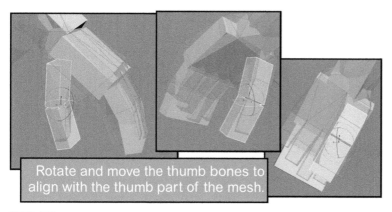

Rotate and move the thumb bones to align with the thumb part of the mesh.

IMAGE 5.53

Position the bone to follow the bend of the thumb on the mesh. The end of the bone should be longer than the mesh, going beyond and outside it. Remember it is alright for the bones to project outside the mesh. When the character is rendered for play in the game, the bones will be hidden.

That completes our arm needs for this rig. Not needing to rig all the individual fingers saves a lot of time. However, if we did need to, we could rig each finger individually.

Select the Pelvis bone Hub, and in the Modify Panel, select the "Add Arm" button. CAT will add a symmetrical arm to the rig, fitting the mesh, opposite the right arm.

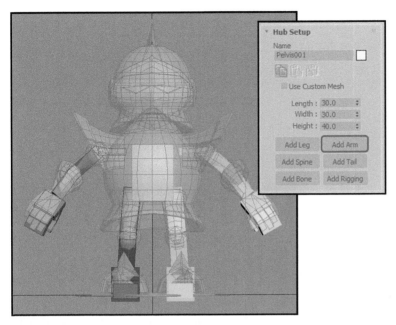

IMAGE 5.54 (3ds Max File Save 5.13)

The last part to rig is the head. Select the Pelvis hub again. This time click on the Add Spine button.

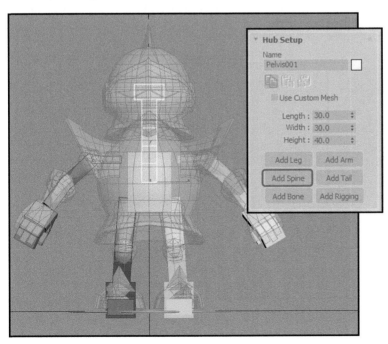

IMAGE 5.55

Our Knight does not really have a neck, so we do not need to create a flexible neck like a human has. Change the number of Bones to 1 in the Modifier Panel.

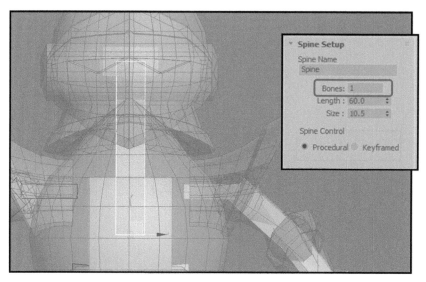

IMAGE 5.56

Scale and position the bone roughly as shown in Image 5.57. Select them both to move them into position, aligning the center with the Visor Hinge mesh in the side view. This will place the pivot point of the helmet in the correct location when it turns and tilts.

When a spine is added to a hub, CAT creates a spine chain of bones capped with a new Pelvis hub. CAT does not know that we are using this as a head bone.

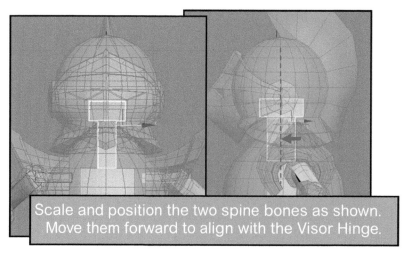

Scale and position the two spine bones as shown. Move them forward to align with the Visor Hinge.

IMAGE 5.57

Rename the bone "HeadHub" in the Name box.

As a hub, we can add arms, legs and tail or another spine. We could also add floating bones, say, for instance, a jawbone to control a character's mouth for talking. We will not be adding any appendages to the head. We just need to resize and position it. Select the HeadHub, and change the settings as shown.

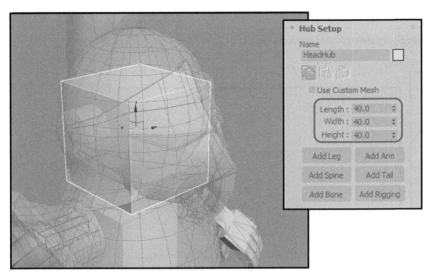

IMAGE 5.58

That completes the rigging needs for the Knight character. If we hide the geometry objects, the meshes, you can see the simplicity of the rig. Now that you know how to create a custom CAT rig, you should be able to create rigs to suit all your character rigging needs.

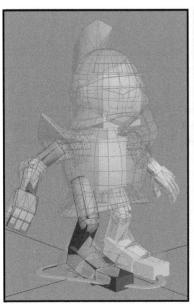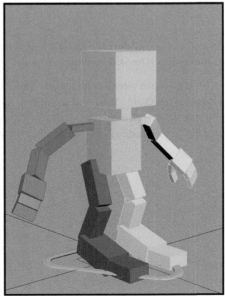

IMAGE 5.59 (3ds Max File Save 5.14)

Adding the Skin Modifier

The next thing we need to do is to add the Skin Modifier to the mesh. Right now, in the Scene Explorer, our CAT rig bones and helpers are in the Knight layer. To make selections easier in the coming steps, create a new layer, Knight Model CAT Rig.

Move or drag the CAT rig components into the new layer.

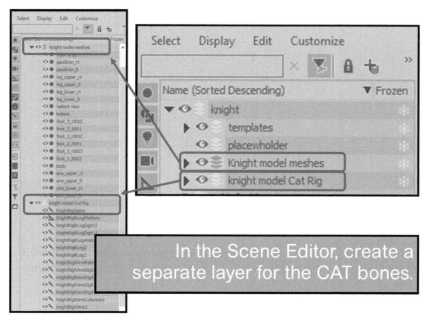

IMAGE 5.60

In the Scene Selector, turn off the CAT Rig layer so just the Knight mesh will be active. We will be needing to select the mesh parts for applying the Skin Modifier.

If the mesh is still frozen, right-click in a viewport and select "Unfreeze All." Select all the knight meshes. Right-click on the mesh to open the Quad Menu, and select the Object Properties window. Uncheck the See-Through option. Select all the Knight mesh objects again if they are not selected. Add a Skin Modifier to them from the Modifier List in the Modify Panel. Notice that the word "*Skin*" is italicized in the Modifier

Stack. When italicized, that indicates that the modifier has been applied to more than one object. In this case, Skin has been applied to every individual mesh as a group. Unhide the Knight model Cat rig in the Scene Explorer to show the bones.

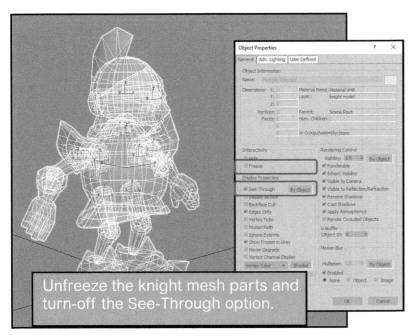

IMAGE 5.61

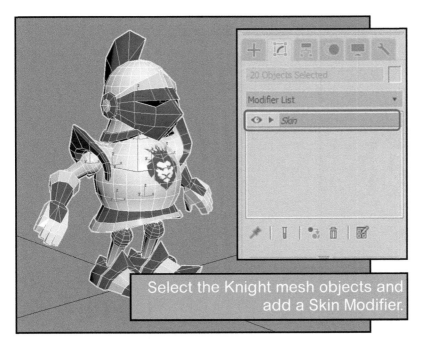

IMAGE 5.62 (3ds Max File Save 5.15)

If you remember, the next step in applying the Skin Modifier to meshes is to add the bones. Scroll down the modifier panel, and click on the Add button next to Bones. The Select Bones window will open. Select the Display tab, and choose the Expand All selection.

 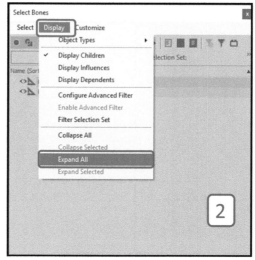

IMAGE 5.63

The list of bones will expand to show all the CAT bone components. Select all the items to add to the Skin Modifier. And then, click the Select button. The CAT bone rig should now be associated with the character meshes.

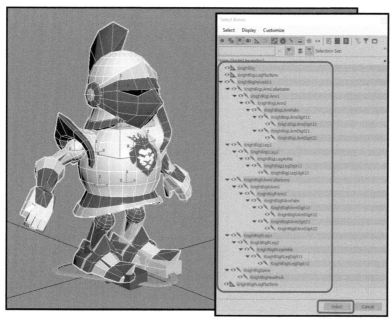

IMAGE 5.64 (3ds Max File Save 5.16)

CAT has a feature, CAT Motion, that automatically applies a walk cycle to the rig, regardless of how many legs or arms the character has. Biped, the other bone system in 3ds Max has a similar feature, but it works only for bipedal figures.

The CATMotion Panel

Click out of the Skin Modifier, selecting one of the CAT bones or the CAT Parent object. Open the Motion Panel tab on the Command Panel. This is where you will control the animation for the CAT Rig.

IMAGE 5.65

Click on the Abs layer button in the Layer Manager to open the drop-down menu of icons. Select the last one in the list to create a new CAT Motion animation layer in the Layer Manager window.

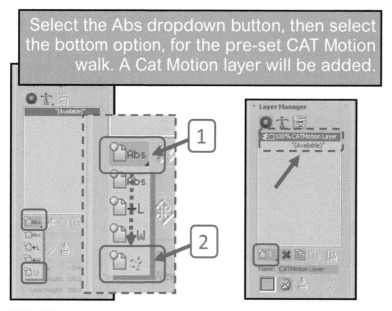

IMAGE 5.66

Next, in the Layer Manager, click on the red "Stop" icon Setup/Animation Mode Toggle button to change it to the green "play" icon, Animation Mode.

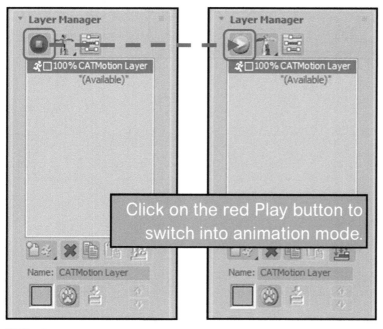

IMAGE 5.67

If you noticed, the character assumed a different position, the meshes following the single frame of the walk cycle pose the rig became.

In Animation Mode, the character assumes the pose.

IMAGE 5.68 (3ds Max File Save 5.17)

If you drag the time slider at the bottom of the UI left or right, the character rig will animate through a walk cycle. It does not look good though… the meshes are not following the rig as we would expect. In a few minutes, with some adjusting of the vertex weights, it will look very different.

IMAGE 5.69

Weighting the Helmet and Torso Vertices

We will begin the adjustments with weighting the vertices of the helmet. Select the Helmet mesh. In the Modify Panel, the modifier stack shows the Skin Modifier at the top of the stack. It is italicized, indicating that Skin was applied to more than one object.

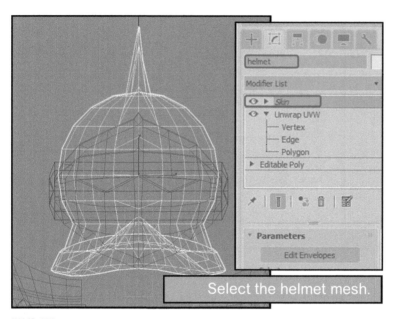

Select the helmet mesh.

IMAGE 5.70

We are going to weight all the vertices of the Helmet mesh to the KnightRigHeadHub bone so that its movement is completely controlled by only that bone. Wherever the head hub bone moves, the helmet will follow it and only it. No other bones will have any influence on the Helmet. Click on the "Edit Envelopes" button in the Modifier Panel. Then, check the "Vertices" tick box below it, under Select.

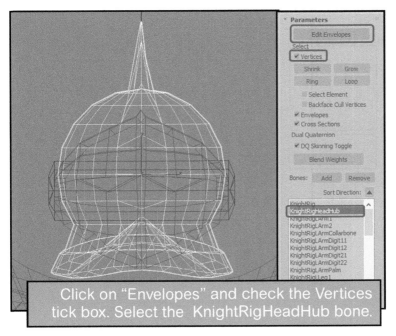

IMAGE 5.71

In the Bones List further down the panel, make sure the KnightRigHeadHub is selected.

Remember we are rigging a character with multiple mesh parts, not a single mesh that needs to deform. Because of that, all our weighting for this figure is greatly simplified.

We just need to weight each mesh part to the corresponding bone at 100% or 1.0. Because of this, the Envelopes are not necessary, there will not be any "approximations," and all weighting will be absolute. Scroll down the modifier panel to the Display section. Click the tick box for "Show No Envelopes" to turn the Envelopes off. We will be able to see the vertices more clearly with them off.

Next, we will open the Weight Tool window. Scroll to the Weight Properties section in the Modify Panel, and click on the Weight Tool button icon.

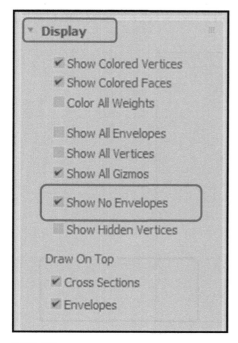

IMAGE 5.72

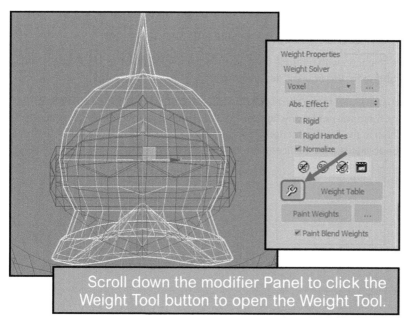

Scroll down the modifier Panel to click the Weight Tool button to open the Weight Tool.

IMAGE 5.73

When the Weight Tool window opens, check the bottom of it to make sure the KnightRigHeadHub is the selected bone. Drag your mouse to select all the vertices of the Helmet. They will be highlighted as shown below. Notice not all the vertices are red. The red vertices are assigned to the selected bone. The orange ones near the center were partially assigned by 3ds Max to the selected bone and are partially assigned to one or more other bones.

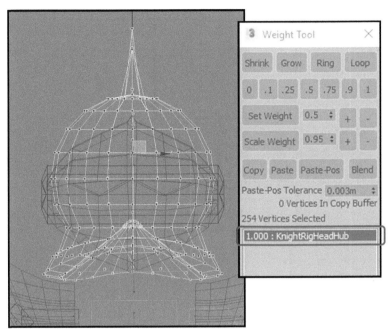

IMAGE 5.74

Assign the selected vertices a weight of 1.0 (100%) by clicking the "1" button in the Weight Tool window. All the vertices will turn red indicating they have 100% of their weight assigned to the selected bone.

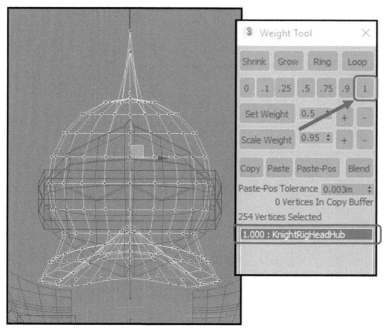

IMAGE 5.75

Click on the Skin layer in the modifier stack to get out of Skin mode. If you were to select the Helmet Visor or the Hinge mesh and check their vertices weights, you would find that all the vertices are all assigned to the KnightRigHeadHub bone. Because of their location, the head hub bone was the closest bone that 3ds Max could assign the vertices to. The next closest bone, the neck spine was in a position too far for the program to consider. Because the vertices of these two meshes are already fully assigned to the head hub, we do not need to assign them.

Click out of the Skin Modifier and select the Torso Mesh.

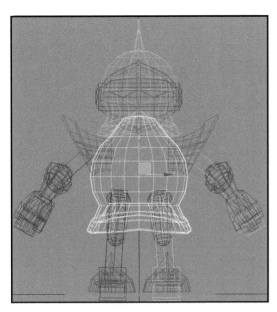

IMAGE 5.76

Click the Edit Envelopes button again as well as the Vertices tick box. This time select the KnightRigPelvis001 bone (if you bone is named differently, just select it).

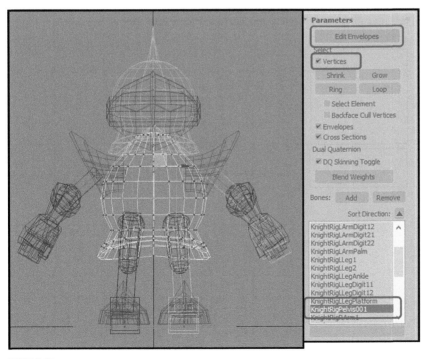

IMAGE 5.77

Open the Weight Tool if it is not open and select all the vertices. The colors of the vertices in the torso indicate the weighting is distributed over two or more bones. Weight them to the selected bone by clicking on the "1" value button.

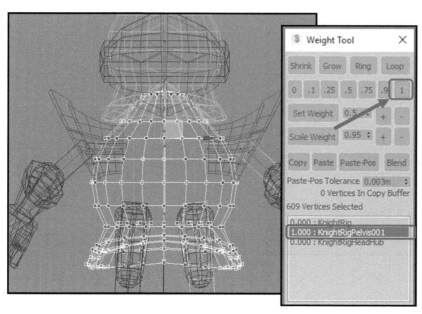

IMAGE 5.78

All the vertices will turn red indicating they are weighted 100% on the selected bone.

IMAGE 5.79

Click out of the Skin Modifier, and select the two Pauldron meshes. We want the two pauldron meshes to move in unison with the torso. Repeat the process to weight these two meshes vertices to the KnightHubPelvis001 bone. Click on the Envelopes, click the Vertices tick box on, select the pelvis bone, select the vertices and weight them to a value of "1."

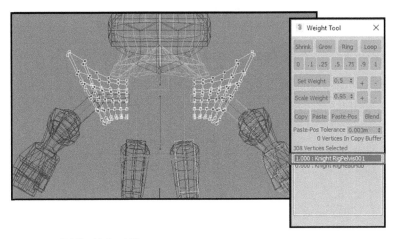

IMAGE 5.80 (3ds Max File Save 5.18)

So far, we have weighted the helmet, torso and pauldron meshes. Click out of the Skin Modifier and go to the Motion Panel. Select any bone object, then click the red Setup/Animation toggle button to change it to Play (green). Scrub the Time Slider to view the walk cycle animation. It should look a lot better with the objects we weighted more under control. There is still weight assigning to be done to the rest of the meshes to help the animation to look even better.

Turn off the Setup/Animation Toggle button in the Modify Panel to get back into Setup mode.

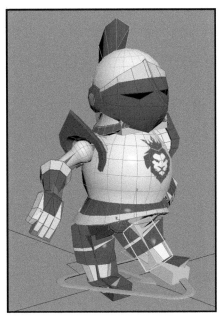

IMAGE 5.81

273

Weighting the Arm Vertices

We will work on weighting the vertices of one of the arms next. Select the upper_arm_rt mesh. In the Modify Panel, select the Edit Envelopes button and the Vertex tick box, so it is active. In the bones list further down the Modify Panel, select the KnightRigRArm1 bone. The vertices that are currently under the influence of the selected bone will be highlighted with a color indicating the weight state.

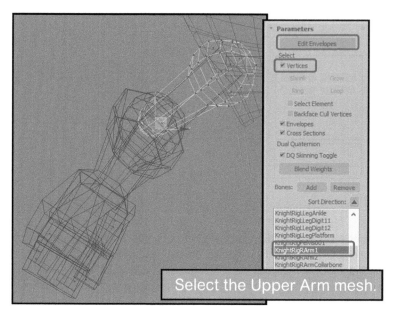

IMAGE 5.82

Select all the vertices of the upper arm mesh. Open the Weight tool if it is not already open and assign the vertices a weight of 1. All the vertices will turn red indicating full weight to the selected bone. Wherever the bone moves, the mesh will follow.

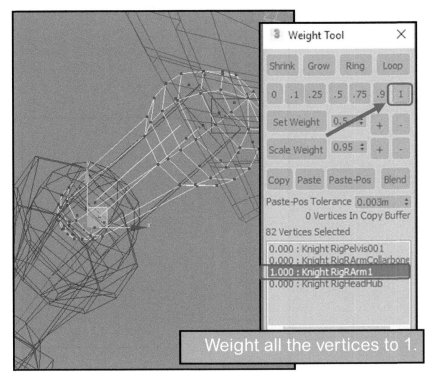

Weight all the vertices to 1.

IMAGE 5.83

The next mesh we will work on is the lower arm mesh. For clarity, I turned off all the other mesh objects in the scene. We will be selecting only certain vertices in this process, so isolating the mesh visually will make it easier to select the correct ones. If you want to, turn off the other meshes in the Scene Selector.

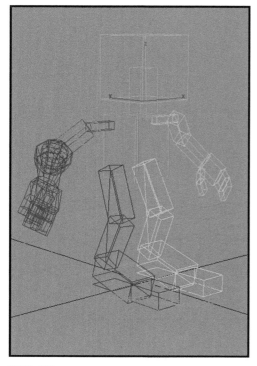

IMAGE 5.84

Select the arm_lower_rt mesh, the hand and lower arm mesh. Rotate the Perspective Viewport so that you have a good view of the mesh with clear sight of the vertices.

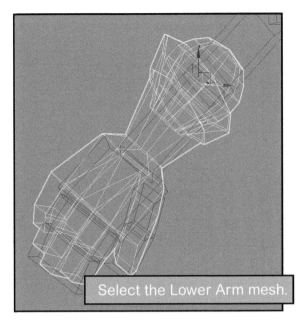

Select the Lower Arm mesh.

IMAGE 5.85 (3ds Max File Save 5.19)

Select the Edit Envelopes button, and select the Vertices tick box. From the Bones list, select the KnightRigRArm2 bone. Note the selected bone will be shown as a yellow line segment with the bone anchors at each end. Note also, the vertices currently being influenced by the selected bone are shown in the range of influence colors. In the bone list, all bones that have these vertices assigned wholly or partially are listed in the bone list. If you select a single vertex, the bones it is assigned to will be listed along with the assigned weight for each bone.

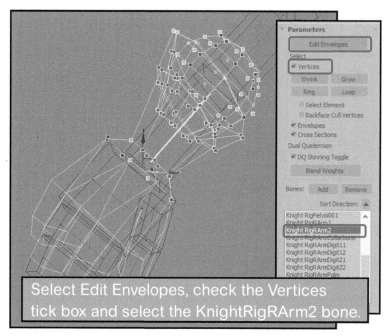

Select Edit Envelopes, check the Vertices tick box and select the KnightRigRArm2 bone.

IMAGE 5.86

Select all the vertices. Assign all these vertices a weight of 1. All the vertices will change to the color red indicating they are weighted 100% on the selected bone.

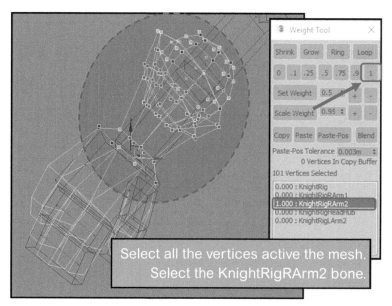

Select all the vertices active the mesh. Select the KnightRigRArm2 bone.

IMAGE 5.87

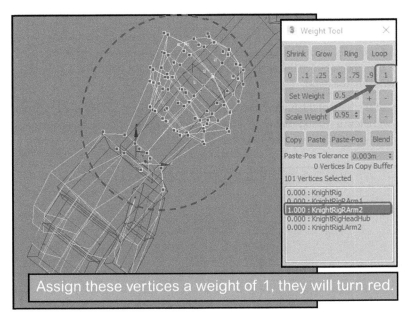

IMAGE 5.88

So far, we have been assigning weights to mesh objects that will not deform or bend. They have been ridged objects. The lower arm is different in that the Palm bone will be able to bend at the wrist, and the mesh will stretch and compress like your skin does at the wrist. The Palm bone will rotate from a pivot point at the wrist. To allow this to happen, the vertices at the wrist need to have equal weighting on both the lower arm bone and the palm bone. We have already assigned the vertices at the wrist a weight of 1 on the KnightRigRArm2 bone. Select just the vertices at the wrist, and select the KnightRigRPalm bone from the bone list in the Modify Panel. Assign a weight of .5 to the selection.

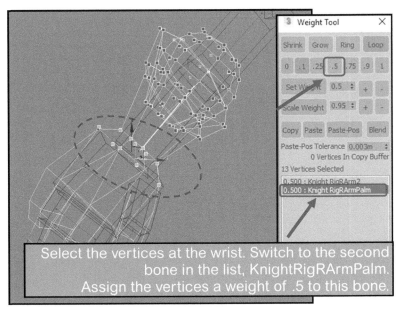

IMAGE 5.89

If you look at the two bones listed at the bottom of the Weight tool, you will notice that the two bones are listed, and each has a weight of .5. We removed .5 from the lower arm bone and reassigned it to the Palm bone. We assigned a weight of 1 initially, so these vertices had a full weighting on the one bone. We could then subtract the .5 from it. If they did not have the weight initially, we could not subtract from it. We will use this process to weight the rest of the hand.

Select the next set of vertices at the base of the fingers and the thumb. Assign them a weight of 1 to insure they are fully weighted. This will allow us to subtract weight by assigning to the digit bone, allowing the mesh to stretch and collapse like your skin does when you bend your fingers.

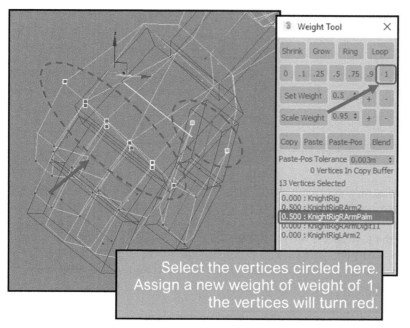

IMAGE 5.90

With the vertices still selected, switch to the KnightRigRArmDigit21 bone and assign a weight of .5. This will leave each bone with .5 influence over the selected vertices.

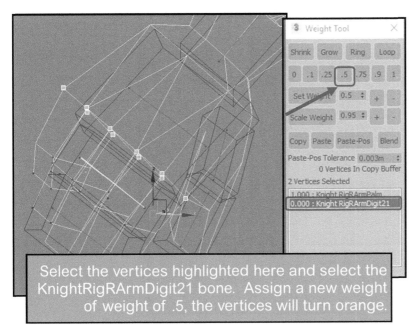

Select the vertices highlighted here and select the KnightRigRArmDigit21 bone. Assign a new weight of weight of .5, the vertices will turn orange.

IMAGE 5.91

Move on to the next finger joint area of the mesh. Select the vertices as shown. Assign them a weight of 1 to establish the full weight assignment for the vertices.

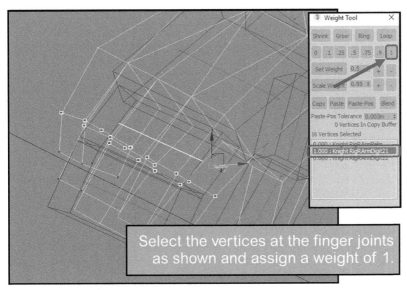

Select the vertices at the finger joints as shown and assign a weight of 1.

IMAGE 5.92

Switch to the KnightRigRArmDigit22 bone and assign a weight of 1. These vertices will now stretch and compress as the fingers bend.

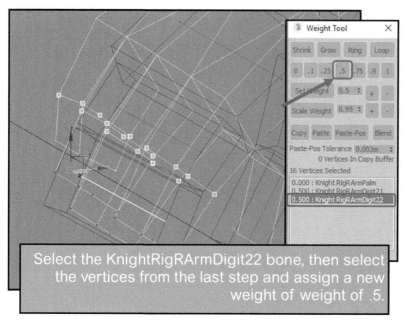

IMAGE 5.93

Next, select the vertices at the end of the fingers and assign them a weight of 1. This will insure they will not be influenced by any other bones in the rig, which can often happen when 3ds Max assigns the vertex weighting.

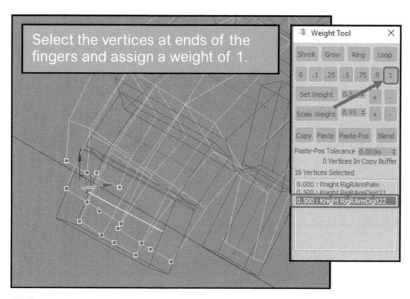

IMAGE 5.94

To finish the weighting of this mesh, we need to assign weight to the thumb vertices. Select the vertices at the base of the thumb where it meets the palm. These vertices should already have a weight assignment of 1 on the KnightRigRArmPalm bone. If they do not, assign them a 1 weight to that bone. Then, subtract half of that weighting by assigning a weight of .5 to the KnightRigRArmDigit11, the first bone in the thumb.

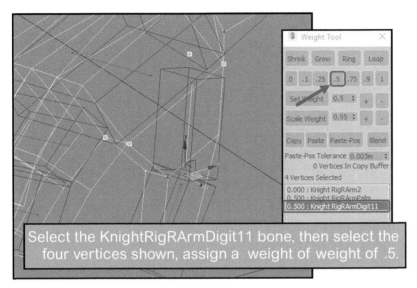

IMAGE 5.95

Select the next set of vertices down the thumb. Assign them a full weight of 1 to the KnightRigRArmDigit12 bone.

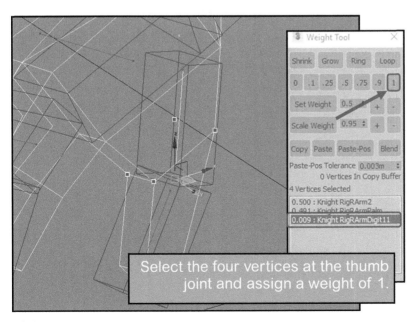

IMAGE 5.96

With the vertices still selected, select the KnightRigRArmDigit12, the end bone of the thumb, and assign a weight of .5 to split the weighting between the two bones.

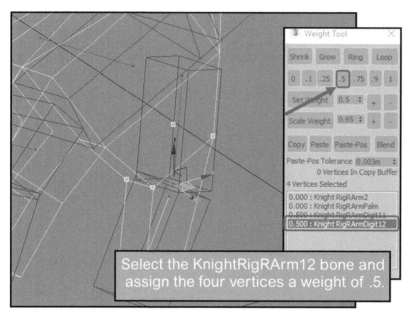

IMAGE 5.97

Lastly, select the four vertices at the end of the thumb. They should be weighted fully to the end bone already, but just to be sure, assign them a weight of 1 to the KnightRigRArmDigit12 bone.

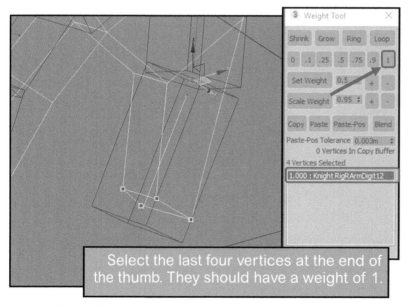

IMAGE 5.98 (3ds Max File Save 5.20)

That completes the weighting of the vertices in the right arm. The next step is for you to weight the vertices of the left arm. Unfortunately, the mirror weights tool in the Skin Modifier will not work with the CAT rig. CAT uses a unique coordinate system from 3ds Max. Remember, it was originally a plugin. On your own, please follow the same steps we did to rig the right arm to rig the left arm beginning with Image 5.82. Take your time, work methodically to keep the steps in order. Continue with the next steps once you have completed the left arm weighting.

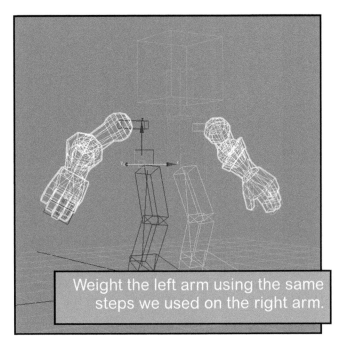

Weight the left arm using the same steps we used on the right arm.

IMAGE 5.99 (3ds Max File Save 5.21)

Weighting the Leg Vertices

Hopefully by now you are getting familiar with the process of simple weighting of the vertices. Next, we will assign weights to the legs. This should go a bit quicker as there are no deforming meshes.

I choose to weight the vertices in the left leg first. For clarity of the images, I turned off all the mesh and bones except for the ones in the left leg. You can do the same if you wish; it is whatever you prefer.

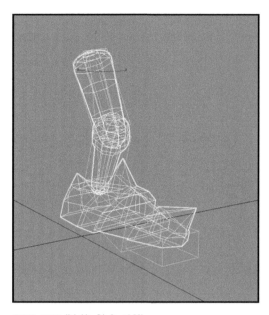

IMAGE 5.100 (3ds Max File Save 5.23)

Select the leg_upper_left, the upper leg mesh. In the Modify Panel, click on the Edit Envelopes and the Vertices tick box. Select the KnightRigLLeg1 bone and all the mesh vertices. Assign a weight of 1.

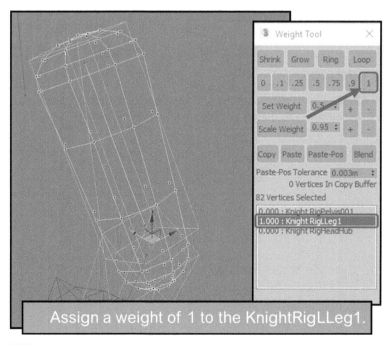

Assign a weight of 1 to the KnightRigLLeg1.

IMAGE 5.101

Get out of the Skin Modifier and move down to select the lower_leg_lt, the lower leg mesh. Again, in the Modify Panel, click on the Edit Envelopes and the Vertices tick box. Select the KnightRigLLeg2 bone and all the mesh vertices. Assign a weight of 1.

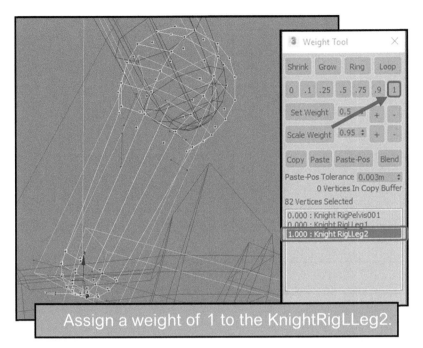

Assign a weight of 1 to the KnightRigLLeg2.

IMAGE 5.102

Next, weight the vertices of the foot_1_lt, the heel section of the foot. Select the heel mesh, and again, in the Modify Panel, click on the Edit Envelopes and the Vertices tick box. Select the KnightRigLLegAnkle bone and all the mesh vertices. Assign a weight of 1.

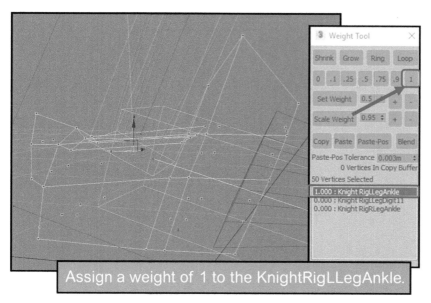

Assign a weight of 1 to the KnightRigLLegAnkle.

IMAGE 5.103

When you weight the vertices of the foot_2_lt, the middle section of the foot, you'll want to assign it also to the KnightRigLLegAnkle bone. Click on the Edit Envelopes and the Vertices tick box. Select the KnightRigLLegAnkle bone and all the mesh vertices. Assign a weight of 1.

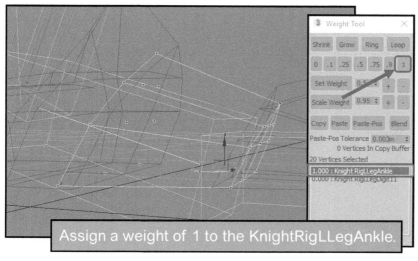

Assign a weight of 1 to the KnightRigLLegAnkle.

IMAGE 5.104

Lastly, Select the toe mesh, foot_3_lt, and weight the vertices with a weight of 1, assigned to the KnightRigLLegDigit11.

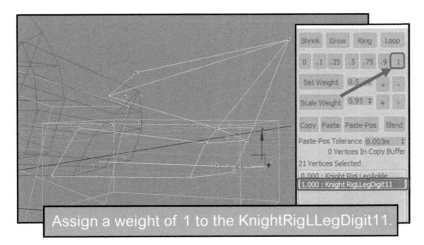

Assign a weight of 1 to the KnightRigLLegDigit11.

IMAGE 5.105 (3ds Max File Save 5.24)

That completes the left leg rig weighting for this character. Repeat the same steps, starting with Image 5.100, to weight the vertices of the right leg of the character. When you complete the procedure, continue with the next part of the text.

Adjusting the CATMotion Animation

With the vertices all weighted properly, go back to the Motion Panel and click on the Setup/Animation Toggle button to the green Amination mode. Click on the Play button to see how the walk cycle plays now. You should see a much better cycle with the meshes more in control. Next, we will make adjustments for a more natural or stylized looking animation.

When we created the Abs Animation Layer earlier, we did not rename the layer in the Layer Manager. Change the name to Knight Walk Cycle. Also, open the Time Configuration window, and change the End time to 89.

IMAGE 5.106 (3ds Max File Save 5.25)

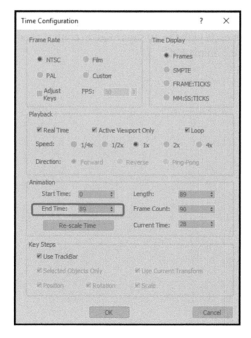

IMAGE 5.107

The CATMotion panel has some interesting features that we can use to adjust the animation movement of the Knight. Next, click on the CAT Motion Editor button icon to open the editor window.

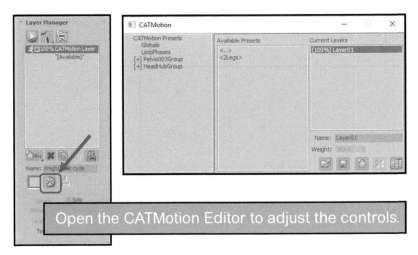

IMAGE 5.108

The CATMotion Editor has a number of preset parameters for the bones in a hub hierarchy that can be adjusted to modify the walk cycle. The bones and their attributes are listed on the left side column of the window. On the right side are the parameters and variables for the item selected in the left side column.

The first in the list is Global. Select it and then change the CATMotion Range setting for "End" to 89. Since there are 30 frames per second, making the range end at 89 will keep the duration of the cycle on a full second of time (the time starts at 0). Increase the Stride Parameters' Max Step Time to 30.0, again keeping it on the full second.

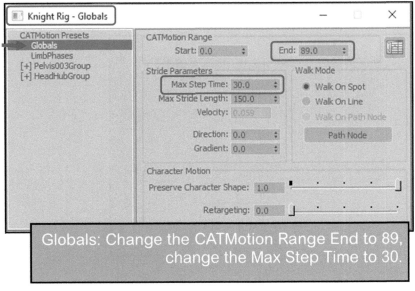

IMAGE 5.109

The next item listed is the Limb Phases. This coordinates the swing of the arms in relation to the swing of the legs. As human bipeds, our arm limbs swing opposite our leg swing motion. When the left foot is forward, the right arm is back. This opposite swinging movement helps us to stay balanced as we move. In the slider section of the Limb Phases, adjust the slider positions to match the image. These positions will set the arms and legs to swing opposite each other.

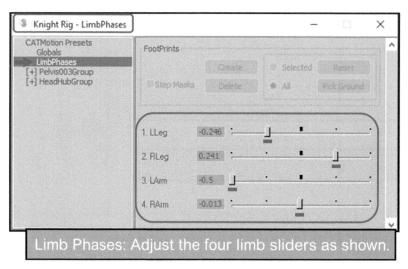

Limb Phases: Adjust the four limb sliders as shown.

IMAGE 5.110

Now we move into the limbs emanating from the Pelvis Hub group. First is the Pelvis. If you noticed in the animation, the torso was swinging wildly back and forth. To control the torso movement, we need to adjust the Twist, Roll and WeightShift. Select the Twist parameter and change the Scale setting from 100 to 30. Then, push enter, which will immediately change the value back to 100 and will change the appearance of the line curve in the window, indicating there was a change.

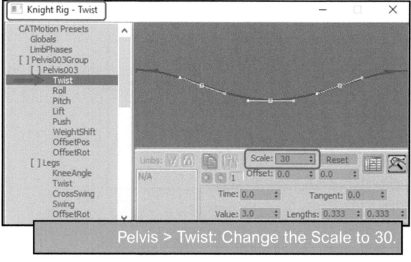

Pelvis > Twist: Change the Scale to 30.

IMAGE 5.111

Next, open the Roll parameter and change the Scale value from 100 to 20. The Scale numbers are percentage numbers. Again, when you hit the enter key, the Scale number will change to 100.0 and the line in the window change to reflect the new 20% Scale number, which is now the full, 100% value.

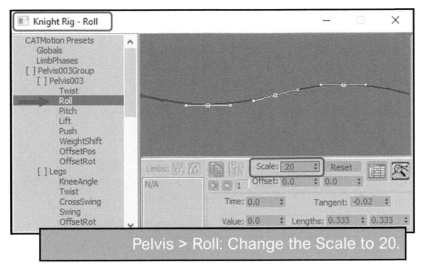

IMAGE 5.112

The last Pelvis adjustment we need to make is in the WeightShift. Select the WeightShift, and change the Scale value to 15. If you were to play the walk cycle animation now, you will find the Torso to be in much more control, with less wild swinging rotations as a bell ringing in a tower.

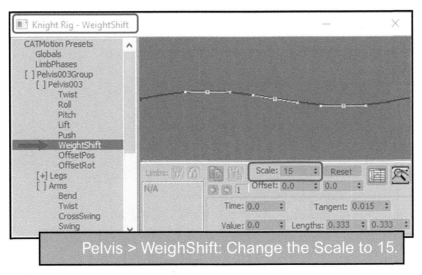

IMAGE 5.113

Move down the Pelvis Hub Group list to the Legs. We will next make some adjustment in the legs and in the ankles. Select the Twist in the lags list. This time change the Value to 0.0. This will stop the twisting rotation that is happening.

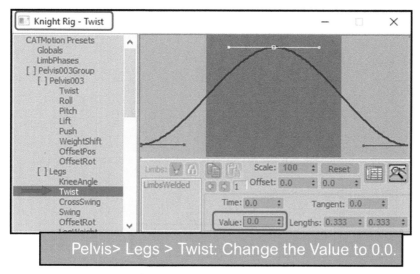

IMAGE 5.114

When the character is walking, the toes are moving through the ground plane instead of staying on top of the ground plane. By adjusting the DigitCurlAngle, we can keep the toes on the surface of the ground. Select the DigitCurlAngle parameter. In the right-side window, find the small phase or keyframe counter. Click the right green arrow once to change it to the second keyframe. Next, adjust the Value to 1.0. This will adjust the toe during the cycle.

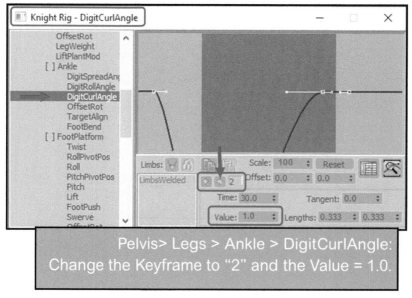

IMAGE 5.115

294

Open the TargetAlign parameter. Change the Value to 1.0. That will take care of the legs. If you were to run the animation now, it will have a normal looking walk cycle.

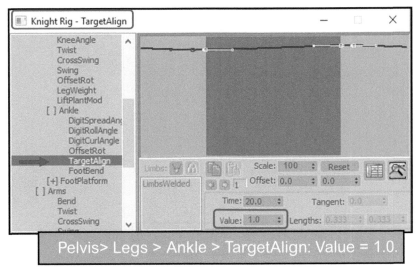

Pelvis> Legs > Ankle > TargetAlign: Value = 1.0.

IMAGE 5.116

The arms are positioned in a semi-raised position instead of a more natural position hanging closer to the body. Move down the Pelvis Hub Group list to the Arms section. Select the OffsetRot parameter. Change the "Y" value to 30.0. This will lower the arms into a better position that still allows the arms to not intersect the Torso as they swing. If you want to, try raising and lowering the spinner arrow values to see how the change in value effects the arm positioning.

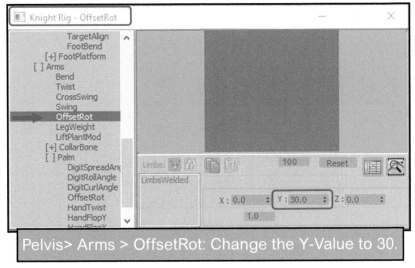

Pelvis> Arms > OffsetRot: Change the Y-Value to 30.

IMAGE 5.117

The hands are over-rotating un-naturally as the arms swing. To create a more natural hand movement, select the HandFlopX parameter and change the Scale value to 30.

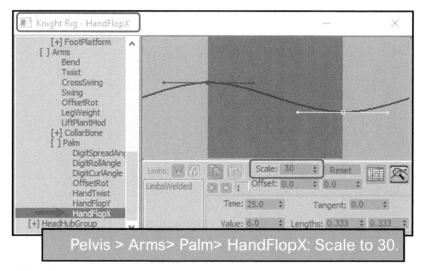

Pelvis > Arms> Palm> HandFlopX: Scale to 30.

IMAGE 5.118

The last two adjustments will be for the Helmet movement. Move to the HeadHubGroup, and open the HeadHubSection. Open the Twist parameter, and change the Scale value from 100 to 20. This will limit the head twist to a slight swivel while still looking forward.

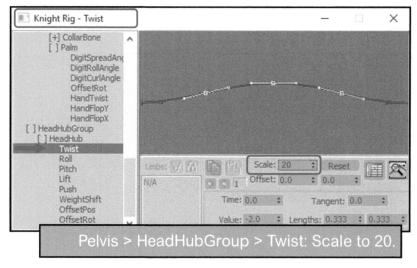

Pelvis > HeadHubGroup > Twist: Scale to 20.

IMAGE 5.119

Lastly, open the Roll Parameter. Change the Scale value to 10. This will limit the "bell ringing" motion to a more natural head roll motion.

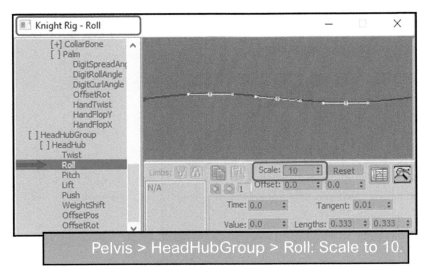

IMAGE 5.120

That completes the major adjusting to the CATMotion parameters. Play the animation of the Walk Cycle again, clicking the Setup/Animation Toggle button, and then the Play button on animation bar at the bottom of the UI. There should be quite a difference in the character motion. It should look rather impressive for no individual keyframing. Do you remember the process of animating the Knight in Chapter 2? Compare your results from the walk cycle exercise to the CATMotion walk cycle. Without having done the earlier exercise, you might not appreciate the value of the CAT rig and CATMotion. Of course, the animation can still use some refining, and it is nowhere near perfect. But, for a beginner at rigging and animating, your results are pretty impressive.

Adjusting the Torso Mesh

While playing the animation, you might have noticed the upper legs passing through the Torso mesh on the lower back side. It is an error that could not really be anticipated. Manually scrub the timeline in the play mode to see the issue. Not a big problem. All we need to do is to reposition the vertices on the back of the Torso to hide the leg as it moves to the rear extreme.

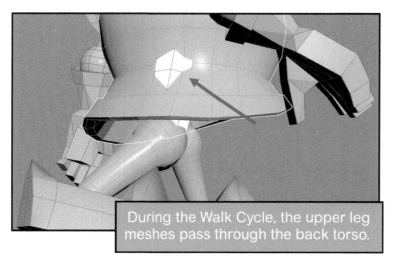

During the Walk Cycle, the upper leg meshes pass through the back torso.

IMAGE 5.121 (3ds Max File Save 5.26)

Select the Torso mesh. In the Modifier Stack the top setting is Skin. Click on the Vertex mode of the Editable Poly (not the vertex in Unwrap!). The warning window will pop-up. Click "OK." Select the row of vertices along the back in the creased area as shown in the next image. Remember, we can move vertices and not lose our mapping coordinates. We cannot add or remove vertices that would break the unwrapping, wiping out all the mapping coordinates.

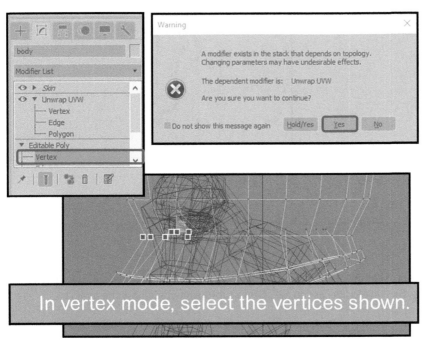

In vertex mode, select the vertices shown.

IMAGE 5.122

In the Top Viewport, use the Select and Scale tool to expand the radius of the vertices selected from the center of the mesh. A small distance will correct the problem. Check the progress in the Perspective Viewport to make sure the upper leg movement is concealed again. When the positions are correct, click the Vertex mode to get out of that state (important).

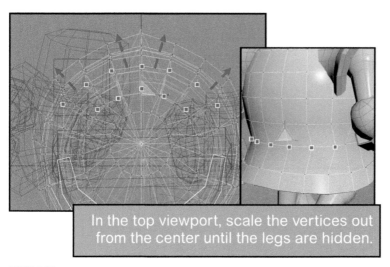

In the top viewport, scale the vertices out from the center until the legs are hidden.

IMAGE 5.123

Then, click back on Skin in the Modifier Stack. If you forget to get out of Vertex mode, only the selected vertices will be used by the Skin Modifier as you are still in a sub-object mode. Save the project.

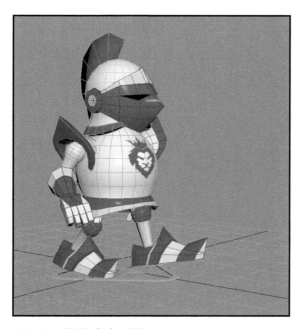

IMAGE 5.124 (3ds Max File Save 5.27)

Chapter 5 Exercise: Walk Variations

Open the last version of the Knight that you just finished in 3ds Max. Save it with a different name to protect the last file. Using the newly named file, alter the walk cycle using the CATMotion Editor to create an entirely different walk. Make it limp, wobble, walk silly, whatever you decide, create a very different walk than what we just completed. By doing this, you will become more familiar with the manipulation of the controllers.

Rigging the Warhorse Knight

Topics in This Chapter

- The Character Animation Tool
- Using a Prefab CAT Rig
- Creating a Custom CAT Rig
- Skin
- Walk Cycle

Concepts/Skills/Tools Introduced in This Chapter

- Weighting Vertices
- The CATMotion Editor

Preparing the Model

In Chapter 4, we modeled the Warhorse Knight. To rig the model, we have a choice: start from scratch or use the rigged Knight model we just finished in the previous chapter to get a head start.

If you would like, you can build a new custom rig from the ground up, starting with the CATParent. Below is an image of the finished rig we will be using. Note that it has a hub for the Horse Body, a hub for the Knight torso and hubs for both the heads of the Knight and the horse. The horse also has a tail bone. The horse has legs, the Knight does not. Our goal is to be able to apply a CATMotion file to the rig so the horse hops in the game as it moves instead of walking. The image below is of the finished CAT bone rig we will be making.

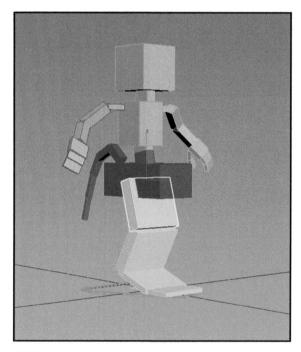

IMAGE 6.1

Since we have already invested the time to rig and weight the vertices of the Knight, we can use it to get a jump start on the Warhorse Knight using everything except the legs. There will be some initial work to be done to set up the model in the scene, but, in the long run, it will save us time. Open the file of the Warhorse Knight that I have provided in the companion files for Chapter 6, Vol2_Save 6.0.max. The companion files can be found online in the website for the book at www.3dsMaxBasics.com. You can also use your last saved version of the project from Chapter 4 if it was completed properly.

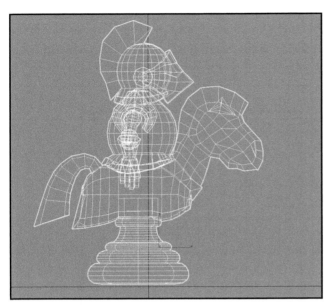

IMAGE 6.2

We will replace the current Knight mesh with the Knight mesh we rigged in the last chapter. Select all the mesh parts of the current Knight and delete them. All that should be left is the Horse Body mesh and the Base mesh.

Next, we will merge the final Knight iteration from Chapter 5 into this scene. Go up to File on the Top Tool Bar, click and select Import. From the flyout menu select Merge. Remember, you merge one .max file into a .max scene file. You import any other appropriate file extension file into a .max scene.

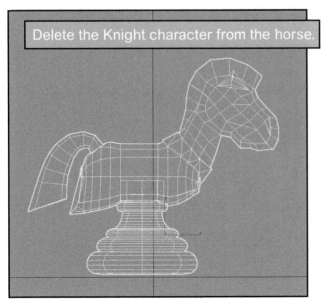

Delete the Knight character from the horse.

IMAGE 6.3

Merging the Knight Model

Select the Vol2_Save 5-27.max file from the companion files for Chapter 6 (there is a saved version there) or the one from Chapter 5 or from your own saved version. When the Merge window opens, select the "All" button, then OK.

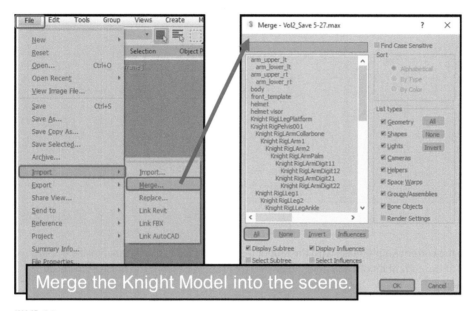

Merge the Knight Model into the scene.

IMAGE 6.4

When the model merges into the scene, it will be located at O, O, O in the X-, Y-, Z-axes. It will be inside the Horse mesh. For clarity, select the CATParent base and move the Knight to the right of the horse to separate them.

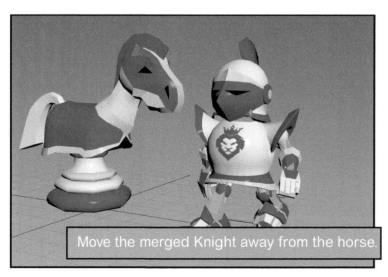

Move the merged Knight away from the horse.

IMAGE 6.5

If you were to go to the Motion panel, select a bone on the Knight and toggle the Setup/Animation Toggle button, the Knight would start the walk cycle we created in the last chapter. We need to remove that animation so we can create a new rig and CATMotion. Select the red "X" delete button to remove the animation layer.

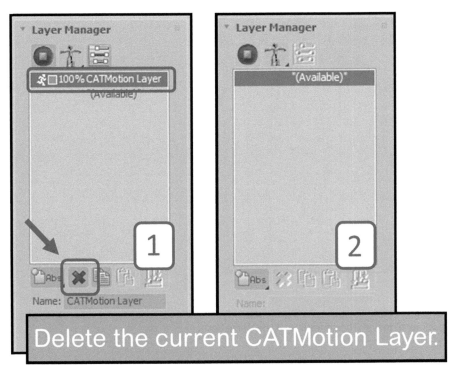

Delete the current CATMotion Layer.

IMAGE 6.6

The Knight on the Warhorse does not have legs, he and the horse are one. Select the four leg meshes, the six foot meshes and the leg bones. Delete them. The meshes being deleted from the model will not affect the Skin Modifier because they were assigned skin separately. The remaining meshes retain their Skin Modifier and vertex weighting.

If the model was a single mesh (not separate pieces), deleting part of the mesh, the legs, would remove all weighting of vertices and the Skin Modifier. Removing parts of the CAT Rig will not affect the functioning of the remaining rig. The remaining bones will still respond to the CATMotion when a new animation layer is created. That is another advantage of the CAT Rig.

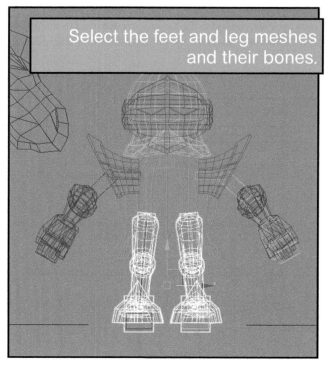

IMAGE 6.7

Move the Knight back to align with the centerline of the Horse Base.

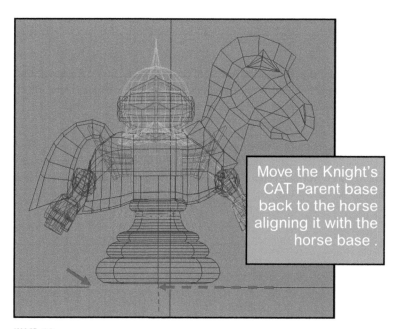

IMAGE 6.8

Select the Knight's Pelvis hub. Move it up, using the Select and Move gizmo Y-axis, to raise the Knight up onto the Warhorse's back. You can adjust the final position later.

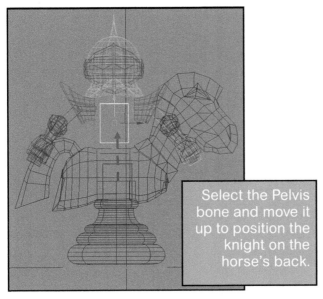

IMAGE 6.9

Creating the Custom CAT Rig

Turn the Knight so he is facing forward on the horse by selecting the CATParent again with the Select and Rotate tool. Change the X-Coordinate box value to −90. If that does not turn him correctly, try the other 90-degree values (0, 90, 270).

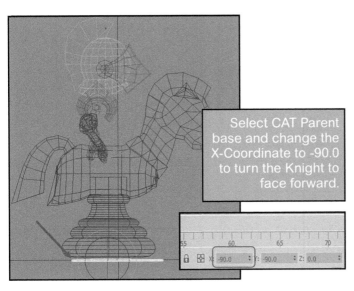

IMAGE 6.10 (3ds Max File Save 6.1)

With the Knight positioned on the Horse's back, we can start adapting its CAT Rig to include the Horse. Select the Knight's Pelvis hub. In the Modifier Panel's Hub Setup, click the Add Spine button.

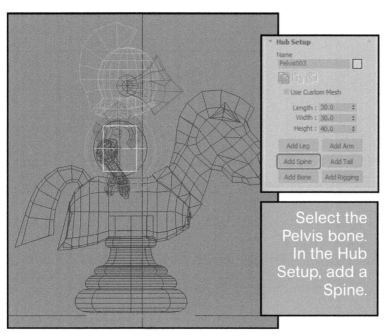

IMAGE 6.11

The new spine is created inside the Pelvis Hub. It is oriented in the direction of the Helmet. At the end of the spine is a new hub.

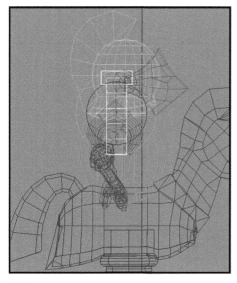

IMAGE 6.12

310

The new hub will be the pelvis hub of the Horse. We need to rotate the entire spine 180-degrees, so it is in the Horse Body. To rotate it successfully, select the root of the spine and with the Select and Rotate tool active, change the Y-axis coordinate value to 90. In the Modify Panel, change the Spine Setup bones to 2.

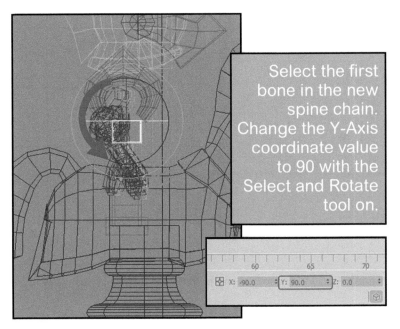

Select the first bone in the new spine chain. Change the Y-Axis coordinate value to 90 with the Select and Rotate tool on.

IMAGE 6.13

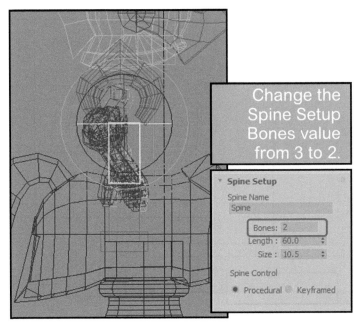

Change the Spine Setup Bones value from 3 to 2.

IMAGE 6.14

Select the new hub and position it so the center aligns with the centerline of the Base mesh. Also, move it slightly upward to center it in the body.

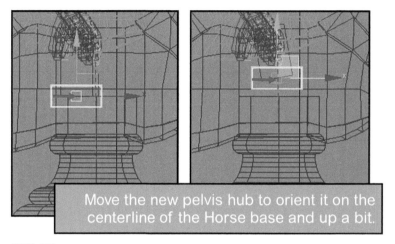

Move the new pelvis hub to orient it on the centerline of the Horse base and up a bit.

IMAGE 6.15

In the Hub Setup, change the Name to HorsePelvis and the Length, Width and Height parameters as shown below.

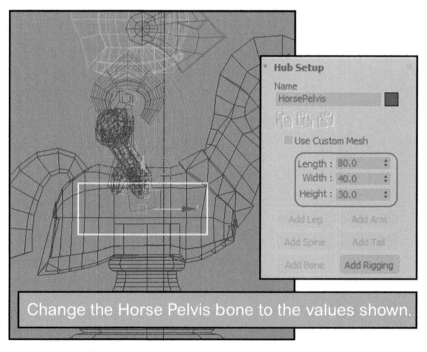

Change the Horse Pelvis bone to the values shown.

IMAGE 6.16 (3ds Max File Save 6.2)

With the HorsePelvis still selected, click on the Add Leg button in the Hub Setup section in the Modify Panel.

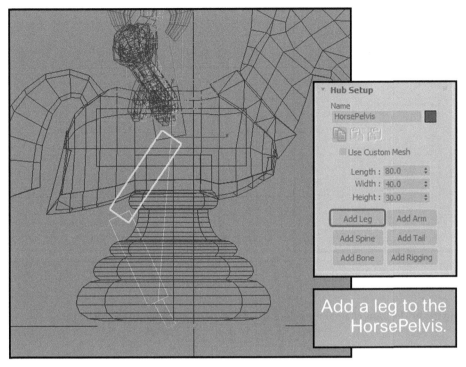

IMAGE 6.17

The new leg is positioned backward like an animal hind leg. We will fix that in a few minutes. It is perfectly fine, no need to panic.

Select a bone on the new leg. The Modify Panel will show the parameters for the leg. Our Warhorse has a chess piece base instead of legs. He only needs one leg for hopping. Click on the "Middle" radio button in the Leg Setup section. This will keep the leg in a straight path as it moves. Choosing the left or right would cause the leg to slightly crossover toward the centerline as it passes through its motion path, like our legs do when we walk.

Select the Ankle bone. Using the Select and Move tool, drag the Ankle to toward the front of the Base, the head end of the Warhorse. Position it roughly where it is in the image. In preparing this tutorial, I have experimented with a lot of different bone placements, sizes, vertex weighting, etc. It took a while to determine the best locations, values, etc., to create a working, animated figure in the end. The measurements are not magic numbers or numbers you should use with other characters. Each character is unique and will require unique solutions. If you would like to experiment with different placements and values as we work along you will be able to see how things work or how they influence the end animations.

313

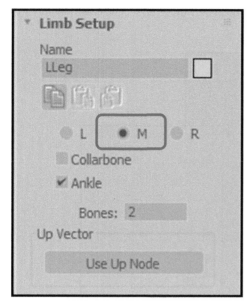

IMAGE 6.18

After positioning the Ankle bone, change the values for its size in the Ankle Setup section of the Modify Panel.

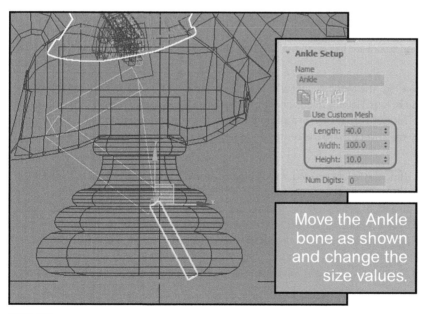

IMAGE 6.19

Switch to the Select and Rotate tool in the Front Viewport. In the Y-axis Coordinate box, change the angle value to 20. If that does not rotate the Ankle into the proper position, just rotate it manually to match the image below.

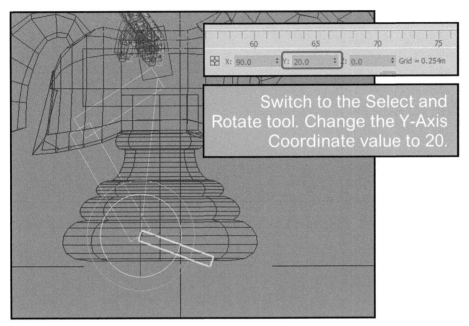

IMAGE 6.20

Now we will address the leg bones looking backward. Select the lower leg, KnightRigLLeg2 with the Select and Move Tool. Drag the gizmo for the bone to the location in the image marked number two below. Note its position, in the middle of the "neck" part of the base and to the front edge.

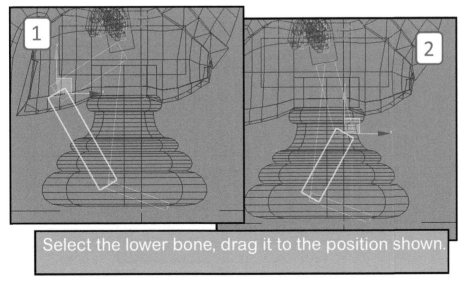

IMAGE 6.21

Once in position, change the size values of the bone as indicated in the next image. This will widen the bone to better fit the mesh and match up with the Ankle bone.

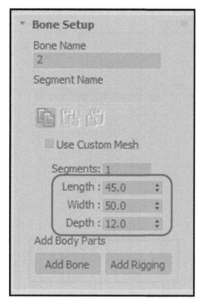

IMAGE 6.22

Next, select the upper bone, KnightRigLeg1. Change the size parameters to be in scale with the lower leg as shown.

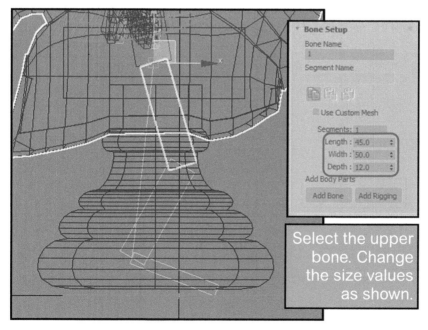

IMAGE 6.23 (3ds Max File Save 6.4)

Select the Ankle bone again. We need to add a toe digit. Change the Num Digits value box to 1.

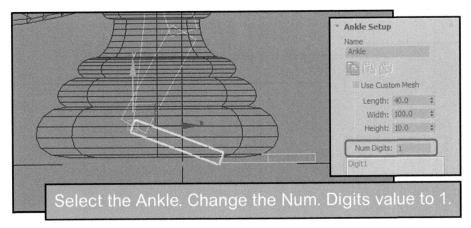

IMAGE 6.24

The default setting for digits is two. We will not be needing bendable toes. Select the Digit that was added to the Ankle bone and in the Modify Panel, change the Digit Setup Bones value to 1. Shorten the length to 25.0.

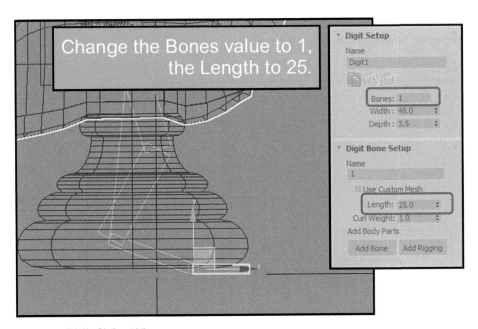

IMAGE 6.25 (3ds Max File Save 6.06)

Remember, we are only using one leg for the rig. Select the bones of the leg and the KnightRigLLegPlatform at the bottom of the bone chain. Use the Select and Move tool gizmo to drag the selection to align the centerline of the leg bones with the centerline of the Horse Base.

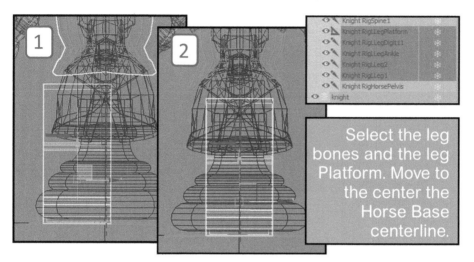

IMAGE 6.26

The last bone we need to add will be the Tail bones. We will not need to add any bones for the Warhorse's neck and head. The movement of the HorsePelvis will move it in the animation. Select the HorsePelvis Hub and add a Tail in the Hub Setup area of the Modify Panel.

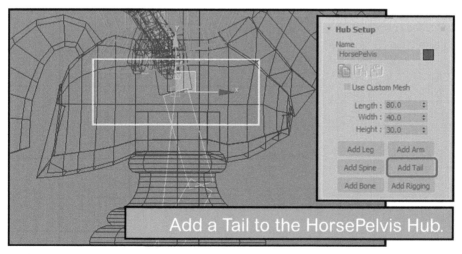

IMAGE 6.27

When the tail gets added it is created at the center of the hub bone, pointing straight up. With the other mesh splines in the area, it can be difficult to see the Tail bones. Select all the Tail bones in the bone chain. If you need to, select them in the Scene Explorer.

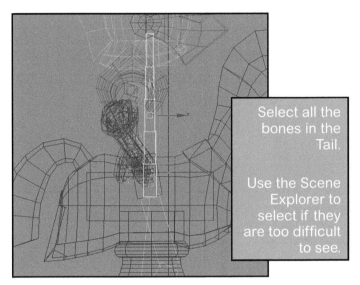

Select all the bones in the Tail.

Use the Scene Explorer to select if they are too difficult to see.

IMAGE 6.28

Once it is all selected, use the Select and Move tool to drag the tail to the tail area of the Warhorse mesh. Position it approximately as shown.

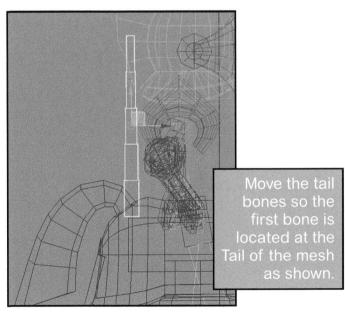

Move the tail bones so the first bone is located at the Tail of the mesh as shown.

IMAGE 6.29

Select the root bone of the chain, the first bone. In the Modify Panel, Change the length of the tail to 110.0. This will ensure that the last bone will extend slightly beyond the end of the tail mesh.

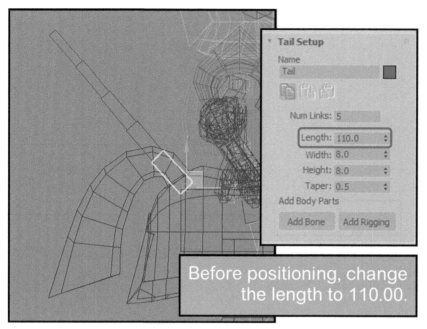

IMAGE 6.30

Next, using the Select and Rotate tool, individually select each bone and rotate them to follow the curvature of the tail as shown. Begin with the first, root bone.

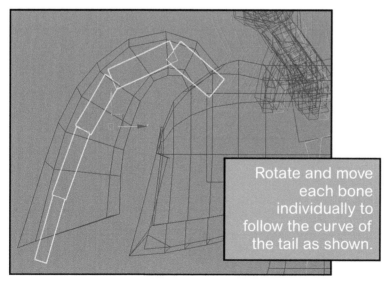

IMAGE 6.31 (3ds Max File Save 6.07)

That completes the rigging. We avoided having to weight the vertices of the Knight, his Torso, Arms and Helmet. We do need to add the Warhorse Body and the Horse Base to the collection of Skinned meshes and weight them.

Begin by selecting the Warhorse Body and the Horse Base. Add A Skin Modifier from the Modifier list in the Modifier Panel.

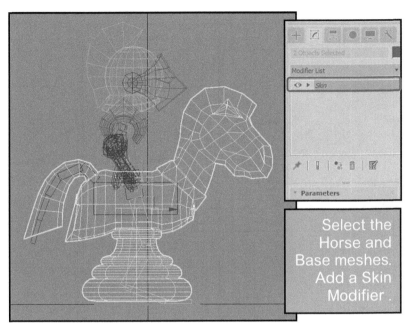

IMAGE 6.32

In the Modifier Panel, scroll down to click on the Bones: Add button to open the Select Bones window. When the window opens, select the Display tab on the top Navigation bar, then open the Expand All selection from the menu. Select the new bones we added to the rig: the HorsePelvis, the Leg and the Tail. We did not need to add the two spine bones between the Knight Pelvis Hub and the HorsePelvis Pub. We will not be assigning any new vertices to them.

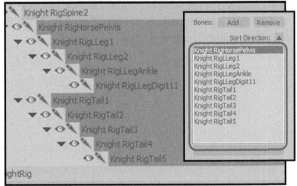

IMAGE 6.33

With all the bones added, you can test the walk cycle animation to see how it looks. Go to the Motion Panel, select a bone. Add an "Abs" CATMotion layer in the Layer Manager. Click the Setup/Animation Toggle button and then the play button on the lower tool bar. Again, it probably looks completely out of control. We need to weight the vertices of the Warhorse Body and base.

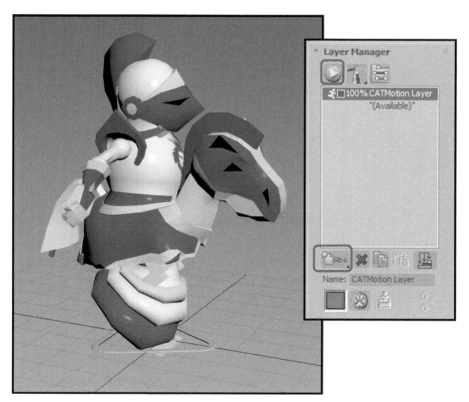

IMAGE 6.34

Weighting the Base Vertices

Just as with the Knight, the weighting of the vertices for the Warhorse will be tedious and will require concentration to keep track of the weighting assignment plan. Select the Horse Base to start. Click the Edit Envelopes and the vertices tick box so they are selectable.

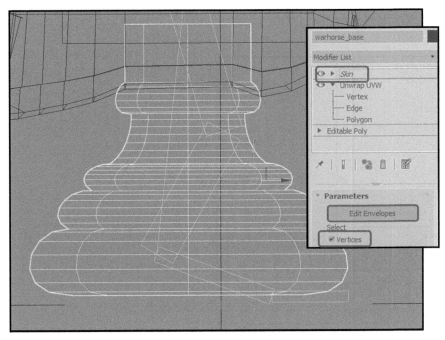

IMAGE 6.35

Enlarge the Front Viewport using the Maximize Viewport Toggle button in the lower right corner of the UI. Working in just this viewport, we will be able to control the vertex selections more easily. You can also scroll down the menu to check the "Show No Envelopes" button. We will be weighting the vertices directly.

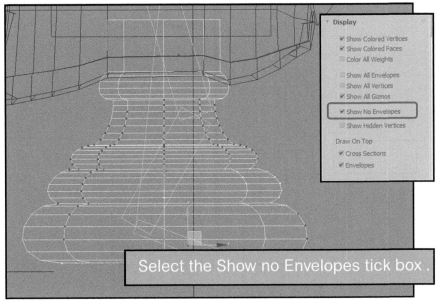

IMAGE 6.36

Open the Weight Tool window by selecting the Weight Tool icon in the Modify Panel.

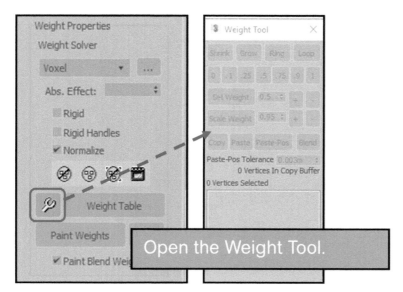

IMAGE 6.37

None of the vertices have weights assigned to them. I like to assign everything with an initial weight to one of the bones so there is something to subtract from if necessary. Select all the vertices of the base and assign them a weight of 1 to the KnightRigLLeg 1, the first bone in the leg Hierarchy Chain.

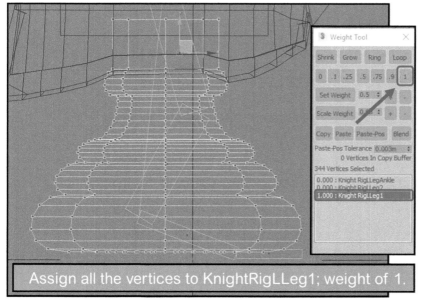

IMAGE 6.38 (3ds Max File Save 6.08)

We are going to assign the vertices in a methodical manner, working from the left side to the right side, top to bottom in the Front Viewport. Select the two columns of vertices on the left side of the mesh as shown below. Select the KnightRigLLeg 2 bone from the list in the Weight Tool or from the Bones list in the Modifier Panel if necessary. We want to distribute the vertex weights evenly between the upper leg bone and the lower leg bone. The upper leg bone already has a weight of 1. So, assign the selected lower leg bone a weight of .5, which will result in each bone having .5 or 50% of the total weight available, the .5 subtracted from the 1.

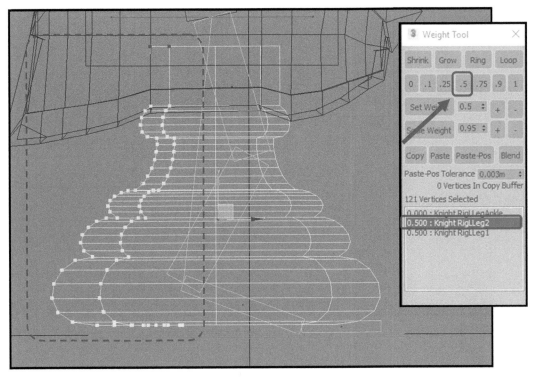

IMAGE 6.39 (3ds Max File Save 6.09)

Next, select the KnightRigLLegAnkle bone. You might need to select it from the Modifier Panel Bone List. Assign it a weight of .5. This will subtract .25 from each of the two previously assigned bone weights, evenly subtracting from all the weighted bones assigned. The selected vertices weights will be influenced by three bones.

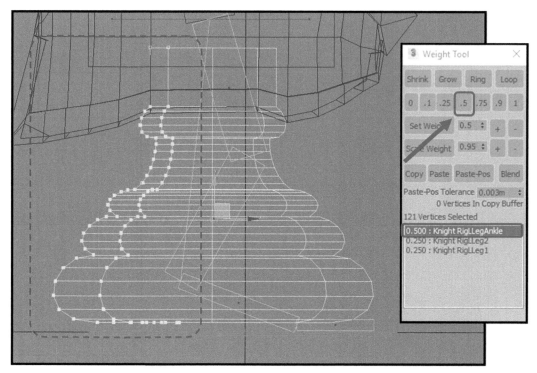

IMAGE 6.40

To summarize what we just did: We selected the vertices and assigned them to the upper leg bone with a weight of 1. Then we selected the lower leg and assigned the same vertices to it with a weight of .5, distributing the vertices between the two bones. We then selected the third bone, the Ankle bone and assigned it a weight of .5. To give it a weight of .5, the program subtracted equal amounts from the two other bones, .25, and transferred the weight to the Ankle bone. The image below has a box with text that describes what we did.

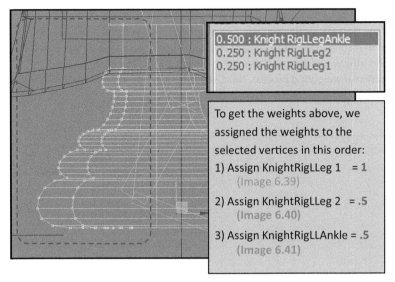

0.500 : Knight RigLLegAnkle
0.250 : Knight RigLLeg2
0.250 : Knight RigLLeg1

To get the weights above, we assigned the weights to the selected vertices in this order:
1) Assign KnightRigLLeg 1   = 1
   (Image 6.39)
2) Assign KnightRigLLeg 2   = .5
   (Image 6.40)
3) Assign KnightRigLLAnkle = .5
   (Image 6.41)

IMAGE 6.41

Moving to the center of the mesh, at the top, select the top vertex and the next six vertices below it that form the top curve shape. The next image has a text box similar to the previous image that has the text box describing our procedural steps. This text box describes the steps you should take to weight this next group of selected vertices. Follow the list in the order presented in the image to weight the vertices. If a bone is not listed, use the Modifier Panel Bone List. First pick the upper leg, assign 1. Then the lower leg, assign .25, then the Ankle, assign .5.

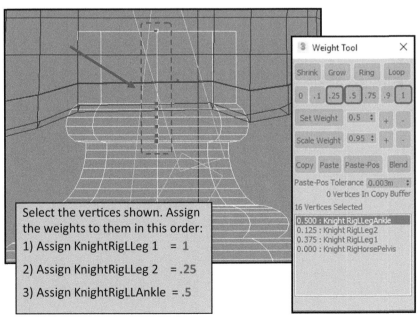

Select the vertices shown. Assign the weights to them in this order:
1) Assign KnightRigLLeg 1   = 1
2) Assign KnightRigLLeg 2   = .25
3) Assign KnightRigLLAnkle = .5

Weight Tool

Shrink   Grow   Ring   Loop

0 .1 .25 .5 .75 .9 1

Set Weight 0.5
Scale Weight 0.95

Copy Paste Paste-Pos Blend

Paste-Pos Tolerance 0.003m
0 Vertices In Copy Buffer
16 Vertices Selected
0.500 : Knight RigLLegAnkle
0.125 : Knight RigLLeg2
0.375 : Knight RigLLeg1
0.000 : Knight RigHorsePelvis

IMAGE 6.42

That is how the next 15 images will work. Follow the order of bone selection and assigned weighting to complete the weighting for the Horse Base. Remember, the weighting I used will result in workable animation in the end. I did a lot of testing of different weights and came up with a workable solution for our use. There are perfectly valid other weight combinations that could be used. We are in a learning situation to understand this particular weighting process. Next, select the next group of vertices below the last group as shown below.

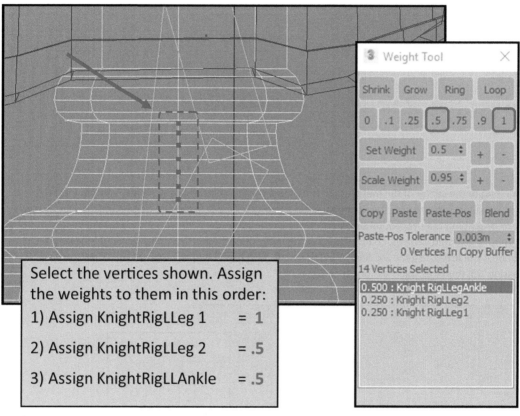

Select the vertices shown. Assign the weights to them in this order:

1) Assign KnightRigLLeg 1   = 1

2) Assign KnightRigLLeg 2   = .5

3) Assign KnightRigLLAnkle   = .5

IMAGE 6.43

On to the next group down the center of the base. This group is the top two curved sections of the bottom three sections.

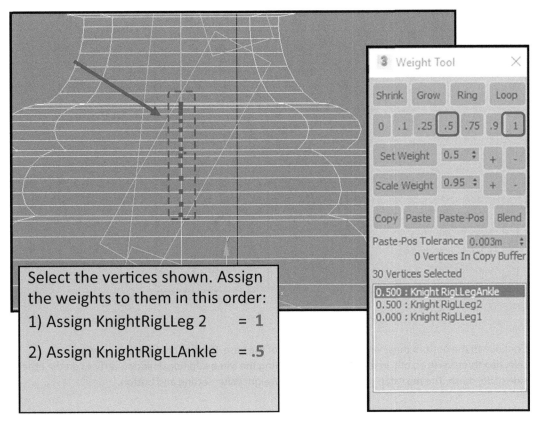

Select the vertices shown. Assign the weights to them in this order:
1) Assign KnightRigLLeg 2   = 1
2) Assign KnightRigLLAnkle   = .5

IMAGE 6.44

The bottom curved section in the center, I split into two, the three upper vertices and three lower vertices. As we approach the bottom, the Ankle bone gets more of the weighting, so it influences the movement to a greater degree. As the walk cycle progresses, the base gets distorted as the foot motion happens. This compensates for it.

In the next image, you will change the "Set Weight" value to .4 and click the Set Weight button to assign a weight not available in the short-cut buttons above it.

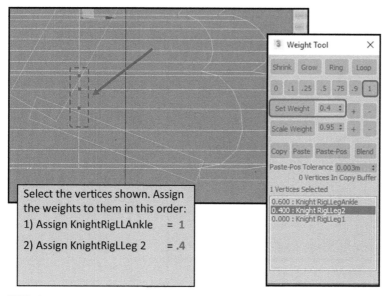

Select the vertices shown. Assign the weights to them in this order:
1) Assign KnightRigLLAnkle   = 1
2) Assign KnightRigLLeg 2   = .4

IMAGE 6.45

Continue to the bottom three vertices in the center of the base. Realize that from this view, you are selecting three vertices, but, in reality, you are selecting the three additional hidden vertices on the other side of the mesh. The next step also utilizes the Set Weight value setting and button.

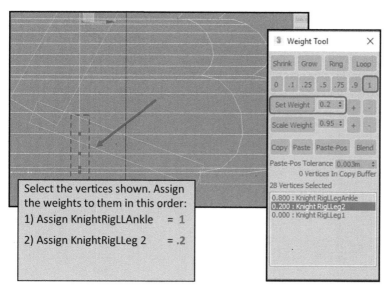

Select the vertices shown. Assign the weights to them in this order:
1) Assign KnightRigLLAnkle   = 1
2) Assign KnightRigLLeg 2   = .2

IMAGE 6.46 (3ds Max File Save 6.10)

Next, move back to the top of the mesh on the right side. Select the vertices shown below and weight as directed.

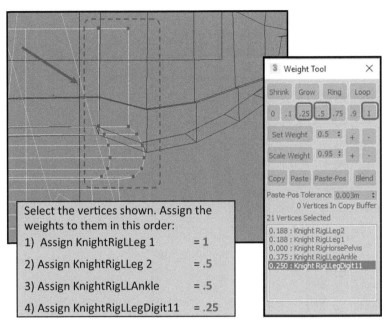

Select the vertices shown. Assign the weights to them in this order:
1) Assign KnightRigLLeg 1   = 1
2) Assign KnightRigLLeg 2   = .5
3) Assign KnightRigLLAnkle   = .5
4) Assign KnightRigLLegDigit11   = .25

IMAGE 6.47

The next section below the last group is the curve.

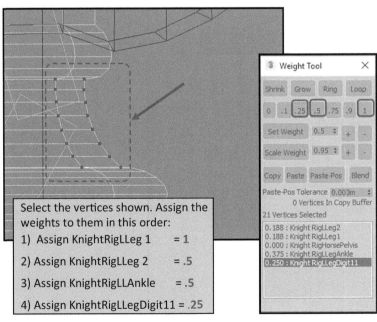

Select the vertices shown. Assign the weights to them in this order:
1) Assign KnightRigLLeg 1   = 1
2) Assign KnightRigLLeg 2   = .5
3) Assign KnightRigLLAnkle   = .5
4) Assign KnightRigLLegDigit11 = .25

IMAGE 6.48

The bottom section has the three curves. We will be weighting them progressively heavier in weight on the Digit bone to help with the walk cycle or in this case, a hop cycle. The front edge of the base does a curl motion like it is digging into the ground to push off on as it hops.

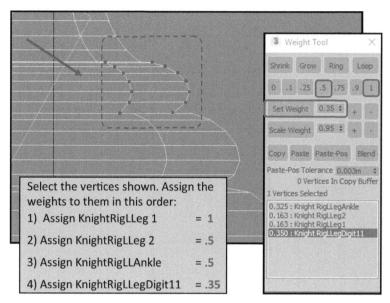

Select the vertices shown. Assign the weights to them in this order:
1) Assign KnightRigLLeg 1 = 1
2) Assign KnightRigLLeg 2 = .5
3) Assign KnightRigLLAnkle = .5
4) Assign KnightRigLLegDigit11 = .35

IMAGE 6.49

Next is the middle section of the three curves.

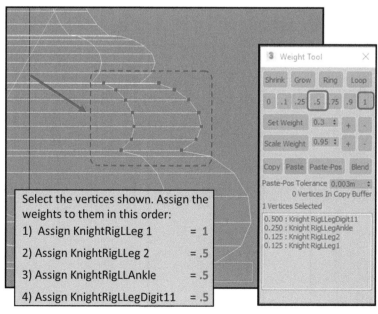

Select the vertices shown. Assign the weights to them in this order:
1) Assign KnightRigLLeg 1 = 1
2) Assign KnightRigLLeg 2 = .5
3) Assign KnightRigLLAnkle = .5
4) Assign KnightRigLLegDigit11 = .5

IMAGE 6.50

The bottom section of the curves gets the largest weighting on the Digit bone, the closest to the vertices.

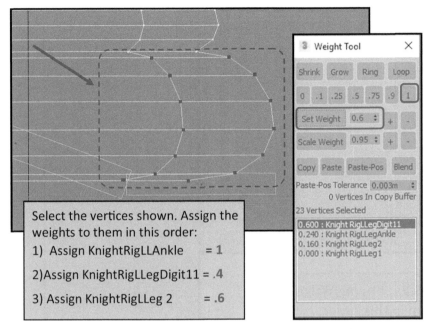

Select the vertices shown. Assign the weights to them in this order:

1) Assign KnightRigLLAnkle   = 1

2)Assign KnightRigLLegDigit11 = .4

3) Assign KnightRigLLeg 2   = .6

3 Weight Tool

Shrink   Grow   Ring   Loop

0   .1   .25   .5   .75   .9   1

Set Weight   0.6

Scale Weight   0.95

Copy   Paste   Paste-Pos   Blend

Paste-Pos Tolerance 0.003m
0 Vertices In Copy Buffer
23 Vertices Selected

0.600 : Knight RigLLegDigit11
0.240 : Knight RigLLegAnkle
0.160 : Knight RigLLeg2
0.000 : Knight RigLLeg1

IMAGE 6.51

We need to weight the vertices on the bottom too. Rotate the viewport with View Cube so you can see the bottom vertices. Select the vertices shown in the image below.

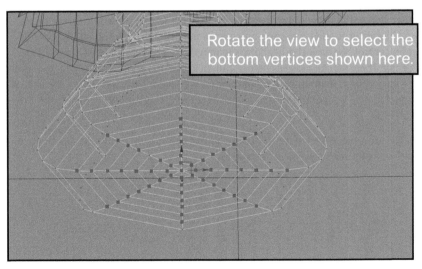

Rotate the view to select the bottom vertices shown here.

IMAGE 6.52

Weight the vertices selected as shown. They will be weighted to the Ankle and lower leg bones.

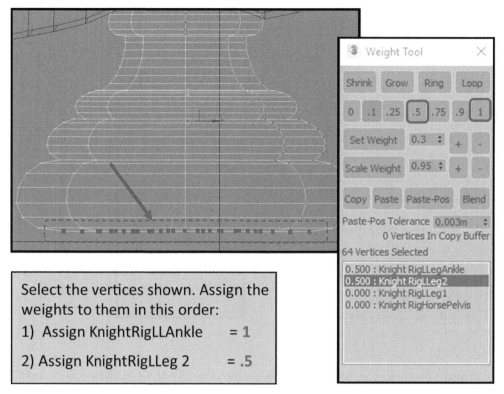

IMAGE 6.53 (3ds Max File Save 6.11)

If we were to play the animation at this point (do so if you like), the selected vertices would be out of place in a few parts of the cycle. The vertices end up passing outside the mesh in the back and out the bottom. To get these vertices under control, the easiest procedure is to move them up into the Base mesh and to scale them toward the center. They will still move as before, but, being within scaled smaller, they are not visible from the outside to the viewer. To do this, we need to go back to the mesh's sub-object level. Click on Vertex mode in the Editable Poly level of the Modifier Stack, below the Unwrap UVW (do not select the Polygon in the Unwrap UVW).

We can move vertices in the sub-object level of the editable poly. We cannot add or subtract anything, or we lose all the skin weighting assignments we have done so far.

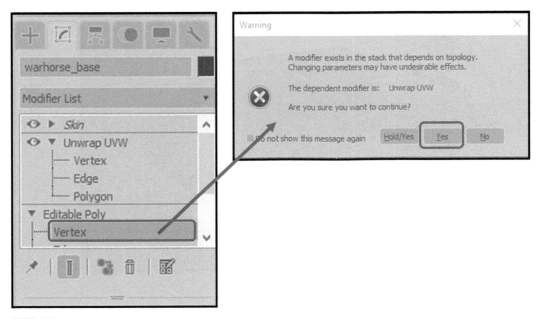

IMAGE 6.54

In Vertex mode, move the selected vertices up into the mesh, almost to the fourth row of vertices from the bottom. Then, switch to the Select and Scale tool and uniformly scale the selection toward the center of the mesh, making the diameter of the selected vertices smaller. This will move them to a safe location for the animation.

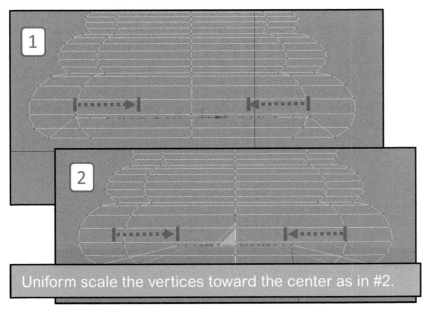

Uniform scale the vertices toward the center as in #2.

IMAGE 6.55

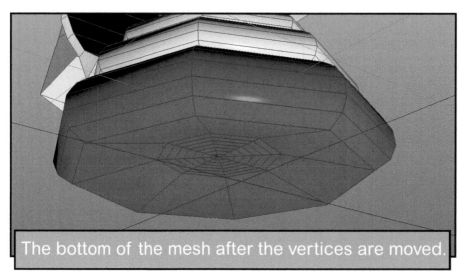

The bottom of the mesh after the vertices are moved.

IMAGE 6.56

Click the Vertex mode button again to leave the sub-object level. This is important to make sure you do. Otherwise everything you do will be applied at a sub-object level and not work.

That completes the weighting of the Horse Base mesh. If you play the animation (click a bone and toggle the Setup/Animation Toggle button in the Motion panel) you will see the base do a rough hopping cycle. We will refine it later once we get the Warhorse Body weighted.

Weighting the Warhorse Body

Weighting the body is somewhat simpler than the Base. To begin, select the entire Warhorse Body mesh. We will weight the mesh using the same process as we did with the base. The images will show the vertices to select and the text box will say which bone to select and how much weight to assign it in the Weight Tool. We will weight the upper half of the mesh to follow the HorsePelvis bone. The CATMotion controller will create the appearance of the head bobbing forward and back like a horse does. The lower half of the mesh will share weighting with the upper leg. This will cause the fringe around the bottom of the "fabric" to move as the legs move, creating more movement and rhythm as the character hops.

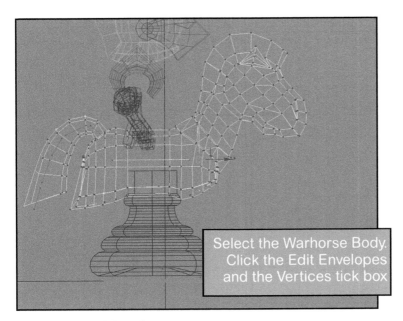

IMAGE **6.57** (3ds Max File Save 6.12)

While in the Skin Modifier, select all the vertices of the Warhorse mesh. Click on WarhorseRigHoesePelvis. Open the Weight tool and assign a weight of 1 to the selected vertices.

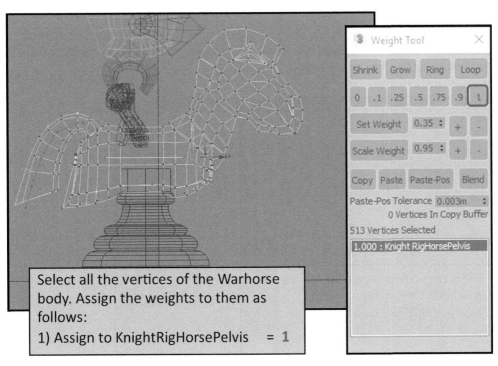

IMAGE **6.58**

Select the vertices on the lower half of the mesh as shown. Select the KnightRigLLeg1 and assign the selected vertices a weight of .1. Ten percent will be enough weight to create some movement in the fabric when the animation is running.

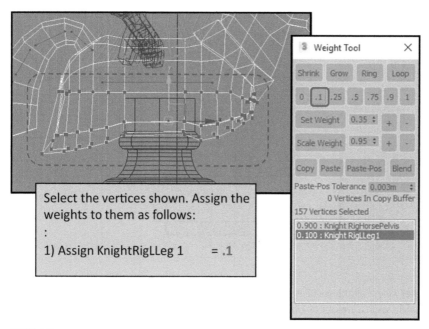

IMAGE 6.59

Next, we will weigh the Tail of the Warhorse. Select the vertices at the base of the tail where it connects with the body as shown in the next image. Put a small amount so weighting, .25, on the first bone of the Tail so it will move slightly when the Tail wags.

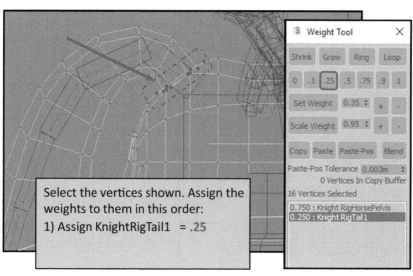

IMAGE 6.60

We will move progressively down the tail by vertex rows, assigning the weights to give the tail fluid movement. To do this, vertices in the middle of a bone will get full weighting to that bone. Vertices where two bones meet, a joint, will get the weight evenly divided to each bone. Start with the next set of vertices from the tail base we just weighted.

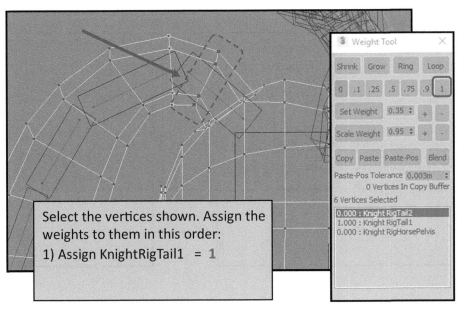

IMAGE 6.61

Continue down the tail assigning the weights to the vertices.

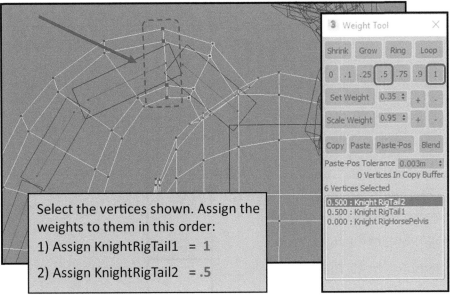

IMAGE 6.62

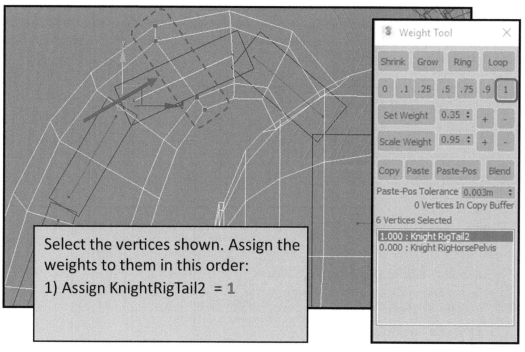

Select the vertices shown. Assign the weights to them in this order:
1) Assign KnightRigTail2 = 1

IMAGE 6.63

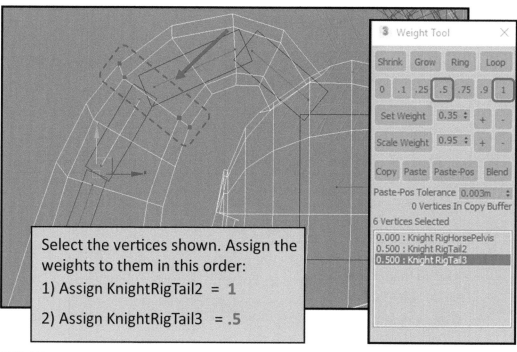

Select the vertices shown. Assign the weights to them in this order:
1) Assign KnightRigTail2 = 1

2) Assign KnightRigTail3 = .5

IMAGE 6.64

Half-way there, continue weighting.

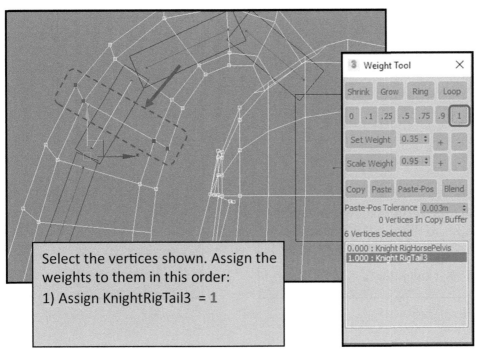

Select the vertices shown. Assign the weights to them in this order:
1) Assign KnightRigTail3 = 1

IMAGE 6.65

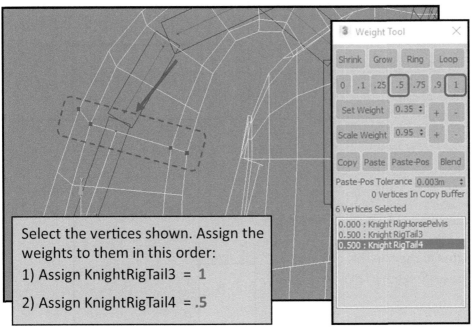

Select the vertices shown. Assign the weights to them in this order:
1) Assign KnightRigTail3 = 1

2) Assign KnightRigTail4 = .5

IMAGE 6.66

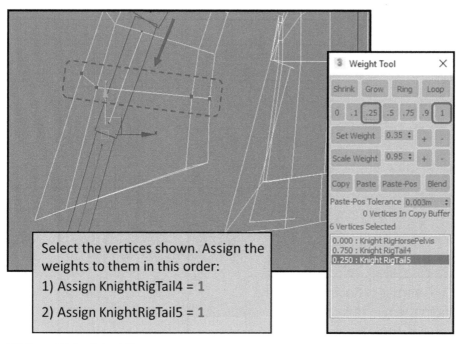

Select the vertices shown. Assign the weights to them in this order:
1) Assign KnightRigTail4 = 1
2) Assign KnightRigTail5 = 1

IMAGE 6.67 (3ds Max File Save 6.13)

The last part, the end of the Tail.

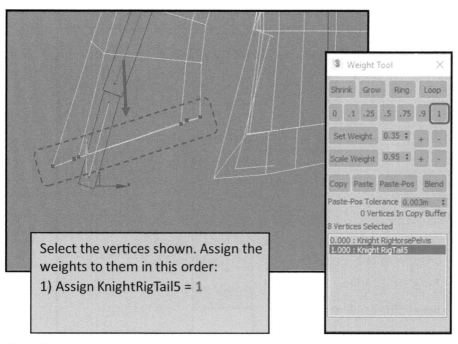

Select the vertices shown. Assign the weights to them in this order:
1) Assign KnightRigTail5 = 1

IMAGE 6.68

That does it for the weighting of the vertices. How can we check our work? Turn on the animated walk cycle. Go to the Motion Panel and toggle the Setup/Animation Toggle button to run the animation. As it runs, activate different viewports to check that everything is as it should be. It will be wild movement; we have not made adjustment to the CATMotion yet.

Stop the animation with the Stop/Play button. Click and drag the Time Slider manually back and forth. Do it slowly. You are looking for stray vertices that did not get weighted correctly. It happens. You will notice it when it happens. The vertex will move out of step with the vertices around it. When you find one. Select a vertex next to it (follow the segment between them). With the Weight Tool open, click on the neighboring vertex to see what the weight assignments are for it.

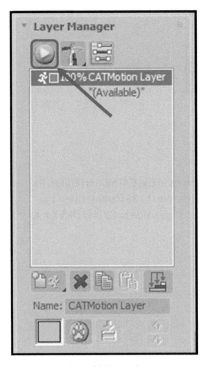

IMAGE 6.69 (3ds Max File Save 6.14)

Make a note of the values and then return to the wild vertex. Click on it and re-assign the vertices to match the neighbors. It should pop back into its correct place. This can be a long slow process on some character rigs because the vertex may be in place from one particular view, and way out of place from another view.

This was a fairly simple rig to work with and I pre-tested all the settings we used, so, hopefully you are in good shape to move on. The image below shows a few stray vertices that need fixing. If you have some strays, take your time, see what the next closest neighbors' weight is and reweight them.

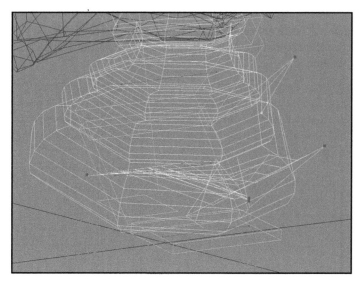

IMAGE 6.70

Adjusting the CATMotion Editor

With the weighting of the vertices finished, it is time to make adjustments in the CATMotion Editor. To start, just like with the Knight, change the overall animation time for the loop to 89 frames. Open the Time Configuration Editor on the bottom tool bar and change the End Time value to 89 and click OK to close the window.

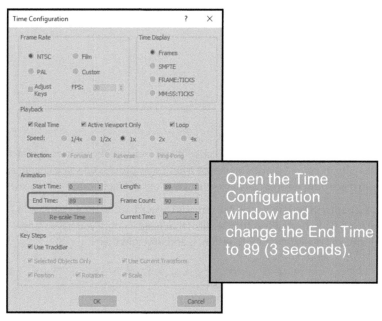

IMAGE 6.71

344

Next, select a bone on the rig. In the Motion Tab of the Command Panel, select the CATMotion Editor in the Layer Manager. Click the Setup/Animation Toggle button to Animation if it is not already (green Play).

We used the CATMotion Editor to get control of the Knight's Walk Cycle. This time we will use it to get the Warhorse into a controlled hopping cycle.

The first Preset in the CATMotion list of Presets is the Global Parameters. Select it and change the End value to 89, so it matches the animation time (the first frame is at 0, not 1). This will ensure we do not get a glitch in motion at the end of the cycle. It will be smooth and continuous.

Change the Max Step Time value to 30 and the Max Stride Length to 140.0. This will shorten the stride a little, so the Base does not appear to be over-stretching as it leaps forward.

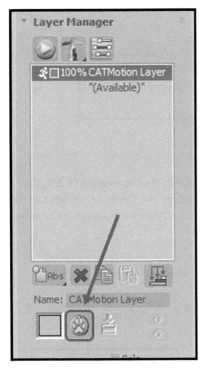

IMAGE 6.72

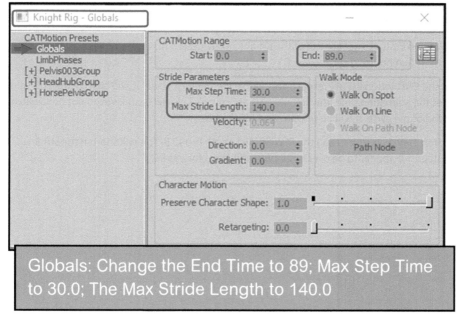

Globals: Change the End Time to 89; Max Step Time to 30.0; The Max Stride Length to 140.0

IMAGE 6.73

Next in the list is the LimbPhases. Select it and adjust the LArm and RArm sliders to a value of 0.257. This will put both the arms in a unified swing motion. Since the Knight is "riding" the Warhorse, the arms would not swig opposite each other like in a walk cycle. To stay balances on top, they would likely move together since we do not have reins to hold.

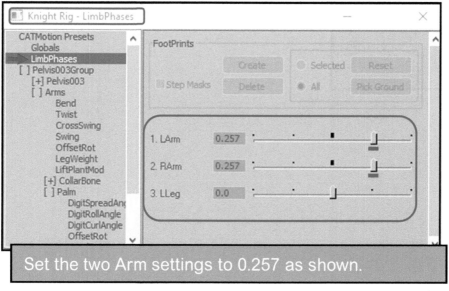

Set the two Arm settings to 0.257 as shown.

IMAGE 6.74

Since the Knight is on the Warhorse, the body does not need a twisting motion like in a walk cycle. Change the Scale value to 10.0 to give the torso a slight twisting motion. A little motion is preferable to give the character some life.

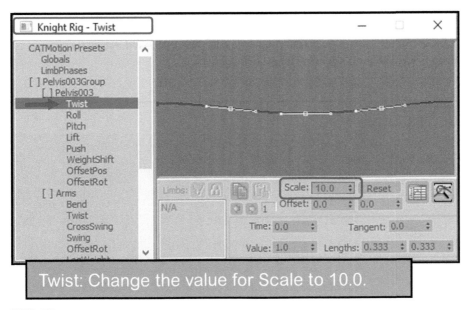

Twist: Change the value for Scale to 10.0.

IMAGE 6.75

In the Roll parameters, change the Scale value setting to 0.0. Again, riding a horse the Roll would be minimized.

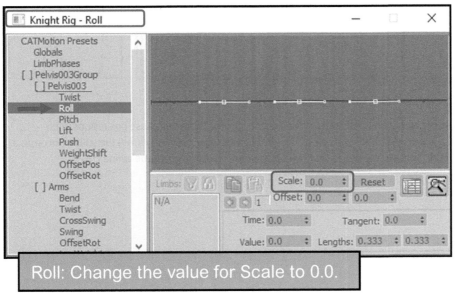

Roll: Change the value for Scale to 0.0.

IMAGE 6.76

With the Pitch, our goal is to get the Knight to move in sync with the Warhorse Body's up and down motion. The four points on the spline in the image are called knots. The spline represents the timeline, so the knots are located at frames along the timeline. Below the spline image are two buttons, Previous and Next and a small window with a number representing which knot in the image is currently selected. Below the Editor image, I have put small snapshots of the four knots and the settings that I used to adjust the motion. Change the setting for the first knot, Time = 10, the Value = 0.0. Next, click the Next arrow button to move to the second knot. Change the values to Time = 35, Value to 2.0. Repeat the steps for the next two knots, 3 and 4, matching the settings in the snapshot images.

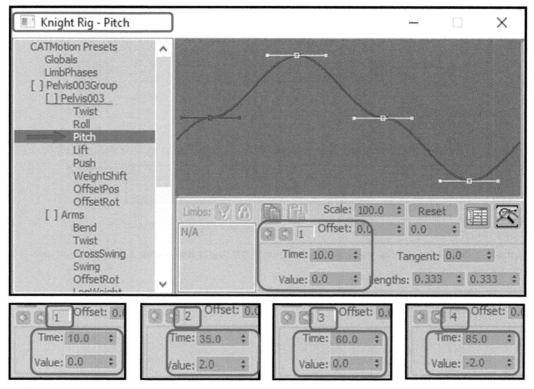

IMAGE 6.77

The Spline in the image now has flat spots at the knot locations. These will cause hesitations in the animation flow. Click on the handle on one of the knots and drag it to rotate it until the spline becomes a continuous, smooth curve as shown. Repeat with each knot, smoothing out the spline curve.

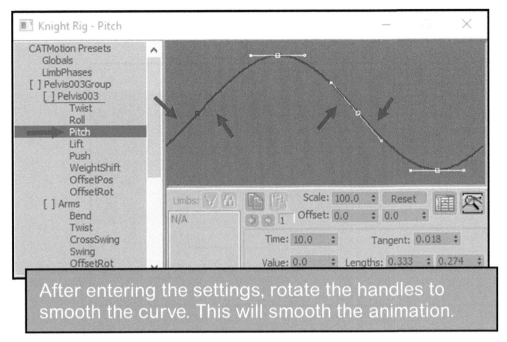

After entering the settings, rotate the handles to smooth the curve. This will smooth the animation.

IMAGE 6.78

Next, in Lift, repeat the same step for adjusting the Time and Value settings for the four knots along the spline in the image.

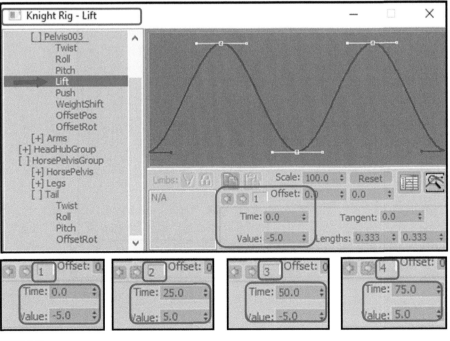

IMAGE 6.79

The WeightShift should be minimized also, but still have some movement to look alive. Change the Scale value to 10.0.

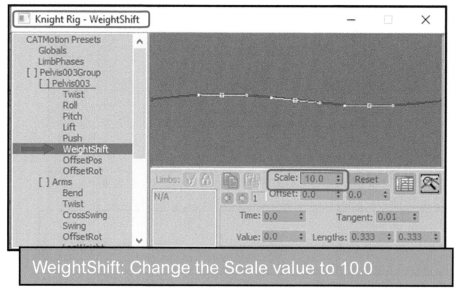

WeightShift: Change the Scale value to 10.0

IMAGE 6.80

Moving on the Knight's arms, select the Bend controller. Change the Scale value to 10.0.

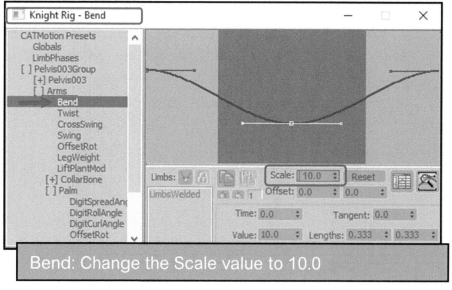

Bend: Change the Scale value to 10.0

IMAGE 6.81

The CrossSwing setting will move the arms toward the Knights back as they swing backwards. To do this, change the value setting to 20.0.

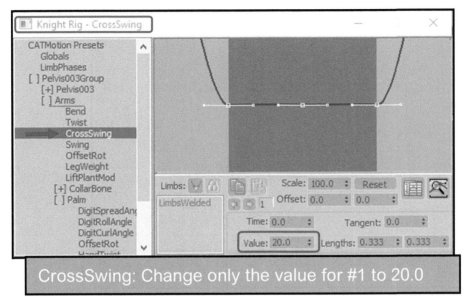

CrossSwing: Change only the value for #1 to 20.0

IMAGE 6.82

Change the OffsetRot "Y" setting to 15.0. This will bring the arms down, closer to the body.

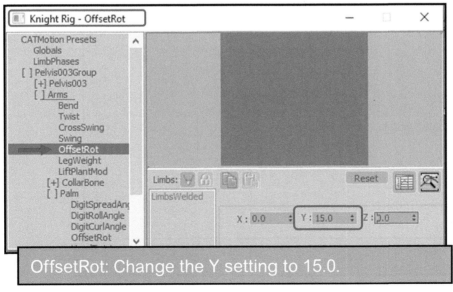

OffsetRot: Change the Y setting to 15.0.

IMAGE 6.83

Move to the Knight's HeadHub next. In the Twist controller, change the scale to 30.0 to control the head motion.

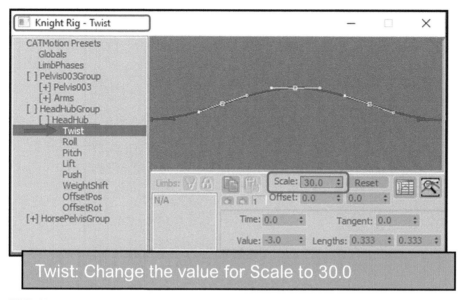

Twist: Change the value for Scale to 30.0

IMAGE 6.84

Adjust the Roll Controller Scale value to 50.0

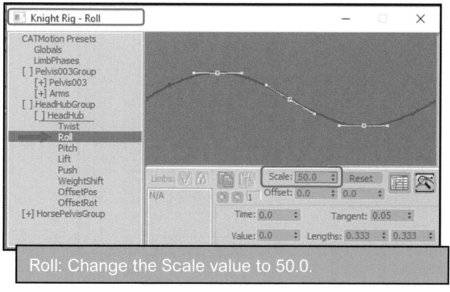

Roll: Change the Scale value to 50.0.

IMAGE 6.85

The head should bob a little as the Knight bounces with the Warhorse. Change the Pitch Time and Value settings for the four knows on the timeline spline.

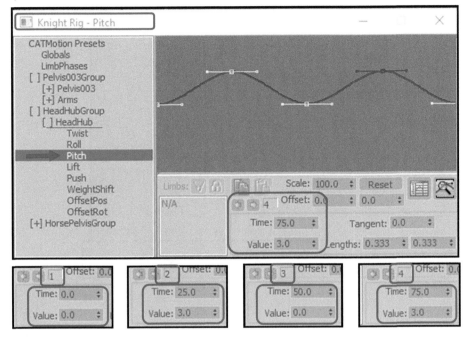

IMAGE 6.86

That takes care of the Knight. Next, adjust the controllers for the Warhorse Body, Legs and Tail. Start with the Horse Pelvis. Change the Scale value to 30.0 to reduce the side-to-side motion.

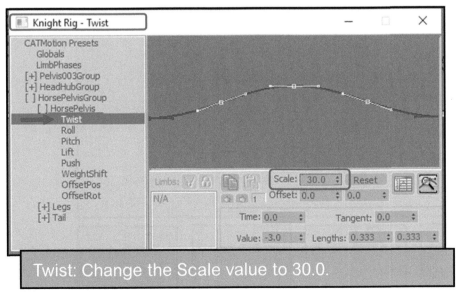

IMAGE 6.87

Adjust the Roll Controller Scale value to 30.

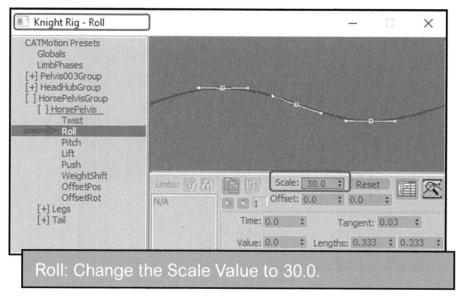

Roll: Change the Scale Value to 30.0.

IMAGE 6.88

Like the Pitch for the Knight's Pelvis, the HorsePelvis requires adjustments for the four knots on the timeline spline. Adjust as shown in the image below.

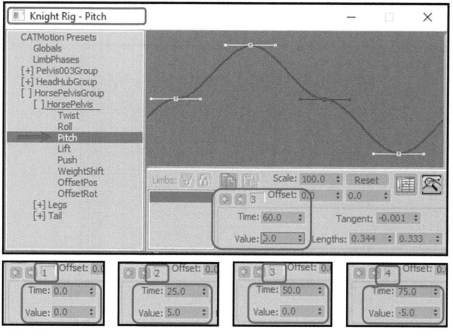

IMAGE 6.89

Adjust the knot handles in the timeline spline area to create smooth transitions from knot to knot.

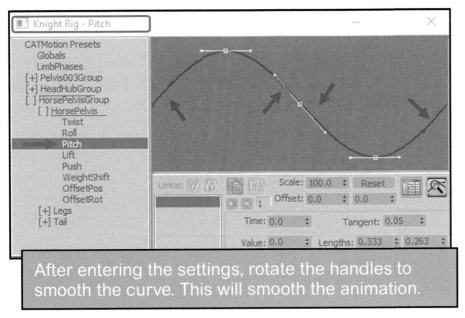

IMAGE 6.90

Move down the list to the Legs. Set the LiftLPlantMod Controller slider to 0.612.

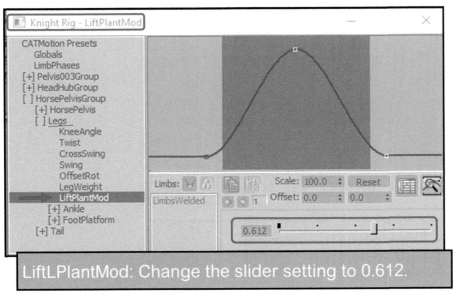

IMAGE 6.91

Next, move down the list to the FootPlatform and select the FootPush. Change Time and Value for the second knot on the timeline spline as shown. This will make the leading toe edge of the Base curl down like it is digging into the ground for traction as the character hops forward.

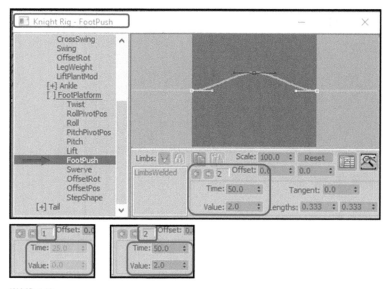

IMAGE 6.92

Last section for adjusting, move to the Tail and select the Twist. Set the four knot values on the timeline spline as shown. This will make the tail movement appear to be a reaction to the body movement.

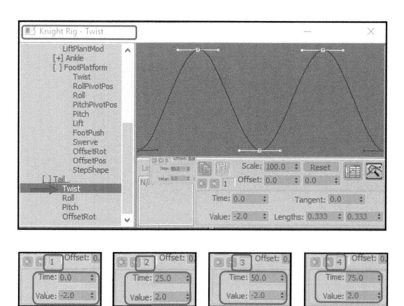

IMAGE 6.93

356

That completes the adjusting to the CATMotion controllers. Click on the Play button to watch the animation. It should look pretty good. Not perfect, but, understand that we did not go into the animation and make detailed keyframe adjustments. His was all done using the CATMotion Editor and the CAT Rig.

Don't like how something is moving? Feel free to go in and make adjustments in the CATMotion Editor to suit your likes. It would be a good way to become more familiar with the controllers. Maybe you would rather position the arms to be up in front of the Knight's torso as if holding reins. You could go back into the rig to add a Spine to the HorsePelvis to rig the horse neck and head. To do so, you just add the Spline, position and resize it. Select the Warhorse Body mesh and add the new bones to the bone list in the Skin Modifier. Add the vertex weights accordingly and then adjust the CATMotion controllers to have the head bob forward as a real horse does when walking. Currently our head and neck are rigid, not realistic, taking away from the animation. We could not add the bones due to the text length required.

IMAGE 6.94 (3ds Max File Save 6.15)

Chapter 6 Exercise: Adding Weapons

Earlier in the book, you made a lance or weapon for an exercise. Merge the weapon into the Warhorse scene just animated and save to a new file name. Position the weapon in the hand of the Warhorse Knight. Link the weapon to the lower arm holding it.

Adjust the CATMotion Editor parameters to enable the Knight to be able to appear to be holding on the weapon as the Warhorse hops. It will take a lot of experimentation to determine which parameters will create the visual control to create a convincing look.

Character Modeling:
The Dragon

Topics in This Chapter

- Character Development
- Preparing the scene: Template planes
- Template images
- Quick Peel Unwrapping

Concepts/Skills/Tools Introduced
in This Chapter

- Polygon Modeling Designing the Character

The next character we will create is the Dragon. From the GGD for the game, the Dragon is described as follows:

Game Castle Keep, Blue Vs. Red	
Character	Character: Dragon
Who	In the game, the Dragon is a common enemy and a threat to both the Red and the Blue Army. All players need to be on the lookout to his attacks What: The Dragon is a lizard-like creature with large wings. He has active, lively movement, and he has four legs, a long tail and a head proportioned like an alligator
When	The mythical creature is typical of those envisioned in medieval times
Where	The Dragon flies in the sky on a looping path over the castle and the land around the castle. Along the path he flies high and swoops low. The Dragon will spew flames that damage players and NPCs
Movement	Flying, no player controls
Animations	Flying, spewing flames
Model	
	Poly limit: 15,000 poly limit
	Size limit: 30 m length, 3 m height (head)
	Complexity: deformable mesh

No one has ever seen a dragon. Our research will be difficult without resources, unless we look at fantasy art. There are lots of interpretations of dragons, a huge range. Starting with something real is often a good place to begin. One clue from the character description is that it is lizard-like. In my searches for imagery, I found the image below, a 3d illustration by Kostyantyn Ivanyshen, to be the major influence in the design.

With this as a starting point, I searched and found images of a Komodo Dragon. They are large, long tail, sort of an alligator-shaped head, and they lumber along with a deliberate walk. All we need to do is add wings! We have a poly limit of 15,000 polygons. I will be creating our design based on this information.

IMAGE 7.1 © Shutterstock. Used with Permission.

Our next step would be to start gathering some reference to base our character design on. The following are some of the images I found to get started.

IMAGE 7.2 © Shutterstock. Used with Permission.

IMAGE 7.3 © Shutterstock. Used with Permission.

IMAGE 7.4 © Shutterstock. Used with Permission.

After some sketching exercises of variations, I settled on the design below for our Dragon. It has a simplicity that would seem to go well with the style of our Knight characters and the level of realism the environment has, a hand-drawn style.

IMAGE 7.5

For the Knight and the Warhorse, we sent through the modeling process step-by-step. By now you should be fairly competent at basic modeling. For the Dragon, the text will move along at a quicker pace, not stating every step, where to click, etc. For the Knight and the Warhorse, I used wireframe images from the models I built. It was fairly easy for you to move your vertices to match the image vertices, almost like paint-by-number easy. For the Dragon, I will just be providing drawn images. You will need to use your skills to determine where to best place your vertices. You will not be able to match the drawings perfectly. That is alright for what we are modeling. Your goal will be to try to get close to the drawing, close enough to create a good interpretation of the image. Do not be obsessed with getting the vertices exactly placed as shown in the drawing. This is how your template will be working in a game company. The scale of the Dragon to the Knight is shown in the image below.

IMAGE 7.6

Setting up the Templates

Just like with the other characters we modeled, create two template planes in a new 3ds Max scene. The three template images are available on the companion website, www.3dsMaxBasics.com, in the companion files tab, Chapter 7. The sizes of the images are written on them. Create the two planes and position in the Front and Left Viewports: two are 7.00 m×4.25 m and one is 4.25 m×4.25 m. Apply the images as textures to the correct planes.

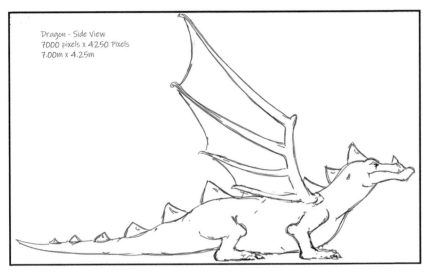

IMAGE 7.7

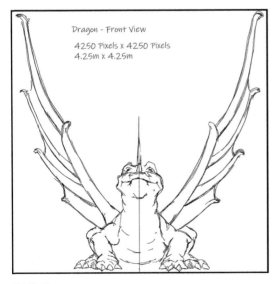

IMAGE 7.8

The next image shows the three templates in the scene ready for modeling. If you are having trouble creating them, please refer back to Chapter 2.

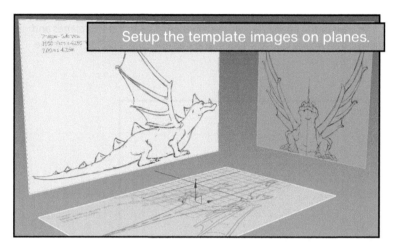

IMAGE 7.9 (3ds Max File Save 7.1)

The Placeholder

Model a rough placeholder for the Dragon using primitives. Use the templates as your guide. No details, just a simple placeholder. Create the proper folders in the Scene Explorer.

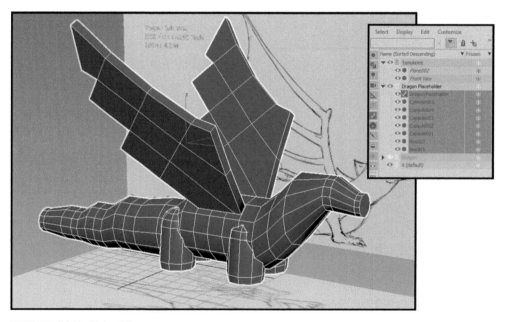

IMAGE 7.10 (3ds Max File Save 7.2)

Modeling the Body

Time to start the Dragon model. Select the two template planes and freeze them (uncheck Show Frozen in Gray in the Object Properties). Create a cylinder in the Left Viewport as shown. Position and change the parameters as shown. Change the cylinder's name to Dragon Body. There should be a separate layer in the Scene Explorer.

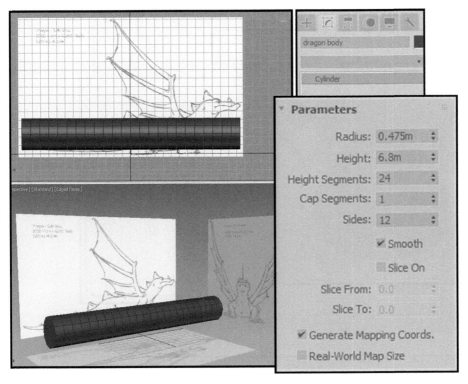

IMAGE 7.11 (3ds Max File Save 7.3)

In the Modify Panel of the Command Panel, add a Taper modifier to the Dragon Body mesh. Change the parameters to as shown in image 7.12.

Convert the cylinder to an Editable Poly. Right click on the mesh to open the Object Properties. Check the See-Through option to on.

In Vertex mode, select each vertical column of vertices individually in the side view and move them vertically so that the center vertex of the group is aligned approximately with the center of the Dragon's body in the image as shown below in Image 7.13.

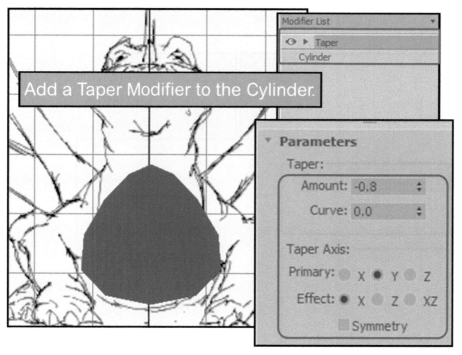

IMAGE 7.12 (3ds Max File Save 7.4)

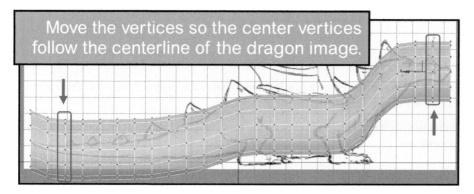

IMAGE 7.13 (3ds Max File Save 7.5)

By moving the vertex columns to the centerline of the body, we can now use the scale tool to scale each column to approximate the Dragon's body outline in the image template. In the Front Viewport, select the columns individually and scale to fit the image size indicated on the template. Use the Select and Move tool to make minor adjustment in position after scaling. Make sure you are scaling uniformly (in the inner yellow are of the gizmo) so you do not create distorted shapes.

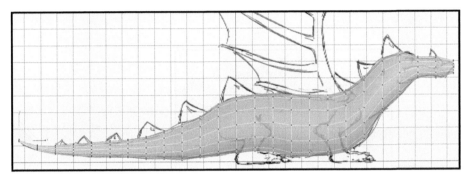

IMAGE 7.14

Switch to the Top Viewport. Repeat the procedure of scaling the rows of vertices individually to fit the Dragon's body outline in the image. Just use the body part of the image.

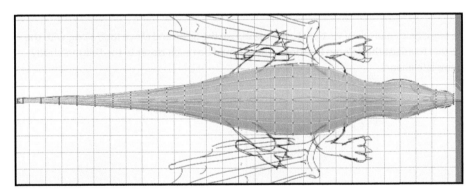

IMAGE 7.15 (3ds Max File Save 7.6)

The neck and head areas of the mesh will be difficult to create the correct shapes with the limited number of vertices from the base cylinder. In Vertex mode, use the Swift Loop Tool in the Modeling Ribbon menu to add new columns of vertices as shown in the image below.

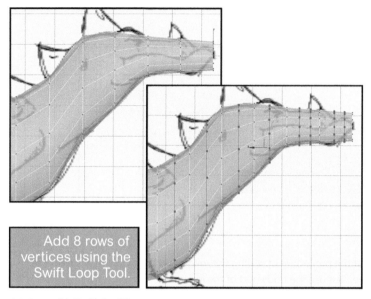

IMAGE 7.16 (3ds Max File Save 7.7)

After adding the eight new columns of vertices to the mesh, use the Scale and Move tool, along with the Select and Move tool to adjust the column locations. They should be much closer to the Dragon's body outline on the template image.

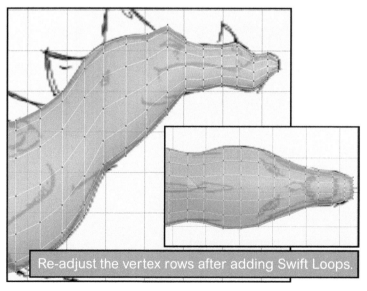

IMAGE 7.17 (3ds Max File Save 7.8)

368

Modeling the Wing as part of the body, at an angle, would be a daunting, frustrating task. We can model it as a separate mesh and attach it when it is complete. We do not need to model it with the curves as seen in the image templates. When we add bones, they will create the curves. Create a new plane for the wing template (2.75 m wide by 3.27 m in length (height)). Create a new texture in the Material Editor using the Dragon Wing.png side view image in the companion files. Freeze the plane.

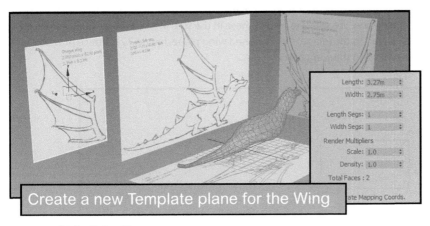

IMAGE 7.18 (3ds Max File Save 7.9)

Modeling the Wing

Next, create a new plane in front of the Wing Template plane that we will use to model the Wing mesh. Create it in the Front Viewport. Change the parameters to match the ones in the image below.

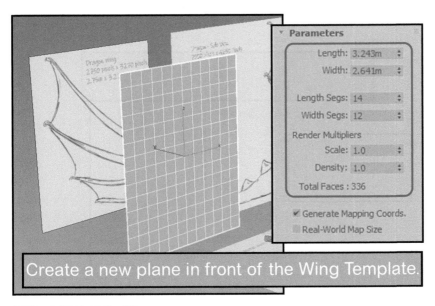

IMAGE 7.19 (3ds Max File Save 7.10)

Convert the plane to an Editable Poly. Start in the lower right corner, moving the corner vertex into position as shown, followed by the vertices to its left, creating the bottom edge of the wing. Try to move vertices using just the Y-axis of the gizmo when possible, sometimes you need to use the X-axis also. If the vertex above the one selected is in the way, move it up out of the way before moving the selected one.

This will be a long process that will require patience. Try to create smooth curves for the rows if possible. There is not just one way to model this wing. You do not need to follow my images exactly. There will be extra vertices to the left of the wing. We will take care of these in the step after all the vertices are placed. Take a few minutes to look ahead to the image of my finished wing plane, Image 7.23. Notice how I broke up the distribution of the vertices in the wing parts.

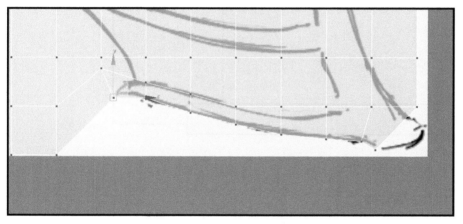

IMAGE 7.20 (3ds Max File Save 7.11)

Continue with the next rows, working your way up the wing methodically, row-by-row as you move vertices.

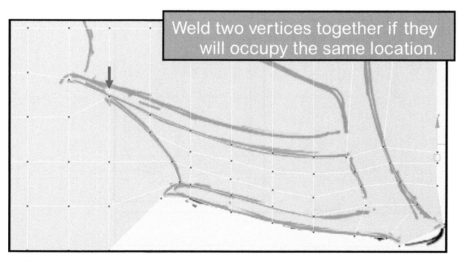

IMAGE 7.21

IMAGE 7.22 (3ds Max File Save 7.12)

Select all the vertices that will not be part of the wing mesh as shown in the image below. Delete them to be left with the wing shape.

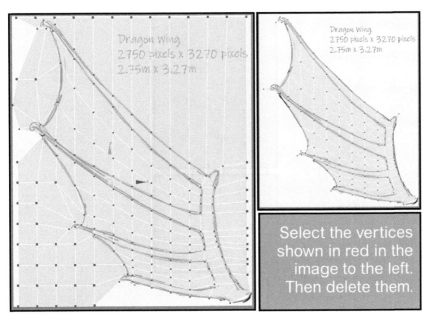

IMAGE 7.23 (3ds Max File Save 7.13)

Next, we will add thickness to our wing and define some shape. Select all the polygons of the wing. Extrude with the Extrude Caddy 0.01 m, very thin.

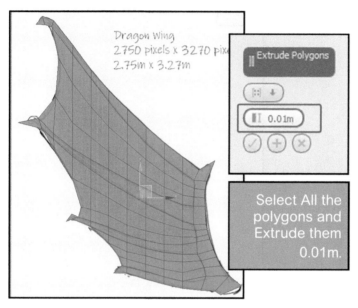

IMAGE 7.24 (3ds Max File Save 7.14)

Select the "bone" polygons as shown below. These will be thicker than the web area of the wing. Extrude them 0.05 m.

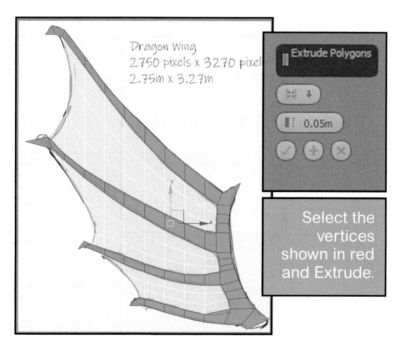

IMAGE 7.25 (3ds Max File Save 7.15)

Turn off the See-Though property in the Object Properties window. Select an Edge on the backside of the Wing mesh. Add a Symmetry Modifier and adjust to the proper setting to create the backside of the mesh.

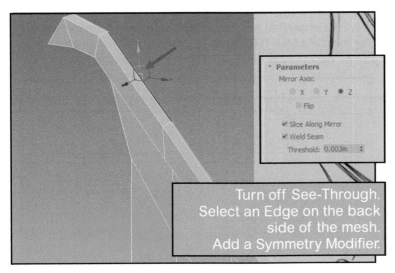

IMAGE 7.26 (3ds Max File Save 7.16)

Next, we will prepare the bottom of the wing so it can be connected to the Dragon Body mesh. Rotate the viewport so you can clearly see the bottom and the side edge as shown below. Notice the arrangement of the vertices, there are no "T" intersections. Use the Target Weld to weld the vertices into the arrangement. You will need to use the Cut tool also. It's a puzzle! The upper section was done just with the Target Weld. For the bottom section, Target Weld the vertices to the left and right of the center vertex to the corners, then Weld the bottom, center vertex to a corner. Use the Cut tool to create the last edge from the other corner to the top center (confusing to describe, but, obviously, it can be done). Do the same procedure to the other end of the bottom. When complete, delete the bottom Polygon.

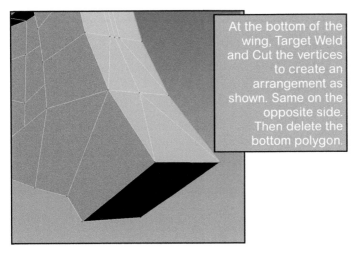

IMAGE 7.27

Attaching the Wing to the Body

Hide the Wing Template in the Scene Explorer. We will not be needing it. Move the new Wing mesh over to the Dragon Body, lined up with the template image. When we modeled the Wing, we do so with the Wing in a vertical position. In reality, the Wing is longer than we made it. The Wing is angled in our templates. With the Wing selected, click on the Select and Scale Tool. Type in new values in the Coordinate boxes at the bottom of the UI: Y = 117 and Z = 75. The 75 value in the Z-Coordinate box will thin the mesh a little.

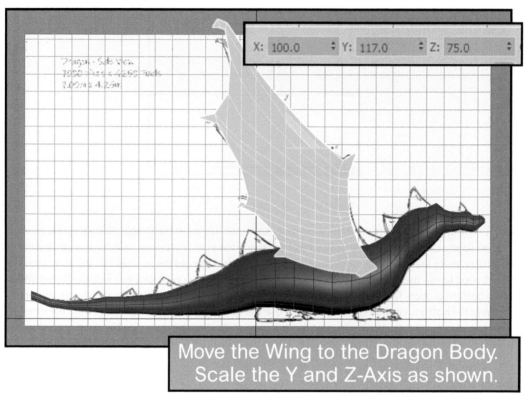

X: 100.0   Y: 117.0   Z: 75.0

Move the Wing to the Dragon Body.
Scale the Y and Z-Axis as shown.

IMAGE 7.28

Move the pivot point of the wing to the bottom of the mesh using the Affect Pivot Only button in the Hierarchy Tab of the Command Panel. Remember to turn it off when done. Then, rotate and move the wing into position as shown. The wing is at a short distance from the body so we can use the Bridge tool to connect the two.

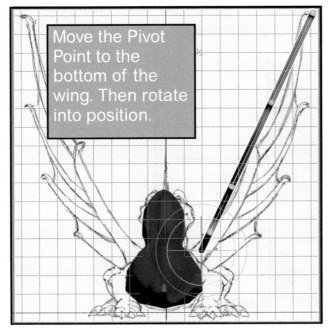

IMAGE 7.29

Select the polygon on the Dragon's Body as shown. This is where the Wing will connect to the body. The front leg will be extruded from the polygon below it. Scale the selected polygon a bit wider, so it is wider than the wing base. When we bridge the wing and the body, this will create a flared base, more anatomical looking. Delete the polygon.

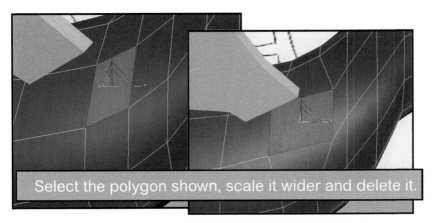

IMAGE 7.30

With an opening on the body and an open end on the wing (we deleted the bottom polygon), we can use the Bridge tool to connect the two. First, we need to attach the Wing mesh to the Dragon Body mesh so they are one mesh. Select the Dragon Body, then click the Attach button in the Edit Geometry section. Click the Wing to Attach. Use the Border tool to select the two openings. Then select the Bridge Caddy. On my model the bridge happened immediately. The settings are shown below.

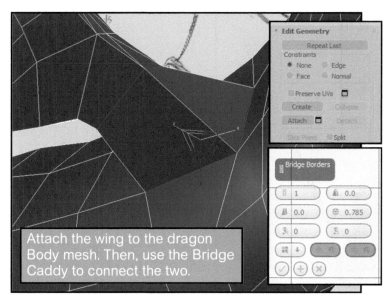

IMAGE 7.31 (3ds Max File Save 7.17)

The wing is now part of the Dragon Body mesh. If you want to adjust the position to be straighter at the connection, select the wing vertices and move them.

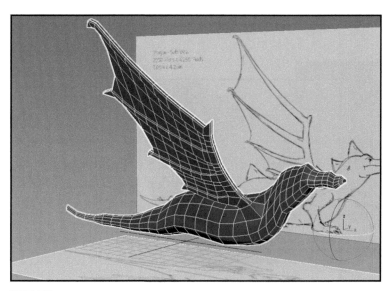

IMAGE 7.32

Modeling the Front Leg

Next, we will model the front leg, well, you will model the front leg. Below is an image of the leg I made, extruding from the polygon just below the wing connection. Use the Extrude Caddy, Hinge from Edge, Rotate and move individual vertices. Use the templates as guides too. There are several ways to get the same result as in the image. You have experience with and command of all the tools, you should be able to create the leg.

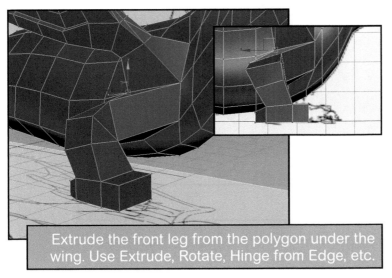

Extrude the front leg from the polygon under the wing. Use Extrude, Rotate, Hinge from Edge, etc.

IMAGE 7.33 (3ds Max File Save 7.18)

To create the three toes, use the Hinge from Edge tool to create three polygons on the front of the foot.

Taper the front end, then Hinge from edge on the two side polygons. Adjust the end vertices toward the back.

IMAGE 7.34

Selected all three polygons and extruded them (by polygons to get individual extrusions) to create three toes. With the toe end polygons still selected, click on Inset. Adjust the size and extrude twice to create the claw nails.

Use Extrude and Inset to create the toes and claws.

IMAGE 7.35

Create a more aggressive demeanor in the toes and claw nails by moving some of the vertices. Look at the image below and move the vertices to create a similar look. It is alright to exaggerate, one of our last procedures will soften everything.

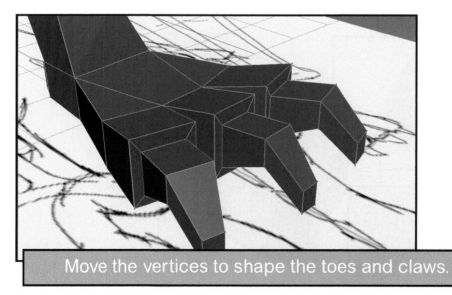

Move the vertices to shape the toes and claws.

IMAGE 7.36 (3ds Max File Save 7.20)

That completes the right front leg. We will use symmetry later to create the left front leg. Using the same procedures you did to create the front leg, now create the back leg. It should look similar, a little larger and the toe of the foot should be angled out a bit.

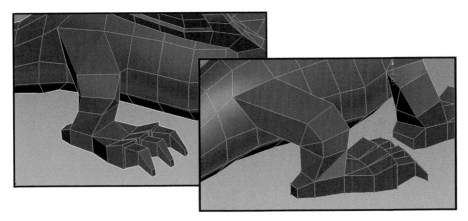

IMAGE 7.37 (3ds Max File Save 7.21)

We now have the basic Dragon shape. Adding details will be the next task.

IMAGE 7.38

Adding Details

Next, select the non-wing half of the mesh. Delete the selected half. Check to ensure the vertices along the centerline are aligned. If they need fixing, select just the centerline vertices, Right-click in the Front Viewport (90-degrees to the Left Viewport) and click the View Align button in Vertex mode. Select an Edge along the centerline and add a Symmetry Modifier.

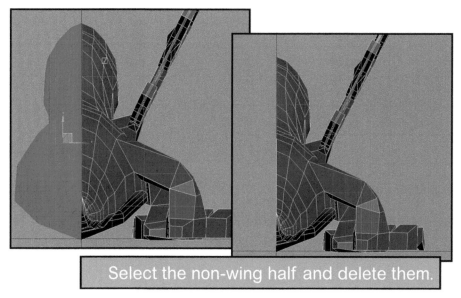

Select the non-wing half and delete them.

IMAGE 7.39 (3ds Max File Save 7.22)

The two ends of our original cylinder are still intact. Select the vertices at the end of the tail and weld them together into a single vertex. Your vertex count might be different than mine as we are not using specific directions. Remember, it is the visual appearance that counts with this model.

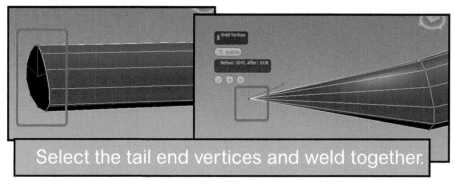

Select the tail end vertices and weld together.

IMAGE 7.40

At the head end, the flat end of the cylinder will be part of the chin that protrudes out past the mouth. Use the Cut tool to make three vertical cuts as shown. Above the end cap, the two Edges on either side of the centerline end in "T" intersections. Weld their two end vertices to the centerline end vertex using the Target Weld.

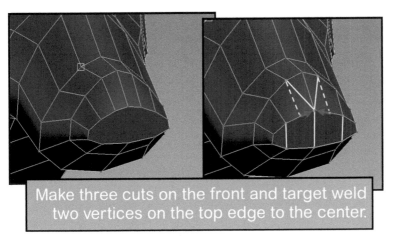

Make three cuts on the front and target weld two vertices on the top edge to the center.

IMAGE 7.41

With the chin segments in place, we can add detailing to the head to look more dragon-like.

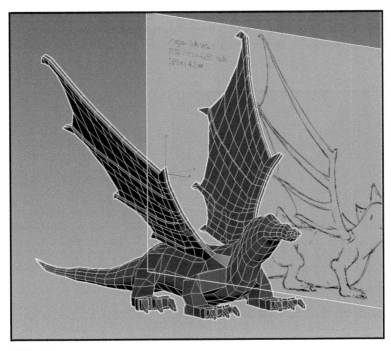

IMAGE 7.42

The Dragon needs to look somewhat menacing, the Dragon in the game is not a friendly soul. One thing that can help create that impression is heavy eyebrows. We will not be modeling eyes with eye lids that close and open. They will be simple spheres. Then select the upper triangular polygon. Locate the polygon on the forehead as shown in the image below. Make a Cut diagonally across the polygon. A simple brow can be created by using the Hinge from Edge tool to create a beveled point. Select the Edge closest to the centerline.

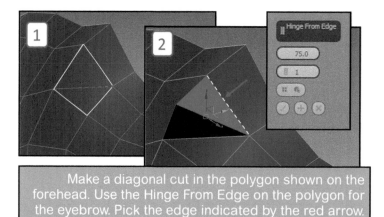

Make a diagonal cut in the polygon shown on the forehead. Use the Hinge From Edge on the polygon for the eyebrow. Pick the edge indicated by the red arrow.

IMAGE 7.43

Eventually, we will be adding a Mesh Smooth or Turbo smooth modifier to the mesh. When that happens, much of the detail will be softened. If we applied the modifier now, the brow would be a small bump in the mesh, not a large brow. To maintain the shape better, we can add more geometry to the edge areas. The added edges will help maintain the desired form. Select each of the three polygons of the raised brow shape and add an Inset using the Inset tool as shown. This adds some polygons to the mesh poly count, but, is necessary to create the look of the model. We will be adding more insets and Swift Loops to the rest of the model to define areas.

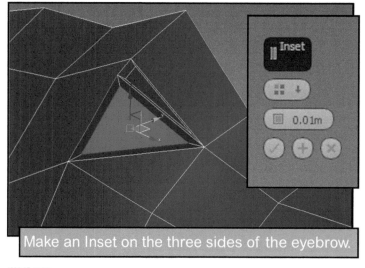

Make an Inset on the three sides of the eyebrow.

IMAGE 7.44

Create a sphere for the eyeball. It should fit in the eye location and not penetrate the top surface of the brows. Orient the Sphere as shown below. Clone the eyeball. Hold the Shift-key and drag the sphere to the position for the left Eye.

Create two spheres for eyes and position.

IMAGE 7.45

Next, create the nostril on the nose. Select the polygon as shown. Create an Inset using the Inset tool. Next, extrude the inner polygon into the mesh to create a depression. Click the green check Mark when set. With the Polygon still selected, switch to the Select and Move tool. Move the Polygon toward the eyes along the X-axis so the nostril appears to go back into the head.

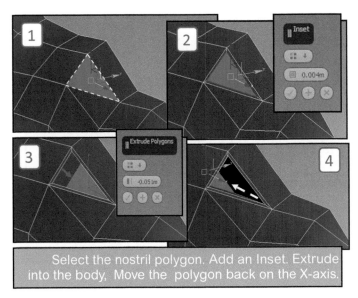

Select the nostril polygon. Add an Inset. Extrude into the body, Move the polygon back on the X-axis.

IMAGE 7.46 (3ds Max File Save 7.24)

The mouth will be created by making a channel between the upper and lower jaw. Create two series of cuts, dividing the polygons along the jaw as shown in the next image.

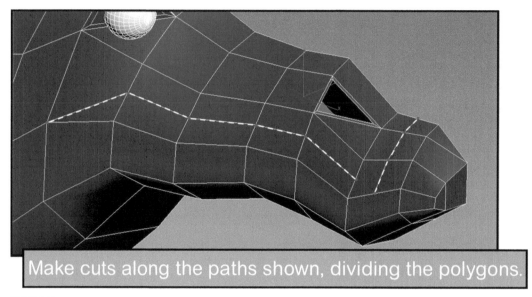

Make cuts along the paths shown, dividing the polygons.

IMAGE 7.47

Select the row of polygons as shown in the image below.

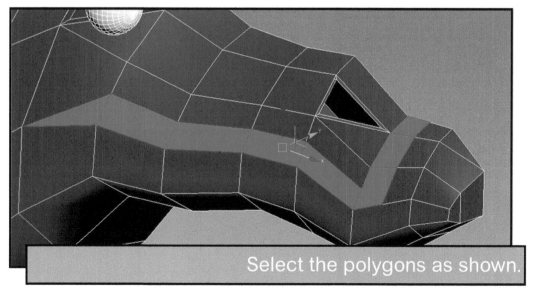

Select the polygons as shown.

IMAGE 7.48

Create an Inset around the perimeter (by Group) of the selection for definition when a Smoothing Modifier is added.

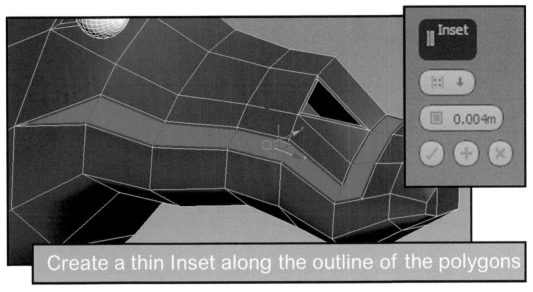

Create a thin Inset along the outline of the polygons

IMAGE 7.49

Extrude the group of Polygons into the mesh to create a channel.

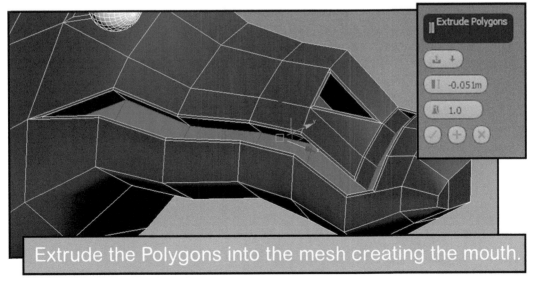

Extrude the Polygons into the mesh creating the mouth.

IMAGE 7.50

Select the two Polygons at the centerline of the mesh at the end of the channel and delete them.

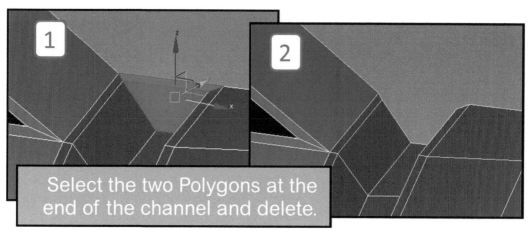

Select the two Polygons at the end of the channel and delete.

IMAGE 7.51

Now would be a good time to check the centerline vertex alignment for stray vertices. In the Left Viewport, select all the centerline vertices again, right click in the Front Viewport (90-degrees to the Left Viewport) and click the View Align button in the Modify Panel.

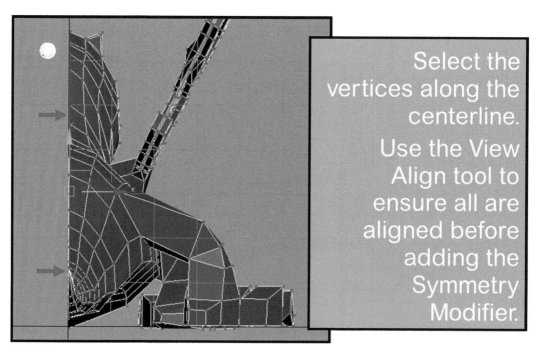

Select the vertices along the centerline. Use the View Align tool to ensure all are aligned before adding the Symmetry Modifier.

IMAGE 7.52

Adding Some Character

Adjust the Perspective Viewport to view the head. In Vertex mode, adjust the vertices to give the Dragon some more character: mean lips like a growl, a protruding chin, etc. It is alright to exaggerate a little, the smooth modifier we apply later will soften features some.

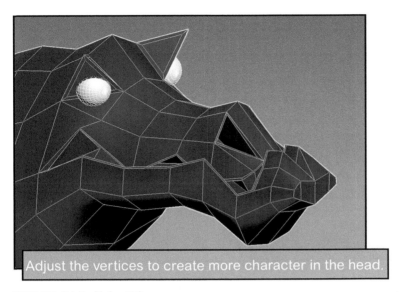

Adjust the vertices to create more character in the head.

IMAGE 7.53 (3ds Max File Save 7.25)

The nostrils could use a bit more shape around them. Select the polygon at the top of the nostril as shown. Use the Hinge from Edge tool to raise the front edge above the nostril.

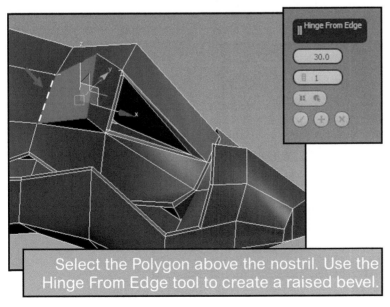

Select the Polygon above the nostril. Use the Hinge From Edge tool to create a raised bevel.

IMAGE 7.54

If you like, add a Mesh Smooth Modifier to the Dragon Body mesh. TurboSmooth will work too, but will add at least a third more vertices. No need to adjust the parameters. You can see how the vertex adjustments will translate with the modifier applied. If something doesn't look the way you like, click down the Modifier Stack to Vertex mode. Make any adjustments and check again with the Mesh Smooth turned on by clicking up in the Stack on it.

With the Mesh Smooth on, the features get created.

IMAGE 7.55

Next, create the fins along the centerline of the Dragon's back. In Vertex mode, make cuts as shown below. Be sure to have the 3D Snaps button on, set only to Midpoint and Endpoint.

Make cuts along the top edge to create the fins along the top of the Dragon's back.

IMAGE 7.56

At the top of the nose, select the vertex along the centerline, between the two angled cuts you just made. Raise the vertex along the Y-axis to create a fin. Switch to Polygon mode. Select the two fin polygons and add an inset using the Inset tool caddy. These will help maintain the fin shape when the Smoothing Modifier is applied.

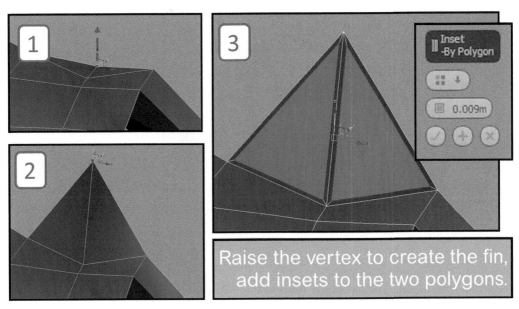

IMAGE 7.57

Repeat the same steps to finish the other fins along the centerline of the back. Be sure to move the vertices only in the Y-axis to keep the centerline alignment.

IMAGE 7.58

Lastly, let's add some definition to the toes so they maintain some structure to their look. Use the Swift Loop tool on the Ribbon in Vertex mode to add a loop around the claws where they connect to the toes on both the front and back legs.

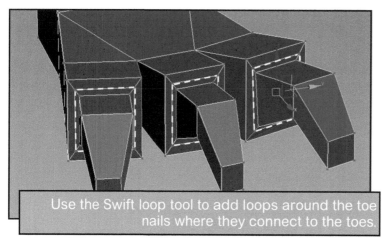

Use the Swift loop tool to add loops around the toe nails where they connect to the toes.

IMAGE 7.59

That completes the modeling of the Dragon. The next step will be to unwrap and texture it.

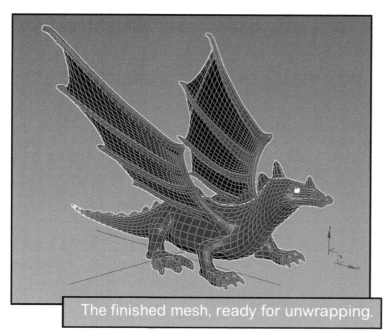

The finished mesh, ready for unwrapping.

IMAGE 7.60 (3ds Max File Save 7.27)

Unwrapping the Dragon

For our past projects, including the environmental pieces in Volume I, we used box mapping process to unwrap the objects. Most of the objects were geometric in nature, often referred to as hard models. The Knights were fairly simple shapes that were symmetrical primitives basically. The Dragon is a bit different. It is a very organic model, or soft model. To use the box unwrapping that we have been using would be difficult. As I mentioned in Volume I, there are several types of unwrapping, all with their individual strengths. By now, you should have a good understanding of what unwrapping, mapping and texturing is all about. With that foundation, we can look at another popular unwrapping method for soft models, Quick Peel.

Quick Peel

We used Quick Peel for the Warhorse Base. For the Dragon, we will utilize Quick Peel more extensively. As a reminder, the main advantage of the Quick Peel method is that it allows the user to establish the seams on the mesh where they are most appropriate for the mesh conditions. Organic meshes can twist and turn in such a way that conventional box mapping does not make sense to use. Look at the Dragon and imagine how you would divide up the surface to create "clusters" of polygons. If you turn back to the first image in this chapter, there is a color image of the finished Dragon. It has an orange underbelly that runs from the tail to the chin. The body is blue. The wings are blue with orange tinged webbing. The eyes are red with black pupils and the inside of the nostrils and mouth is very dark blue. The claws are also very dark blue with orange highlights across the claw tops. You can see how the mesh was divided up. Box mapping these clusters would be an all-day proposition. Using Quick Peel, the job can be done in far less time.

Learning the basics of Quick Peel is not overly complicated. At first you might have some hit or miss efforts that might need re-doing. With limited text space available, I will give you a quick run through of the procedure involved so you can acquire an understanding of what is happening. The space required in the text is just not available with everything else that needs to be covered. As a supplement to the text, there is a full video of the unwrapping of the Dragon using Quick Peel available on the Companion website, www.3dsMaxBasics.com in the Chapter 7 section of Volume 2, with the whole process being done and explained, step-by-step. To start the Quick Peel process, add an Unwrap Modifier to the Modifier Stack for the Dragon Body, place it above the Editable Poly in the Stack, but below the Mesh Smooth or Turbo Smooth if you added one of those previously.

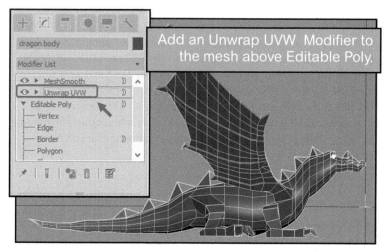

IMAGE 7.61

When the Unwrap UVW was added, it applied some seams to the mesh automatically. Those need to be removed so the seams are only where you assign them. Open the UVW Edit window. Select to Polygon in the Unwrapping modifier (not in Editable Poly) and uncheck the Ignore Backfacing button. Select all the Polygons in the Dragon Body mesh. Go to the Mapping tab on the UVW Edit window. Select "Flatten Mapping" from the drop-down menu.

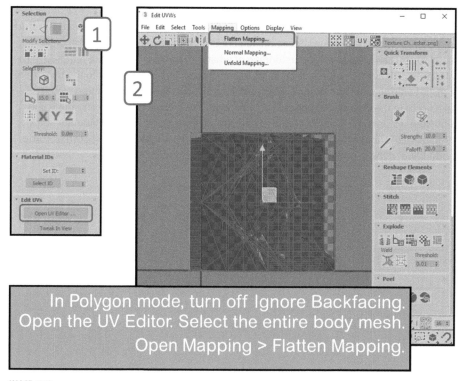

IMAGE 7.62

Clicking the Flatten Mapping button will open a dialog box. In the top value, Polygon Angle Threshold, change the setting to 180 and click OK. This will remove all the seams from the mesh.

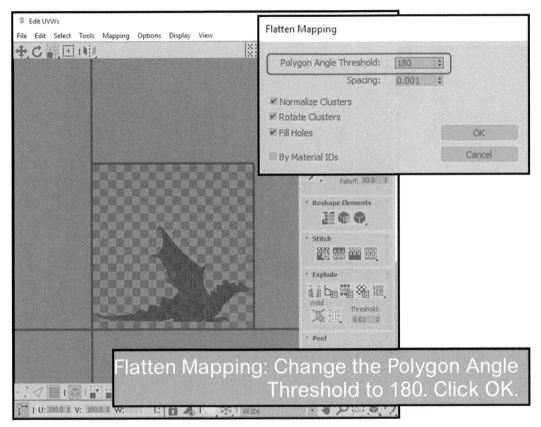

IMAGE 7.63 (3ds Max File Save 7.28)

In the Modify Panel, scroll down to the Peel section. In that section is a button called Point-to-Point, select it. Define the parting line seams for the polygon clusters by selecting vertices along a line of segments. Start with the vertex under the chin as shown. Follow the path of segments selecting the vertices as shown. Continue to the tip of the tail. The tool does allow you to skip vertices, connecting all those along the path that were skipped.

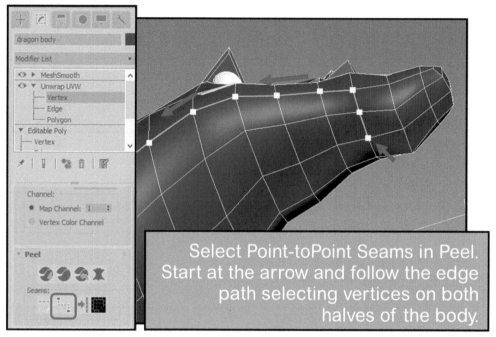

Select Point-toPoint Seams in Peel. Start at the arrow and follow the edge path selecting vertices on both halves of the body.

IMAGE 7.64

When you click on the tip of the tail, follow with a right click to end the seam. Repeat the procedure on the opposite side of the body beginning at the chin and continuing to the tip of the tail. This will define the belly/underside cluster of polygons.

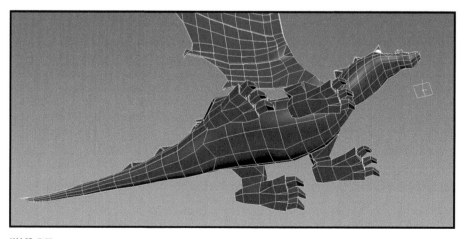

IMAGE 7.65

394

Continue creating seams, following the images for guidance. It might be difficult to see every seam. Please view the video instruction on the Companion Site for a detailed description. All the seams are covered.

IMAGE 7.66 (3ds Max File Save 7.30)

The image above has Edged Faces turned off, leaving only the seams. The legs are all separate Polygon clusters with a seam down the back inside from the connection with the body down to the inside corner of the heel. The claws at the end of each toe are all separate polygon clusters. The two polygons on top of each claw are further separated into separate clusters. Follow the segments around the perimeters creating the seams for each toe as shown in Image 7.67.

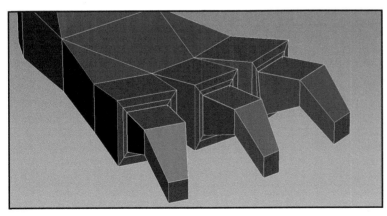

IMAGE 7.67

The head of the Dragon has some interesting seams. The perimeter of each nostril is a seam. The outside perimeter line of segments for the mouth are a seam. You might have some trouble selecting the seams where we overlapped the polygons for character expression. Stick with it, they can be selected. The edges around the base of each fin are a seam as well as the edges along the centerline of the fin.

IMAGE 7.68

When all the seams are established, it is time to use the Quick Peel. Scroll down the Modifier Panel again and select the Quick Peel icon button. The polygons will be separated into clusters within the UVW Edit window box. The clusters will work for creating a template for use in Photoshop or other image editing software. However, some of the clusters will be difficult to paint due to their positioning (Image 7.69). Move the clusters outside the box and group common shapes together.

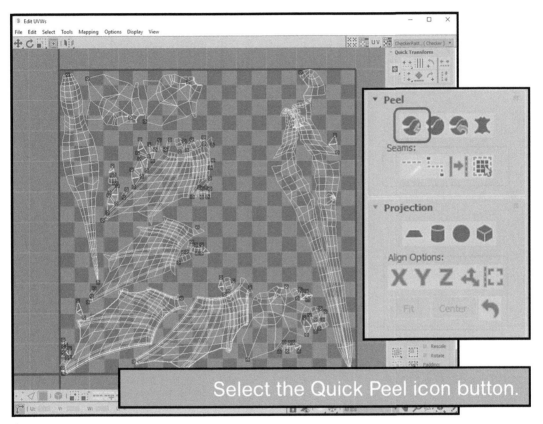

IMAGE 7.69

All the fins can be stacked together with their points aligned. Rotate the wings and legs to orient them better. Export a UVW Template using the Render UV's tool in the Tools tab.

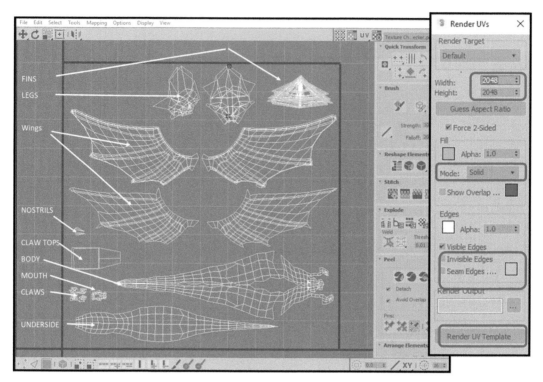

IMAGE 7.70 (3ds Max File Save 7.31)

Below is the UVW Template that was exported from the UVW Edit window. The Template was taken into Photoshop and the colors were added using layers above the Template base layer. The eye, created in the upper left, will be unwrapped separately but will use this texture image. An important step in packing the UVW Edit window is to not change the scale of the major clusters. The body, wings and legs should all stay the same scale so the surface texture will be consistent across the seams.

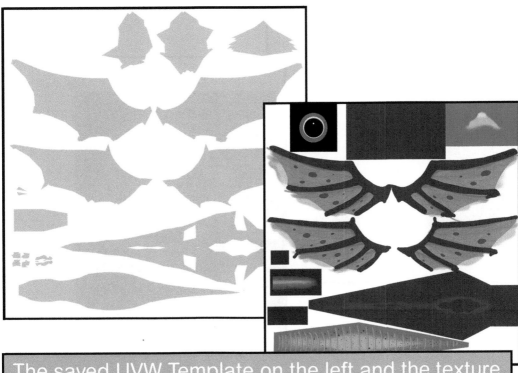

The saved UVW Template on the left and the texture made on layers above the Template in Photoshop.

IMAGE 7.71

Add an Unwrap UVW modifier to an eye sphere. Unwrap using Box mapping. Place the front half over the eye image and the back, scale down and locate on the red of the image. Clone the sphere and replace the other eye. As mentioned before, this was a quick explanation of the Quick Peel Process. Please review the Chapter 7 video on Quick Peel for more complete instructions.

The Dragon is complete, ready for rigging.

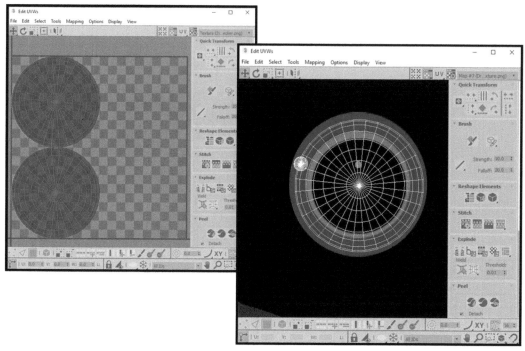

IMAGE 7.72

Chapter 7 Exercise: Color Variations

Create a second texture for the Dragon using different colors and accents. You might have noticed that the Dragon texture I created uses complimentary colors. You might want to try the same thing with other complimentary colors. The texture used is bold colors that go along with the Knight characters.

IMAGE 7.73

Rigging the Dragon

Topics in This Chapter

- CAT Rigging
- Preset Rigs

Concepts/Skills/Tools Introduced in This Chapter

- Rigging a Quadruped
- CATMotion with Quadrupeds Setting up the Rig

Our next task is to rig and animate the Dragon mesh. We will again by using the CAT rigging system. This time, we will be able to utilize one of the preset rigs that come in the CAT library of rigs, the Lizard. This will save a lot of time. We will need to customize it for the wings.

Open your last 3ds Max file version of the Dragon, or you can access the file I will be using on the Companion website, www.3dsMaxBasics.com in Chapter 8 of Volume II. If the model is not already there, start by zeroing the model, setting the X-, Y- and Z-coordinates to 0. Move the Pivot Point to the center of the figure.

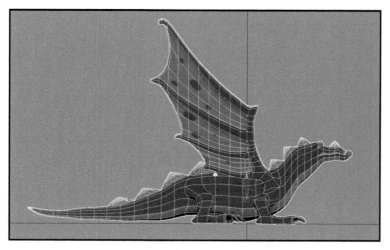

IMAGE 8.1 (3ds Max File Save 8.1)

In the Command Panel, open the Geometry Panel and then click on the Helpers tab icon. From the drop-down menu, select CAT Objects. Select the CATParent option in the Object Type section, then go down to the "CATRig Load and Save" list and select "English Dragon."

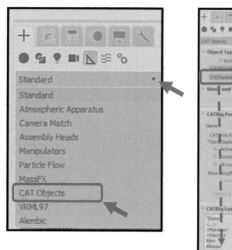

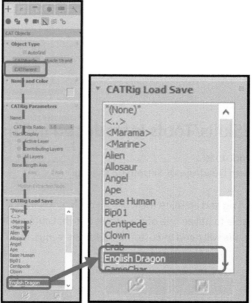

IMAGE 8.2

Click and drag the mouse to create an English Dragon rig next to your Dragon Mesh. After creating the rig, you will notice that the wings are in a different position than those on our mesh. The wings were positioned in a more upright position on the mesh to allow easy access to the legs without the mesh covering up the vertices. The wings on the rig will not stop our progress. We will just deal with the problem with our tools and skills to correct things.

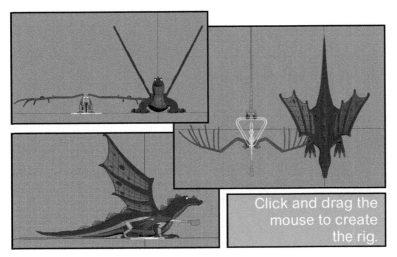

Click and drag the mouse to create the rig.

IMAGE 8.3

Before making any adjustments to the mesh, we need to save the UVWs that we created in the previous chapter. Open the Unwrap UVW modifier in the Modifier Stack of the Command Panel. Scroll down the panel to the Channel section. Click on Save and save the UVWs file in the pop-up window with an appropriate name.

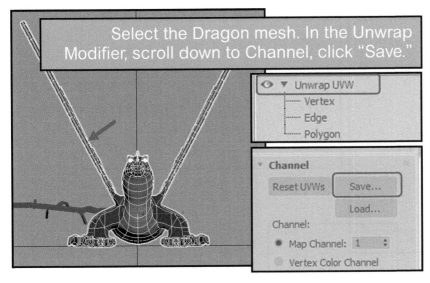

Select the Dragon mesh. In the Unwrap Modifier, scroll down to Channel, click "Save."

IMAGE 8.4

Next, move the rig over, centering it into the Dragon Mesh.

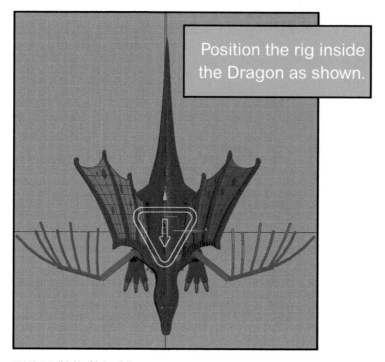

IMAGE 8.5 (3ds Max File Save 8.2)

Now we will correct the wing position issue. In the Editable Poly layer of the Modifier Stack, select Polygon. Click "Yes" in the popup Warning window.

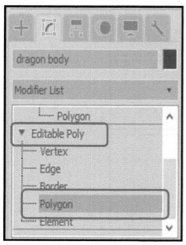

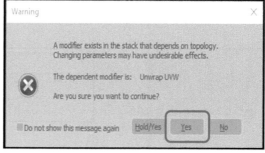

IMAGE 8.6

Adjusting the Wings

Next, select all the Polygons on the Left Wing, except for the polygons at the base of the wing as shown. Be sure to select all the polygons, there might be a few along the bottom edge of the Wing that did not get selected. If you miss them, you will need to come back to this step later to correct the selection. Once selected, rotate the group of polygons to a horizontal alignment. They will pivot from the center of the group. The edges along the left side will stretch from the body mesh, they are not broken. Use the Select and Move tool to lower the selection and position so the Wing is aligned with the base of the Wing on the Body mesh.

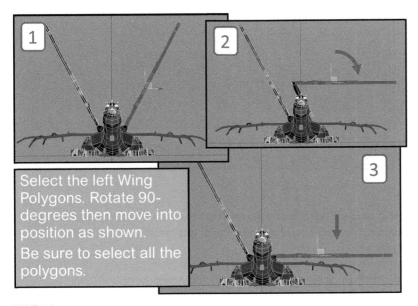

Select the left Wing Polygons. Rotate 90-degrees then move into position as shown.
Be sure to select all the polygons.

IMAGE 8.7

In the Top Viewport, use the Select and Rotate tool to rotate the polygon group so they align with the rig wing bones. Again, check that the wing is aligned so it looks like it emanates from the base polygons on the body. We will adjust the bones later to fit the mesh.

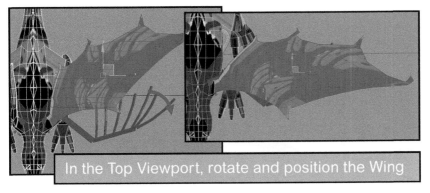

In the Top Viewport, rotate and position the Wing

IMAGE 8.8

When the polygons are in proper position, deselect the group. Repeat the same procedure on the Right Wing. When both wings are in position, you can leave the Editable Poly level of the Modifier Stack. Make sure that you unclick the Polygon mode so you are not in a Sub-Object level. The texture on the mesh is all messed up from going into the Sub-Object level. Restore the texture by returning to the Channel Section of the Unwrap UVWs modifier panel. Select "Load" this time. Select the file you saved previously in the popup file window. The textures should all return to their proper placement.

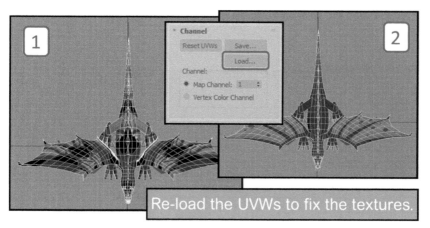

IMAGE 8.9

As you have done with previous projects, right click on the mesh to open the Object Properties window. Select the Freeze, See-Through and uncheck Show Frozen in Gray. Select the CATParent and rename the rig to Dragon in the CAT Rig Parameters.

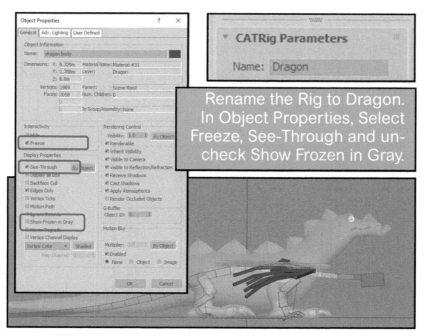

IMAGE 8.10

Note: When CAT creates limbs on Hubs, it does so in a specific order: first the left side of the Hub, then the right side of the Hub. Sometimes, if you adjust the pose of a right limb, it will not copy to the left side when the Add a Leg or Add a Arm is selected. To make sure we work on the left side of the Hub first, select the right two legs and wing and delete them.

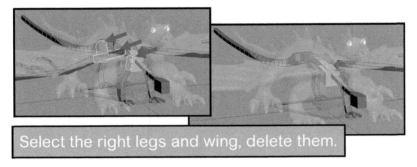

Select the right legs and wing, delete them.

IMAGE 8.11 (3ds Max File Save 8.3)

Next, begin adapting the rig to our mesh by adjusting the positions of the Pelvis, Ribcage and Head Hubs as shown below.

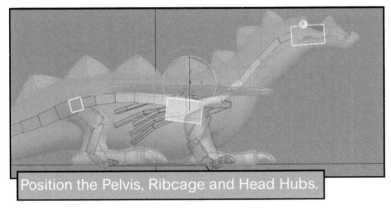

Position the Pelvis, Ribcage and Head Hubs.

IMAGE 8.12

Select the root bone of the Tail and adjust the length to match the mesh.

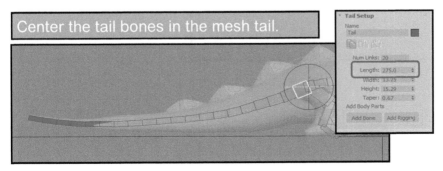

Center the tail bones in the mesh tail.

IMAGE 8.13

The height location of the wing bones on the CAT Rig needs to be moved to match the Dragon mesh. You will need to adjust them in Front Viewports (a front view). Select the entire wing, including the small collar bone.

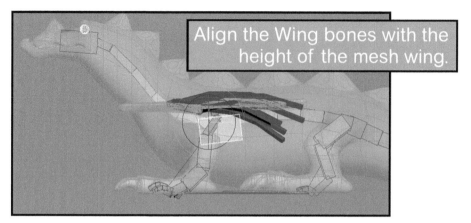

IMAGE 8.14

Select the bones on the Front Leg and move it to the right as shown to align the top bone of the leg with the mesh where the leg meets the body. Repeat with the Rear Leg.

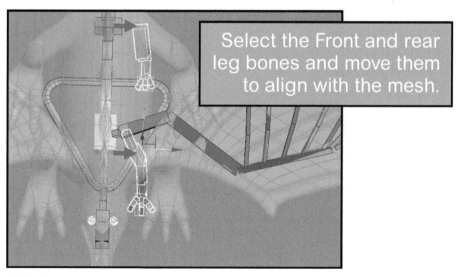

IMAGE 8.15

Adjusting the Front Left Leg

The next step will take a little more time and concentration. Adjust the Front Leg and toe bones to fit properly inside the mesh. Begin by moving the DragonRLegPlatform into position inside the bottom center of the foot part of the mesh. Look at the next image for reference.

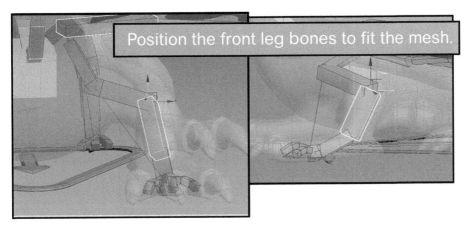

IMAGE 8.16

NOTE: When positioning the foot bones, the Palm bone will appear to be twisted, the toes twisting with it. Do not attempt to untwist it. Do not rotate it. Doing so will throw off the animations. The animations apparently adjust for the twisting. Move the toes as you normally would, fitting them to the toe areas of the mesh.

Carefully adjust the bones, checking and rechecking the positions in the Front and Left Viewports as well as rotating the view in the Perspective Viewport. Once the bones are in position, select each bone individually and rescale them to fill 70% of the mesh.

For the toes, scaling the first bone in the chain will automatically scale the others in the chain.

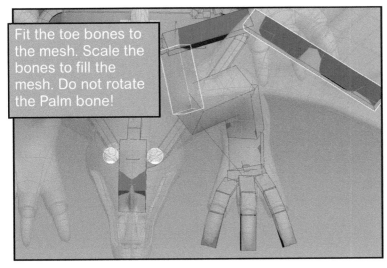

IMAGE 8.17

Creating a Mirrored Right Leg

With the Front Leg adjusted, make a mirrored copy of the leg on the right side of the Ribcage Hub. Normally, all you would need to do is select the Hub, then click the Add Leg button to create the mirrored leg. For some reason, that feature was not working on my rig. To work around the problem if your rig is also not responding correctly, Select the Ribcage Hub and click on the Add Leg button twice. First it will create a standard shape on the left side, then a mirror of that leg on the right side of the Hub.

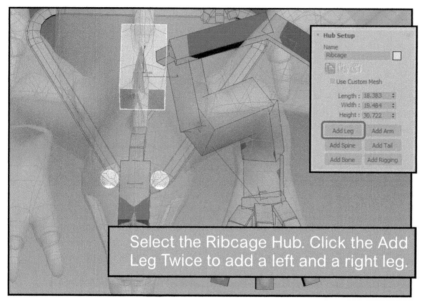

IMAGE 8.18

Select the first leg created on the left side of the Hub. Delete the new left side leg.

Next, select a bone on the modified Left Leg. In the Limb Setup section of the Modify Panel, select the "copy" icon button. Select a bone on the new Right Leg. Click the "Paste" icon button, two buttons to the right of the "Copy" icon button. The new leg will be a mirror image of the modified Left Leg (Image 8.21).

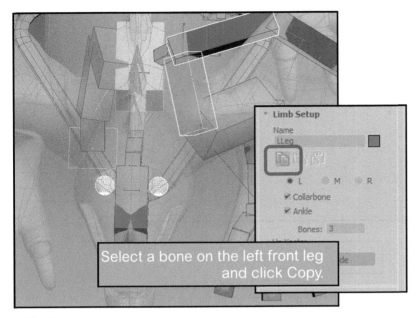

IMAGE 8.19

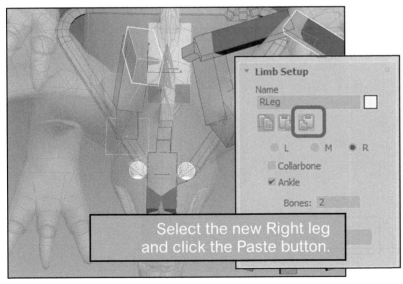

IMAGE 8.20

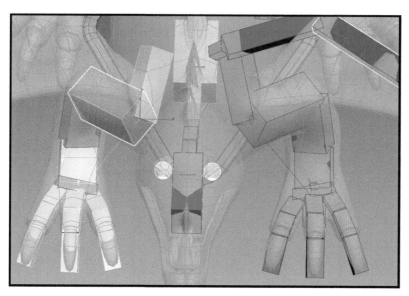

IMAGE 8.21

That completes the two Front Legs. Repeat the process of rigging the Front Leg to the two Back Legs. Be sure to start with the Left Rear Leg. On my rig, when the time came to copy the modified Left Rear Leg to the right side of the Hub, the normal "Add Leg" worked, creating a mirrored modified Rear Right Leg.

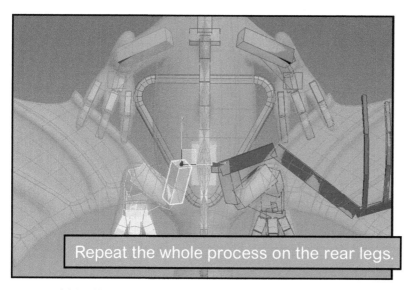

Repeat the whole process on the rear legs.

IMAGE 8.22 (3ds Max File Save 8.4)

Rebuilding the Wings

Time to take care of the wing bones. The English Dragon has wings that do not match our Dragon's wing structure. The wing is really an arm coming off the Ribcage Hub. It starts with a small collar bone. We will use the collar bone and the first two bones coming off it. Select all the other bones, creating a fan shape, and delete them.

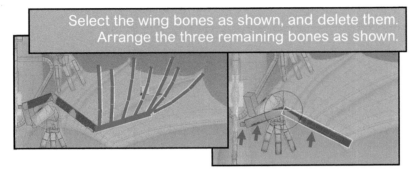

IMAGE 8.23

Select the second bone and add a bone to it using the Add Bone button. A new, small bone will be created at the end of the second bone. It is a floating bone, meaning it can be repositioned. Move the bone to the root end of the bone and orient it so it follows the first rib of the wing, about half of its length as shown in the next image. Add a new bone to the bone you just positioned and position it. For the next three ribs on the wing, use the third bone as the root bone for the ribs. Add the three remaining bone chains as shown.

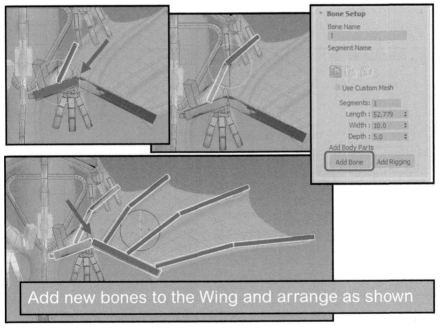

IMAGE 8.24

When complete, a mirrored wing needs to be created on the right side of the body. Select the Hub, and then Add Arm. If the wing generates on the opposite side, great. If a regular arm appears, Copy and Paste the modified Wing to the regular arm just as you did with the Front Leg.

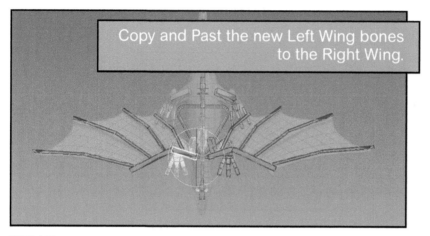

Copy and Past the new Left Wing bones to the Right Wing.

IMAGE 8.25

The Body Bones

With the limbs complete, the last thing to do is to scale the bones so they fill approximately 70% of the mesh mass. Remember, the reason for this is to ensure 3ds Max assigns weights more accurately to the vertices. Select each bone of the spines individually and rescale as shown in both the Top and a Side Viewport.

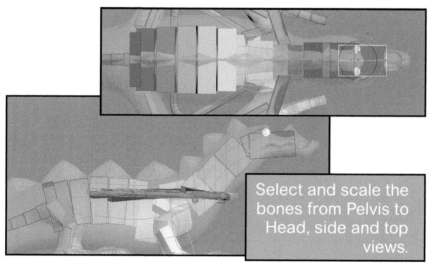

Select and scale the bones from Pelvis to Head, side and top views.

IMAGE 8.26 (3ds Max File Save 8.5)

Scaling the Tail is an easy task. Select the root tail bone next to the Pelvis. Scaling this bone will scale the others in the chain. Scale the bone using the Length, Width, Height and Taper values of the Tail Setup in the Modifier Panel.

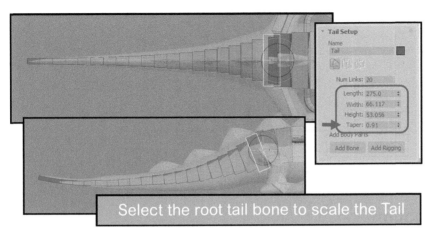

IMAGE 8.27 (3ds Max File Save 8.6)

Linking the Eyes

The eyes are separate objects from the Dragon Body mesh. Link them to the Head Hub bone.

IMAGE 8.28

Add a CATMotion layer to the Layer Manager. Test the Animation, then turn off the Setup/Animation toggle.

IMAGE 8.29 (3ds Max File Save 8.7)

Adding CATMotion

Test the animation of the CAT Rig. Add a CATMotion layer to the Layer Manager in the Motion Panel. Remember, it is the last layer type in the Abs flyout button. Next, click the red Setup/Animation Toggle button to turn on the animation mode. Click the Play button to run the animation. Once you see everything working, toggle the animation off and stop the Play button. You are ready to Skin the character.

Adding Skin and Weighting the Vertices

Select the Dragon Mesh. In the Modifier Stack add a Skin Modifier above the Unwrap UVW modifier. Put it below the Mesh Smooth or Turbo Smooth modifier if you have one. Once added, scroll down to the Bones; Add button and select it. Expand the bones list in the Select Bones list. Select all the Dragon Boned except the Dragon (CATParent) and Platforms.

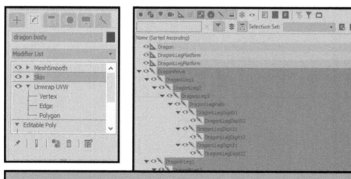

Unfreeze the Dragon Mesh. Add a Skin Modifier to the Modifier Stack.
Add the bones to the Skin.

IMAGE 8.30

418

Go to the Motion Panel and turn on the Setup/Animation Toggle button. Play the Walk Cycle to see if there are stray, unassigned vertices. For my Dragon, the only problems were the heels of each foot that were not weighted, creating an elongated mesh as it walked. In the last chapter, we weighted the individual vertices. A time-consuming job. You developed an understanding of how weighting of vertices worked. This time, we will use a relatively new feature in 3ds Max.

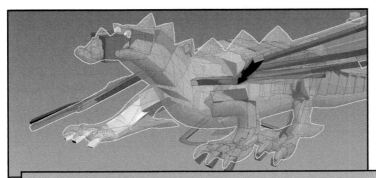

Toggle the Setup/Animation toggle to evaluate the vertex assignments by 3ds Max during animation. Note the vertices dragging at the heels.

IMAGE 8.31

Scroll down the Skin Modifier Panel to the Weight Solver. This is the magic button! Click on the small icon button with three dots. The Geodesic Voxel Solver window will popup. Just click on the Apply button, no need to for adjustments.

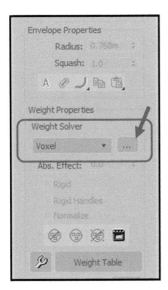
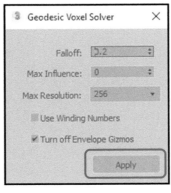

IMAGE 8.32 (3ds Max File Save 8.8)

When you click in the scene, the Popup window will close and some of the mesh vertices may shift. The Weight Solver will correct some of the stray vertex weighting. It is not really a magic button, but it is helpful. Your eye is still required to make aesthetic decisions. Play the animation again. The solver did fix the heel issues. Remember, our mesh was very close to the proportions of the rig before we began the adjustments. The scaling up of the bones filled the mesh nicely. That is the main reason we do not need to spend hours weighting vertices.

Chapter 8 Exercise: Walk Cycle Refinement

As the animation plays, notice that the wings are very active as well as the pelvis. Open the CATMotion Editor. We used it to modify the Walk Cycle for the Knight. I made a few adjustments to my Dragon. For the Bend in the Arms (the Wings) I changed the Value to 2.0. The Scale of the Head Twist, I changed to 10%. The body is in more control, but still moving a bit wildly. For this exercise, make adjustment to the CATMotion Editor to create a controlled Walk Cycle for the Dragon.

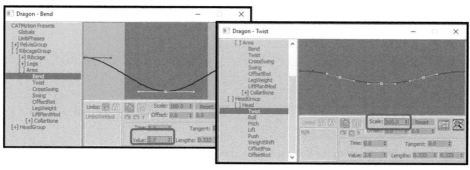

IMAGE 8.33

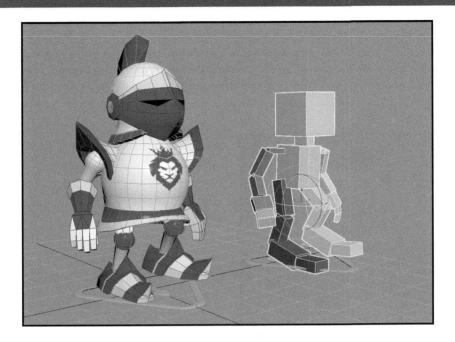

Character Animations

Topics in This Chapter

- The Character Animation Tool
- Using a Prefab CAT Rig
- Creating a Custom CAT Rig

Concepts/Skills/Tools Introduced in This Chapter

- Creating and assigning materials with the Slate Editor
- Review of using the basic tools from Volume I

Game Character Animations

Having watched CG and hand-drawn animated films, video and games all your life, you are likely familiar with the noticeable and subtle differences between them. In video games, the player typically initiates their character's movement through an input device, a game controller, keystroke, etc. When the input is activated, the program runs the appropriate animation clip until the sequence ends or the input signal is ended. A character can have any number of animation clips: run, walk, attack, idle, crouch, jump, die, etc.

For our game, due to limited text space, we will set up just two animation clips for the Knight character: Idle and Walk. Open the last version of the 3ds Max file of the Knight you modeled from Chapter 5. The file Vol2_Save 5-27.max can be found in the Companion files online at www.3dsMaxBasics.com if you would like to use it.

IMAGE 9.1

When the file opens, click on the CATParent at the base of the rig. Select the Motion Panel in the Command Panel and scroll down to the Layer Manager. Previously, we used the Layer Manager to add the CATMotion layer with the Walk Cycle. We used the CATMotion Editor to control the animation.

So, we have our walk cycle completed. We need to create an Idle state for when the character is not walking. After we have our two cycles completed, we will save each as a CATMotion file. Next, we will combine the two cycles in one animation for the FBX file we will export to Unity 3d.

Saving the Walk Cycle

Having the Walk Cycle completed will save us some time. We need to save the cycle so we can import it into a new animation sequence.

Click on the CATParent. In the Layer Manager, make sure the current CATMotion Layer is selected. Scroll down to the Clip Manager section and select the Save button. The Save As window will open to the Clips folder. In the Filename box, enter the name "knightWalk" for the file. Click the Save button.

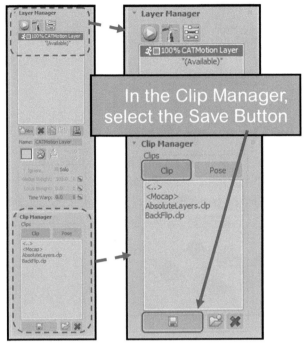

IMAGE 9.2

A new Save Cat Clip window will popup. In that window, we need to enter the Start and End time for the clip. Our Timeline runs until frame 89. Leave the Start setting at 0. Change the End setting to 29, which will create a 30-frame cycle. The 89-frame timeline is three, 30-frame cycles keep the Save Entire Layer Stack checked. There is only the one cycle in the Layer Manager. Click Save. The new Clip will appear in the Clip Manager list as shown.

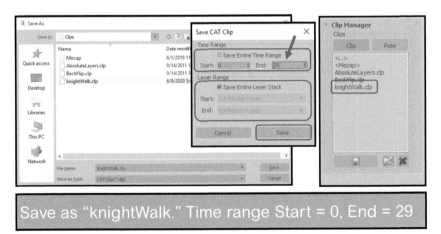

IMAGE 9.3

With the Walk cycle clip saved, we can delete it, clearing the animation layer stack. Click on the red "X" below the Layer Manager list window to delete the layer.

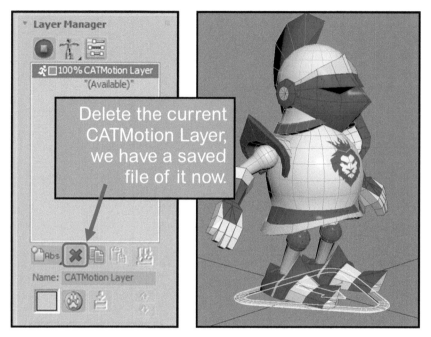

IMAGE 9.4 (3ds Max File Save 9.1)

Creating the Idle Animation

With the Layer Manager list clear, we can create a new layer for the Idle state. Click on the word "(Available)" in the Layer Manager list to make it active. Next, click and hold the Layer type flyout list. Select the bottom type, the CATMotion layer. The layer will appear at the top of the list as shown in the next image.

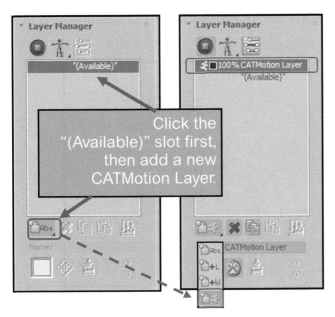

IMAGE 9.5

Toggle the Setup/Animation Toggle button to the green Animation state. Rename the CATMotion Layer "knightIdle" in the name box below the layer creator button. So do not change the name of the layer up in the list, only change it in the Name box. Next, open the CATMotion Editor.

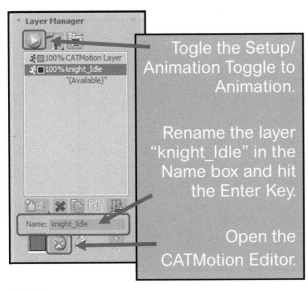

IMAGE 9.6

425

The CATMotion Walk Cycle is a preset that has default settings. When we worked on the walk cycle in Chapter 5, our goal was to get the Preset Walk cycle under control using the CATMotion Editor. We will be doing that process again, only this time, we need to greatly restrict the movements to create an idle: the character standing in one place, no foot movement and a rhythmic shifting of balance to keep the figure looking alive and in this case, alert.

Start with the Globals panel. Set the animation to Start at 0 and End at 89. The Max Step can be set to 30 and the Max Stride length set to 2.0.

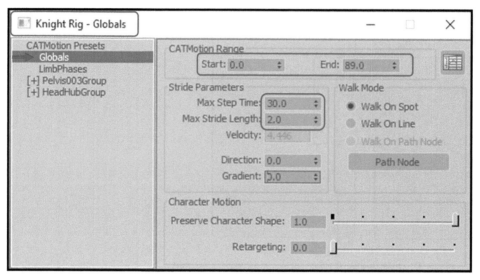

IMAGE 9.7 (3ds Max File Save 9.2)

Next, adjust the LimbPhases. We do not want the legs "walking," so set them both to the neutral position at 0.0. Set the limbs to −0.25 and 0.25.

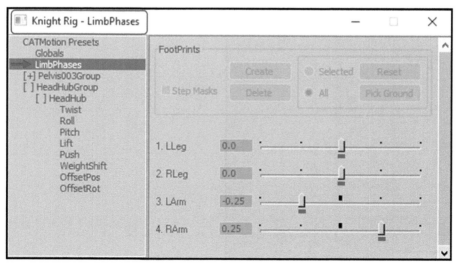

IMAGE 9.8 (3ds Max File Save 9.3)

Moving to the Pelvis Group, in Pelvis, the first four controllers need to change: Twist, Roll, Pitch and Lift. Select each one individually and change the Scale value of each to 0.0. They cannot be changed as a group. After changing, all their timeline splines should be flat.

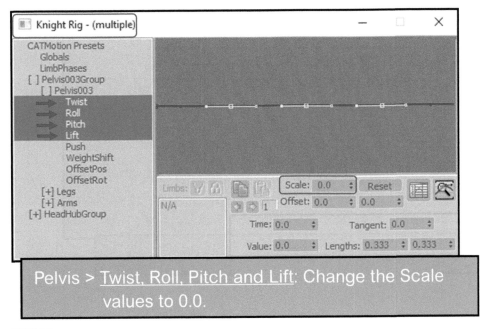

Pelvis > Twist, Roll, Pitch and Lift: Change the Scale values to 0.0.

IMAGE 9.9

Next, change the WeightShift controller Scale value to 10.0. This will create a rocking motion in the hips.

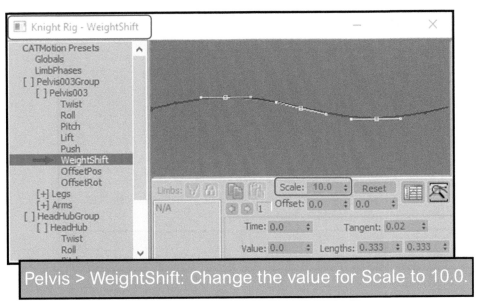

Pelvis > WeightShift: Change the value for Scale to 10.0.

IMAGE 9.10

Moved down to the Legs. In the Twist controller, stop any twisting by setting the Scale value to 20.0.

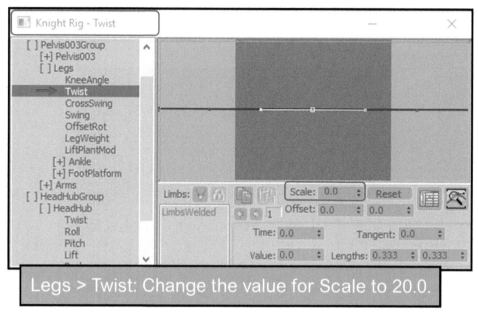

Legs > Twist: Change the value for Scale to 20.0.

IMAGE 9.11

The Swing in the Legs section gets a slight movement, change the Scale value to 5.0.

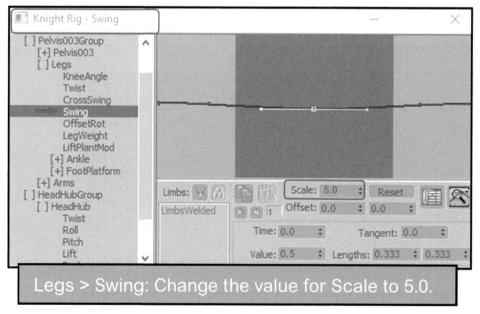

Legs > Swing: Change the value for Scale to 5.0.

IMAGE 9.12

To keep the heels of the feet from rising, set the Slider setting in the LiftPlantMod controller to the extreme right for a value of 1.0.

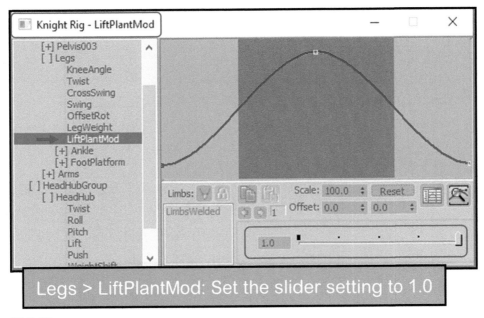

Legs > LiftPlantMod: Set the slider setting to 1.0

IMAGE 9.13

To keep the feet from moving forward in an inching movement, set the TargetAlign controller Value to 1. The timeline spline will flatten.

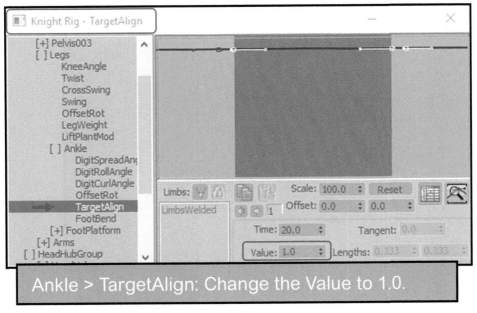

Ankle > TargetAlign: Change the Value to 1.0.

IMAGE 9.14

In the FootPlatform section, change the Pitch, Lift and Swerve Scale values all to 0.0. Change each controller separately, not as a group.

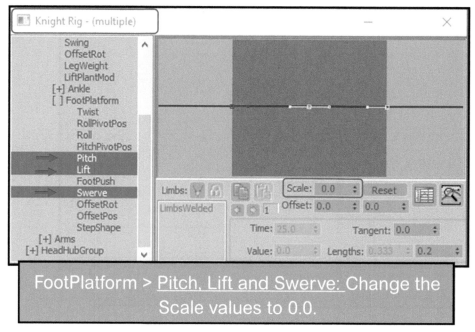

FootPlatform > Pitch, Lift and Swerve: Change the Scale values to 0.0.

IMAGE 9.15

In the Arms section, both the Bend and the Twist Scale values need to be changed to a setting of 0.0, minimizing the motion.

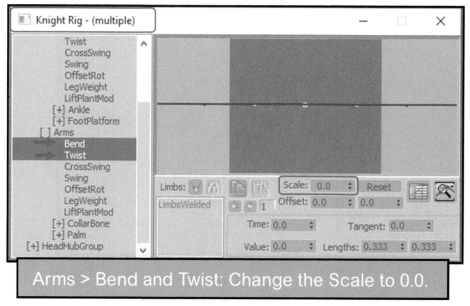

Arms > Bend and Twist: Change the Scale to 0.0.

IMAGE 9.16

430

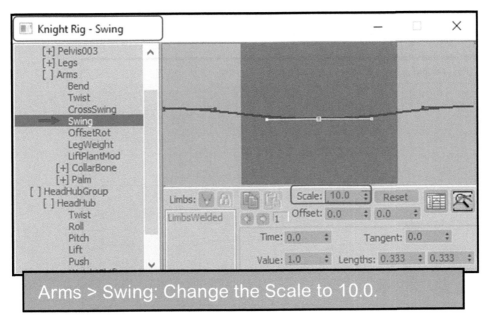

Arms > Swing: Change the Scale to 10.0.

IMAGE 9.17

Also, in the Arms section, Change the "y" axis setting to 30.0 to bring the arms in closer to the body.

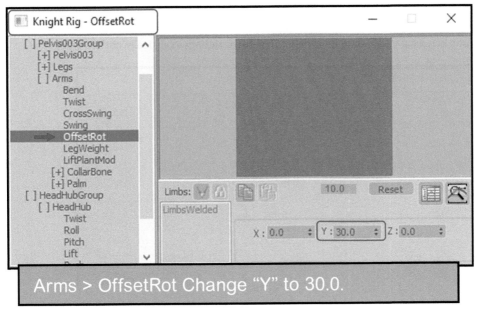

Arms > OffsetRot Change "Y" to 30.0.

IMAGE 9.18

To limit the shoulder motion, change the Motion Z, Motion Y and Motion X Scale settings to 0.0 in the CollarBone section. Change them individually, not as a group.

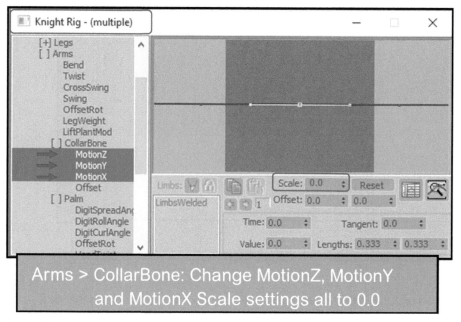

Arms > CollarBone: Change MotionZ, MotionY and MotionX Scale settings all to 0.0

IMAGE 9.19

The Palms need a lot of restriction, they are moving all over the place. Change the DigitCurlAngle, HandTwist, HandFlopY and HandFlopX Scale settings all to 0.0. Change the settings individually, not as a group.

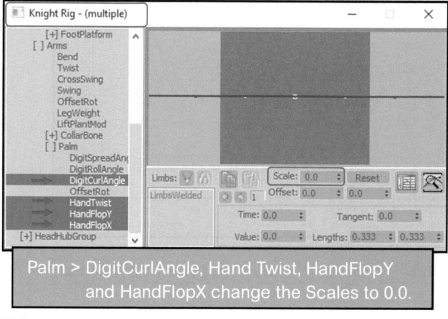

Palm > DigitCurlAngle, Hand Twist, HandFlopY and HandFlopX change the Scales to 0.0.

IMAGE 9.20

432

Lastly, get the Head movement under control. Change both the Twist and the Roll controllers Scale value to 10.0. This will keep the head slightly moving, looking alert.

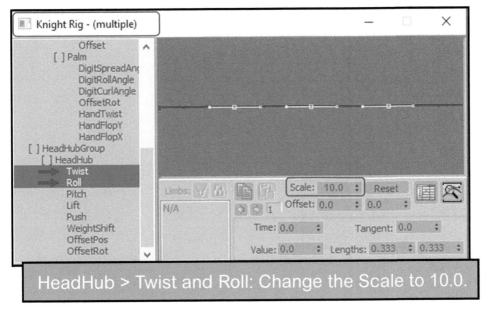

IMAGE 9.21

That completes the adjustments for the Idle state. Play the animation. If there are any large movements, there must be a wrong setting for one of the controllers. Try to determine which mesh is out of step and adjust that mesh's controller.

Saving the Idle Clip

We are ready to save the Idle to a clip like we did at the start of the chapter, saving the Walk Cycle. Click on the CATParent. Scroll down the Motion Panel to the Clip Manager. Click on the Save button.

The Save As window will open with the Clips folder. Name the file "knightIdle." Click Save. The Save CAT Clip popup window will open. In this window, we can specify how what part of the entire timeline we want to save. We only want one complete cycle. Set the Start to 0 and the End to 29, making the clip 30 frames long or 1 second. In the Layer Range, leave the Save Entire Layer Stack tick box checked. Click Save. The clip will be added to the list. Delete the CATMotion layer from the Layer Manager.

IMAGE 9.22

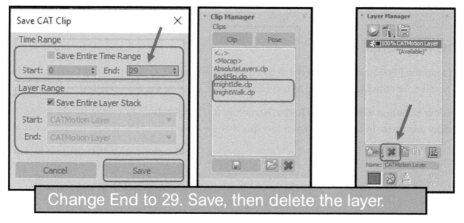

IMAGE 9.23

Creating the New Motion Clip

With the two motion clips saved and the Layer Manager empty, we can create our single animation to include with the FBX file when the character is exported to the game engine Unity. The new animation clip will be a combination of the knightIdle, 30 frames and the knightWalk, 30 frames. Open the Time Configuration window using the icon button on the lower tool bar.

IMAGE 9.24

In the Time Configuration window, change the End Time to 59. Notice that the Frame count number will be 60. Click Ok to close the window.

In Unity, when we setup the character in the game engine we will split the animation clip up according to the two time durations of the Idle and Walk. The program will call on the clips when needed.

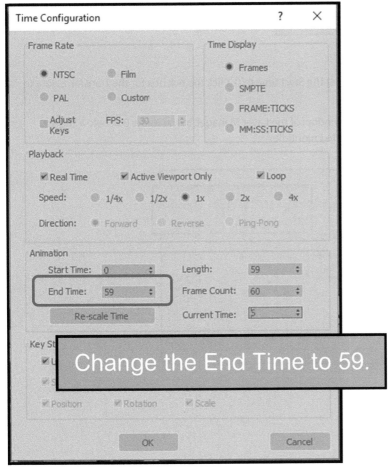

IMAGE 9.25

Next, add the knightIdle clip to the Layer Manager. Double-click on the knightIdle file in the Clip Manager section.

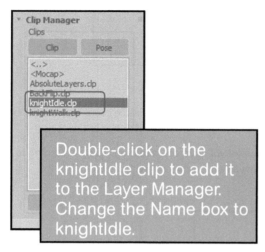

Double-click on the knightIdle clip to add it to the Layer Manager. Change the Name box to knightIdle.

IMAGE 9.26

The Clip Options window will popup. Set the Start time to 0. Click the tick box for the Transform data to current position option.

The motion clip will appear in the list window of the Layer Manager. In the Name Box below the list window, change the name of the layer to knightIdle.

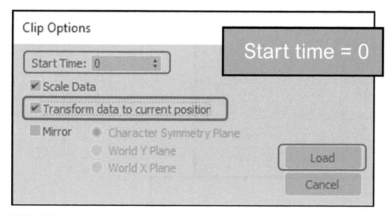

IMAGE 9.27

Repeat the process to add the knightWalk to the Layer Manager as a new layer. Double-click on the knightWalk clip in the Clip Manager and change the name in the Name box.

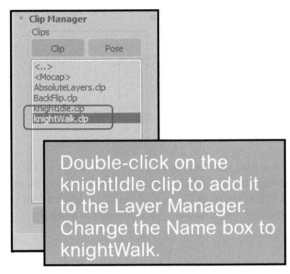

IMAGE 9.28

When the Clip Options window pops up, change the Start Time to 30 and check the Transform data to current position tick box.

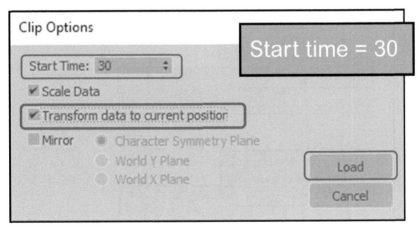

IMAGE 9.29

With the two clips now in the Layer Manager we can proceed to adjusting the Global Weights to make the two clips play in the timeline properly. If you play the animation now, only the Walk animation will be displayed.

Click the Auto Key to turn on the Animation Mode. The timeline area and the active viewport outline will turn red. Click on the knightWalk layer in the Layer Manager if it is not selected already.

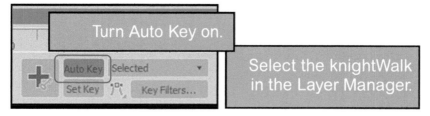

IMAGE 9.30

Move the Time Slider to frame 0. In the lower section of the Layer Manager, set the Global Weight to 0.0. This will essentially turn off the Walk Cycle clip, allowing the Idle clip to play. Move the Time Slider to frame 29 and set the Global Weight to 0.0. Move the Time Slider to frame 30 and adjust the Global Weight setting to 100. Click the Play button to run the animation. The Idle should run for 1 second, then the walk for 1 second. Both complete cycles.

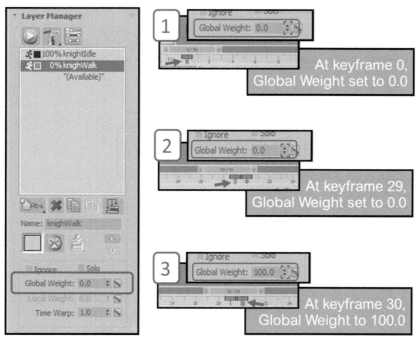

IMAGE 9.31 (3ds Max File Save 9.4)

That completes the clip setup. We are ready to Export the character to Unity.

Creating the FBX File for Export

Select the entire Knight model including the CAT Rig. From the File tab of the Main Menu, select the Export option and from the Export flyout, click on Export Selected.

We are using the Export Selected instead of the Export option because if we used the Export option, 3ds Max would create an FBX file that includes the Template Planes we used to set up the initial meshes back in Chapter 3. They are still in the Scene Explorer. Using the Export Selected, we can control the objects that are included.

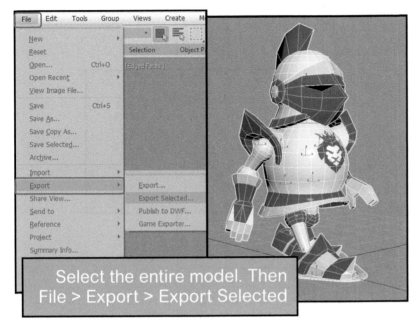

IMAGE 9.32

When the Select File to Export window opens, save the file as knightAnimated. Later you might want to import other Knight characters with different features, so we will use a descriptive name.

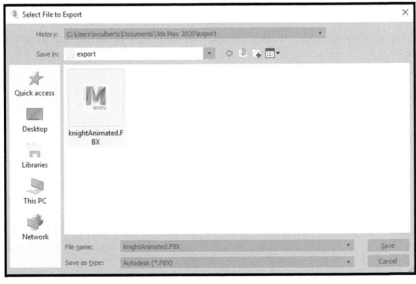

IMAGE 9.33

The FBX Export window will open. Most of the settings are fine the way they are by default. We do need to adjust three settings. Open the Animation drop down menu and check the tick box on. Do the same for the Bake Animation and the Embed Media, checking their tick boxes.

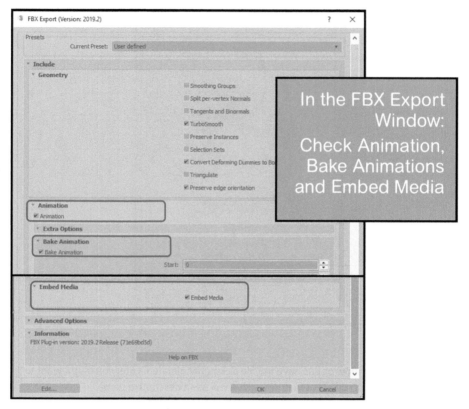

IMAGE 9.34

When you click OK, another window will open with errors listed. They will not affect our use in Unity, so it is alright to continue, click OK.

An FBX file of the model and the animation has been created for export to Unity or other game engines.

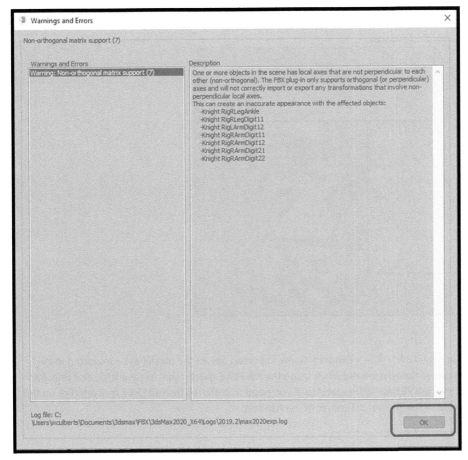

IMAGE 9.35

A recent addition to 3ds Max is the Game Exporter utility. This is a streamlined utility for exporting your character or model as an .FBX file to import into a game engine. It is not that different from the exporter we just used, but it does have a nice feature for separating the animation clips. Having just completed exporting your character using the full FBX Export utility, you might want to try the Game Exporter Utility.

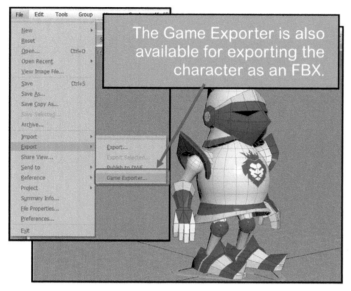

The Game Exporter is also available for exporting the character as an FBX.

IMAGE 9.36

Open the FBX Exporter Utility (File > Export > Game Exporter). Select the model to be exported in the scene. Use the same settings as we did when using the full FBX Exporter that are available and select an export path for the new FBX file to be saved to. If you need to switch to the full FBX Exporter, click on the "Advanced" button in the lower right corner of the window.

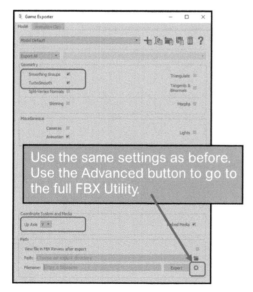

Use the same settings as before. Use the Advanced button to go to the full FBX Utility.

IMAGE 9.37

442

If the model has animations, use the animation tab at the top of the window before exporting to add the animation clips. List the separate animation clips for the model, their start and end frames in the Animation Clips section. Click the play button that appears to the right of the clip to view the animation. Be sure to check the Export box at the end of the row. Export the model.

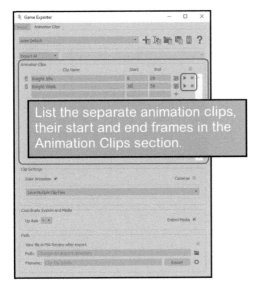

IMAGE 9.38

Chapter 9 Exercise: Exporting Characters

For this exercise, export the Warhorse Knight and the Dragon as FBX files, ready for import to the game Engine.

IMAGE 9.39

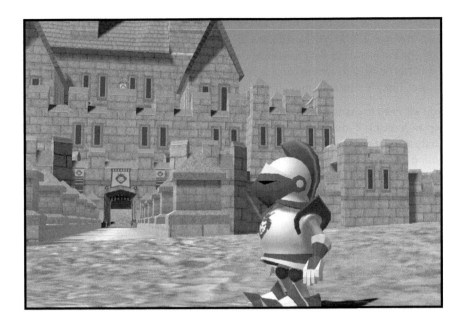

Exporting to the Game Engine

Topics in This Chapter

- Opening Unity
- Importing the Asset Package
- Importing the Character

Concepts/Skills/Tools Introduced in This Chapter

- Linking to the Character Controller
- Review of using the basic tools from Volume I

Setting Up the Game Engine File

In Volume I, we modeled the Castle environment and exported it to the Unity Game Engine. The characters we modeled in this text were designed to go with that environment. In this chapter, we will take the .FBX files of the characters that we exported and import them into our Castle Scene. We will link the characters and their animations in the character controller in the game engine so the character can run around the environment. The characters will be in the game scene. If you do not already have a Unity Account and a current version of the game engine, go to www.Unity3d.com and navigate to the "Get Unity" button. Downloading and installing is straight forward and simple. You might want to consider downloading the Unity Hub also. The Unity Hub helps to manage the various versions of Unity you might end up installing and your project. Unity is constantly upgrading with new and revised features.

To begin, you will need to create an account on the Unity site. The Unity website has beginner interactive tutorials that are available if you are new to the product. Before continuing here, make sure you have created a Unity account and have downloaded and installed the program on your computer. For this text, we will be using the Unity 19.3 version, the most current one available at this time. Open the Unity Hub that you installed. As mentioned before, in this tutorial, we will be bringing our character, the Knight, into the Castle Scene. Jordan Dubreuil, who prepared out Unity scene for the Castle, also prepared the packages we will be importing. In the packages that we will bring into Unity, Jordan prepared the code scripts needed to integrate the character and animations into the scene. He has done the bulk of the work needed to be done for this tutorial to work. It allows you to insert the character and link it up without needing to write the code for the controllers, etc. This is not a Unity book, so we cannot go into depth on working in Unity. However, we can accomplish the task and see the character in the game environment.

Opening Unity

When the Hub opens, you can create a new project or open an existing one. If you have more than one version of Unity, any existing projects listed will have the corresponding version of Unity that it was made with. To the right of the "New" button is a small drop-down menu button. If you have multiple versions of unity, select the 19.3 version or download it so you can work on this project.

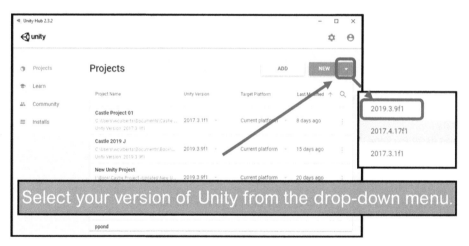

IMAGE 10.1

Then create a new project with Unity window will open. Select the 3D Template and give the project and name and location to create files. Then select the Create button. Unity will take a minute or two to create the project.

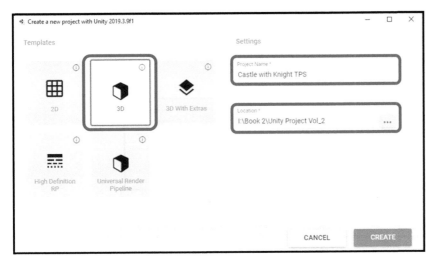

IMAGE 10.2

Import Cinemachine

The first thing we need to do once the Unity project opens is to import the Cinemachine Package into the Scene. The Cinemachine is a third-person camera system that we will be utilizing with the animated character. Cinemachine must be imported into the scene prior to the asset packages and the assets (the meshes and textures) to work properly in the scene.

IMAGE 10.3

To import the Cinemachine, click on the Windows tab on the top tool bar. In the drop-down menu, select "Package Manager." A new window, the Package Manager will open. In the search box, type in "cine" to get the Cinemachine to top the list on the left side of the window. At the bottom of the window, click install.

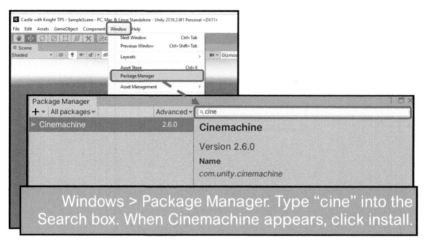

Windows > Package Manager. Type "cine" into the Search box. When Cinemachine appears, click install.

IMAGE 10.4

Install the Scene Package

The next item to install is the ThirdPersonCameraStat.unitypackage file. Download the file from the Companion Site, www.3dsMaxBasics.com, from Chapter 10, Volume II. Locate the download file where you can easily access it. Unzip it. To import into the scene, use the same procedure we used to bring the castle into the scene in Volume I. Click on the Assets tab to open its drop-down menu. Select Import Package and its flyout, Custom Package. The Import Unity Package window will open. Click on the "All" button in the lower left corner of the window, then the "Import" button in the lower right corner.

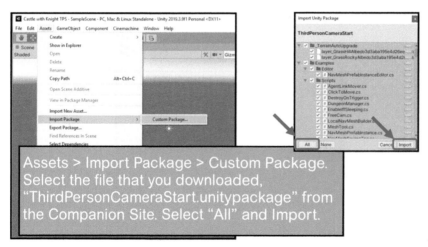

Assets > Import Package > Custom Package. Select the file that you downloaded, "ThirdPersonCameraStart.unitypackage" from the Companion Site. Select "All" and Import.

IMAGE 10.5

Open the Scene

When the Unity is done importing the package, we can open the scene. In the Project Panel, expand the Assets item by clicking the small triangle next to it if it is not already expanded. Expand the Scenes item. Inside Scenes is the Unity scene, ThirdPersonSceneStart. Double-click on it. If your Project panel looks differently than mine, that is alright. In the upper right corner, click on the three vertical dots. There is an option to show the panel in a single or double column.

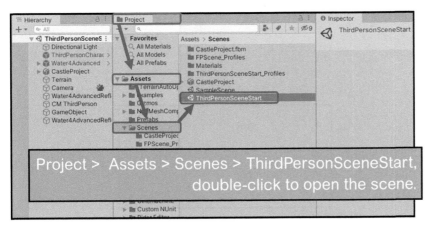

IMAGE 10.6

After you double-click on the ThirdPersonSceneStart, the scene will open. Double-click on the ThirdPersonCharacter listed in the Hierarchy Panel. The scene view will shift to the character. The Cinecamera and castle should be visible in the scene.

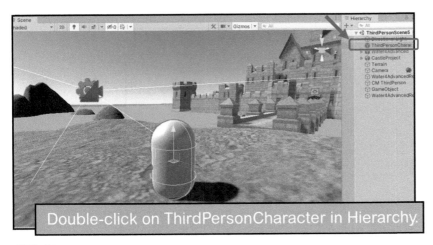

IMAGE 10.7

The white capsule is the character. You can make it move about the scene using the WASD keys to move the character and move the mouse to rotate the camera view around the character. Click the Play button or press the CTRL + "P" keys to run and stop the scene.

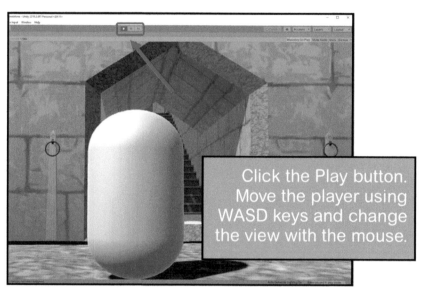

IMAGE 10.8

Import the Character

We are ready to bring the Knight into the scene. Right-Click in the Project Panel or go up to

IMAGE 10.9

Assets on the top tool bar. From the dropdown menu, select "Import New Asset."

The Import New Asset window will open. There should be two files listed, The knightAnimated.FBX and the texture file for the Knight. Select them both and then import.

You will be importing the Knight I made and animated. If you want to import your Knight (I hope you do), navigate to the .FBX exported Knight you created and animated in Chapter 9, and select it and its texture instead of mine. For the text, I will keep referring to my model.

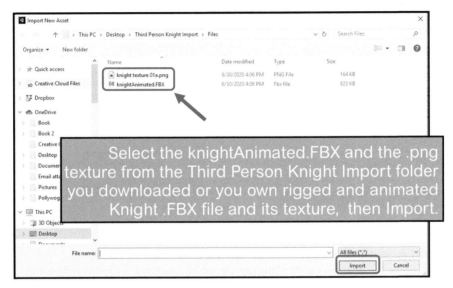

IMAGE 10.10

The model and texture were imported into the Project Panel inside the Scene folder. Drag the knightAnimated model over into the Hierarchy Panel inside the ThirdPersonCharacter.

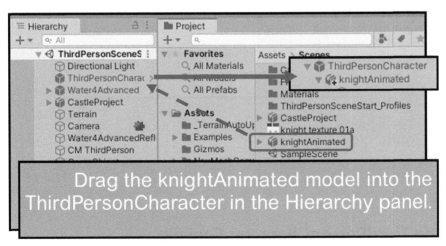

IMAGE 10.11

Next, select the knightAnimated model in the Hierarchy Panel. The Knight will appear in the capsule, the Parent object it is liked to. The Knight is likely too high up in the capsule.

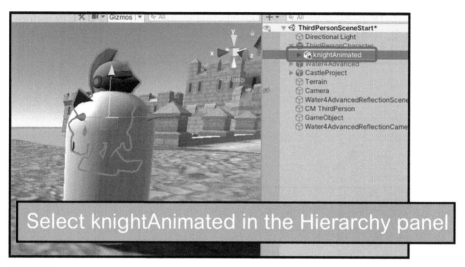

IMAGE 10.12

With the Knight selected, move it down inside the capsule near the ground. We will make finer adjustments later. It fits inside the boundary walls of the capsule, which is good. The capsule will be the collider for the figure.

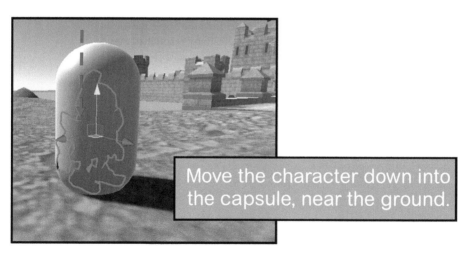

IMAGE 10.13

Adjusting the ThirdPersonCharacter Capsule

We will adjust the capsule next to better fit the character. Select the ThirdPersonCharacter in the Hierarchy Panel. To the right, in the Inspector Panel, uncheck the Mesh Renderer's box so the capsule does not render, revealing the character. In the Capsule Collider section, click on the Edit Collider button as shown in the next image.

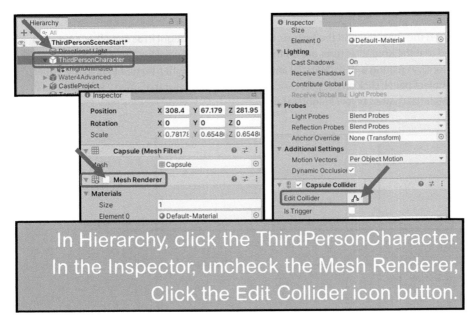

In Hierarchy, click the ThirdPersonCharacter.
In the Inspector, uncheck the Mesh Renderer,
Click the Edit Collider icon button.

IMAGE 10.14

With the Capsule not rendering, it is easy to see the cage of the Capsule and note its position relative to the Figure. Adjust the height of the capsule by selecting the small handle at the top and move it down toward the helmet crest using the Move tool.

IMAGE 10.15

The sides are relatively close to the body and arms, so we can leave them as they are.

Correcting the Texture

When Unity imported the character and the texture, the texture was brought in as any other asset. You might have noticed that the Knight textures are on the dark side. The original texture is much brighter. We can fix the texture by creating a Unity Material and assigning the Knight's texture to it. In the upper left corner of the Project panel, click on the plus (+) icon. From the menu list that opens, select Material. Rename the new Material created below knightMaterial.

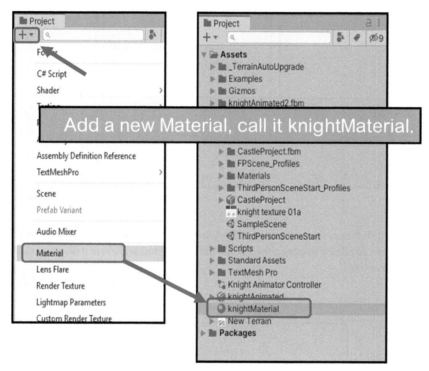

IMAGE 10.16

Click on the new Material if not already selected. In the Inspector, the panel contains a number of parameters that can be adjusted to optimize the texture in the game. Assign the Knight's texture by dragging the Knight texture 01a in the Project panel to the small box next to the Albedo heading in the inspector. Albedo is the measure of the diffuse reflection of light from a surface. Adjusting the albedo in the Inspector changes how the calculation for the light reflected off a surface is interpreted. A shinny surface projects an image of a smooth surface, like metal. Adjust the Metalic and Smoothness as shown below.

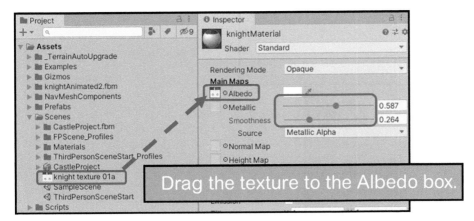

IMAGE 10.17

Image 10.18 shows a before and after image of the material.

IMAGE 10.18

Fixing Flipped Faces in Unity

With the texture more visible, look at the pauldron and limbs on the left side of the character. If they look funny, they were probably created using the Mirror Tool in 3ds Max. If they were, the faces have been flipped inside out. If you used the Mirror Modifier, this should not happen. In case this has happened to your model, there is a fix. You might want to know about this fix for the future, even if it does not apply to your current model.

Faces on the left, mirrored meshes are flipped, inside out.

IMAGE 10.19

Select one of the meshes with the problem, the Left Pauldron in the image below. In the Inspector, scroll down to the Skinned Mesh Renderer. Change the box value next to the Root Bone listing by selecting the small circle with a dot inside it all the way to the right of the value box. When selected a window called Select Transform opens. Scroll to the top of the list and select the value "None." This will essentially flip the normals of the mesh, allowing the texture to be mapped on the outside of the mesh where they belong.

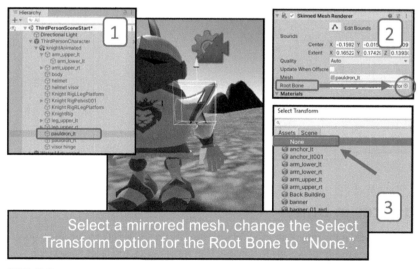

Select a mirrored mesh, change the Select Transform option for the Root Bone to "None.".

IMAGE 10.20

Repeat the same steps for any other meshes that have the same problem. In the sample mesh, in addition to the Left Pauldron, the Left Upper Arm, Left Lower Arm, Left Upper Leg and Left Lower Leg as well as the three left foot meshes need to be flipped.

Setting up the Animations in Unity

In 3ds Max, we created two animations for the Knight, an Idle and a Walk cycle. We exported them as one animation, 59 frames long. With the animations now in Unity with the character, we need to separate the two animations so the program can call on them as needed when called by the player input by pressing the keyboard keys.

Click on the knightAnimated in the Project Panel to open the Inspector with its attributes. Click on the Animation tab at the top of the Inspector if it is not already selected. In the Animation tab there are tools to separate our single animation into two separate clips. At the very bottom of the panel is an image of the Knight on a grid. If the image is not visible, grab the top edge of the bottom item and raise it to show the character. There is a Play button that will play the full animation clip. First the Idle will play, then the Walk Cycle, and repeat.

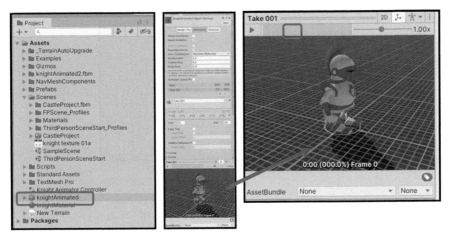

IMAGE 10.21

Scroll down the panel to find the value box with the name "Take 001" in it. Unity has named the animation clip associated with this model as default. Take 001 has both the Idle and the Walk animation clips in it. Rename "Take 001" to "Idle." The Start value of "0" is correct. Change the End value to 29, the end of the Idle cycle. Check the boxes for Loop Time and Loop Pose. Loop Time will loop the cycle continuously, Loop Pose will try to make a smooth transition at the loop End and Start if there is an inconsistent transition.

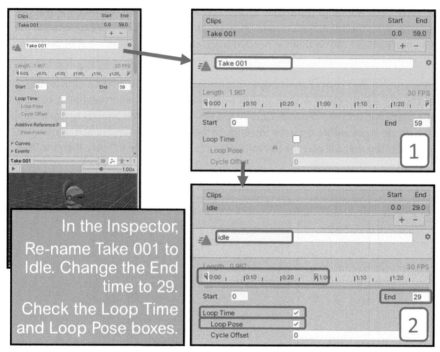

IMAGE 10.22

Next, create a new Take 001 by clicking the plus (+) sign. Change the name "Take 001" to "Walk Cycle." Change the Start value to 30 and the end value to 59, the start and end of the Walk Cycle. Again, check the Loop Time and Loop Pose check boxes.

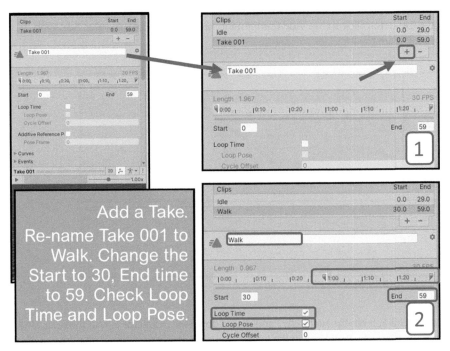

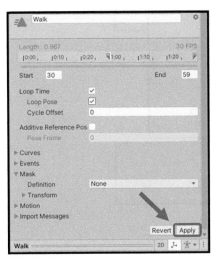

IMAGE 10.23

The new setting will not become active until you scroll down to the bottom of the panel and click on the Apply button. Click on the Apply button before proceeding.

IMAGE 10.24

We have imported the character and texture. Adjusted the ThirdPlayerCharacter capsule size to fit the character and separated the animation clips. Next, we need to connect the scripts, the code, to our character and animations to get everything working. One of the Scripts we need to connect is the Basic Motor Script.

Next, we need to add an Animator Component to the knightAnimated. Select the knightAnimated in the Hierarchy Panel. In the Inspector, click on the "Add Component" button. In the Search value box, type "anim." Select "Animator" from the list.

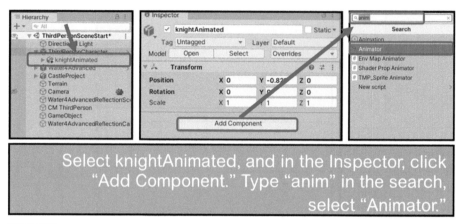

Select knightAnimated, and in the Inspector, click "Add Component." Type "anim" in the search, select "Animator."

IMAGE 10.25

Click on the ThirdPersonCharacter in the Hierarchy Panel. Scroll down the inspector to find the Basic Motor Script section. Back in the Hierarchy Panel, select the knightAnimated object and drag it into the value box next to "Anim" as shown.

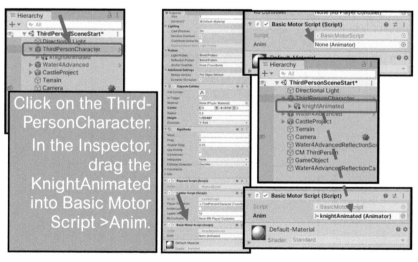

Click on the Third-PersonCharacter. In the Inspector, drag the KnightAnimated into Basic Motor Script >Anim.

IMAGE 10.26

Now that there is an Animator Component, we can assign the controller. Select the Knight Animator Controller in the Project Panel and drag it into the value box for the Controller.

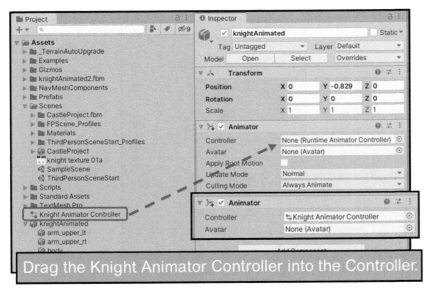

IMAGE 10.27

The Animator

The next task is to connect the two animation clips with the Animator. From the top tool bar, select the Window tab. From the Window menu, select Animation and then click on the Animation fly-out, Animator. The Animator window will open. If it opens in the upper left window with the Scene, drag the Animator tab down next to the Game tab in the lower window. This will make it easier to work, still having access to the Scene window.

The Animator window is a visual depiction of the Animation Controller with all the associated elements involved. In the Animation Controller, the transitions between animation clips can be set up. The Animation Controller that Jordan Dubreuil set up for this tutorial is visible in the window. Without getting into the Boolean statements and code scripts, not within the indicate transitions between the two, which will occur as we move the player. If we made other animations, such as, run, jump, crouch, die, they would each have a state box in the Animator window and have transitions between them. We kept this really simple with just two states, Idle and Walk.

The connections we made in the past few pages, the Knight Animator Controller into the Controller, the knightAnimator into the Basic Motor Script and the separation of the animation clips all come together here in the Animator.

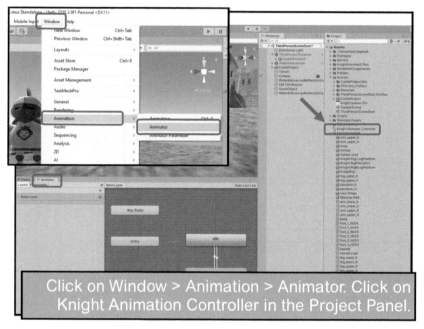

Click on Window > Animation > Animator. Click on Knight Animation Controller in the Project Panel.

IMAGE 10.28

Select the orange "Idle" box in the Animator. In the Project Panel, expand the knightAnimated object. Drag the "Idle" to the Motion Value box as seen in number two of the image below.

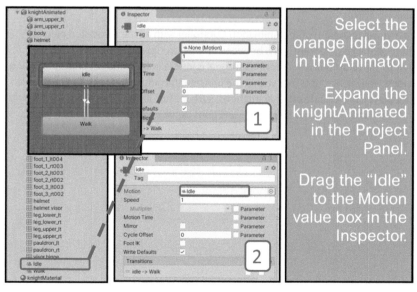

Select the orange Idle box in the Animator.

Expand the knightAnimated in the Project Panel.

Drag the "Idle" to the Motion value box in the Inspector.

IMAGE 10.29

Next, select the gray "Walk" box in the Animator. Drag the "Walk" into the Motion value box in the Inspector.

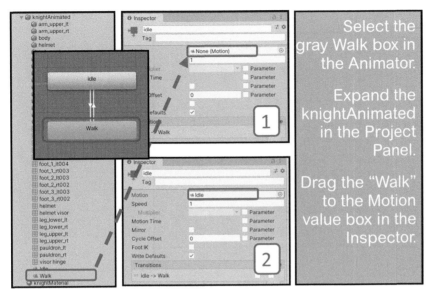

Select the gray Walk box in the Animator.

Expand the knightAnimated in the Project Panel.

Drag the "Walk" to the Motion value box in the Inspector.

IMAGE 10.30

That should complete the connections. The player should be ready to get moving. Click on the Play button at the top of the UI. Use the W and S keys on the keyboard to move forward and backward, the A and D keys to turn left and right. Move the mouse to rotate the camera view around the character.

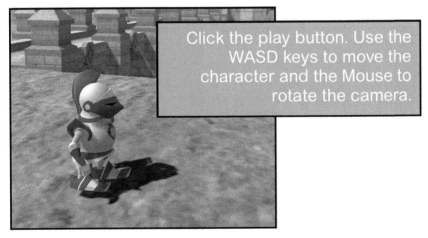

Click the play button. Use the WASD keys to move the character and the Mouse to rotate the camera.

IMAGE 10.31

The Knight is not touching the ground as it walks. Select the knightAnimated object in the Hierarchy. Move the Knight down toward the bottom of the Capsule cage. The Capsule cage will not penetrate the terrain when the game is active.

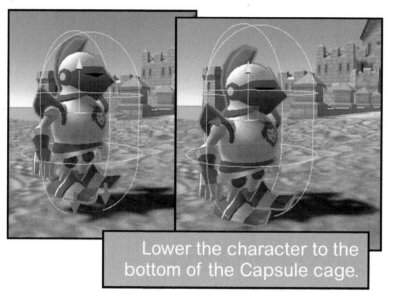

IMAGE 10.32

As it moves, the player seems to be out of sync – the footsteps are floating across the ground. It moves too far for each step taken. We can fix this in the Animator. Select the gray Walk box in the Animator. Over in the Inspector, change the speed value of 1 to a value of 2, making quicker footsteps.

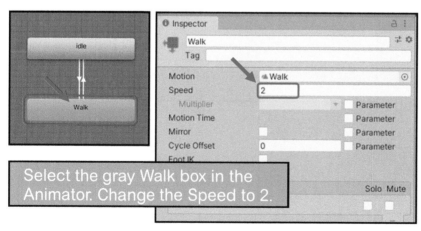

IMAGE 10.33

Play the game again. The Knight should look more realistic walking at a quicker pace for the distance it covers. It should be walking on the ground too.

That completes the importing of the character you created into the environment you created in a game engine, Unity. Well done!

IMAGE 10.34

Chapter 10 Exercise: Importing the Warhorse Knight and Dragon

You successfully imported the Knight into the game. What about the Warhorse Knight that you animated? What about the Dragon? Import them both into additional scenes using the same steps we used for the Knight. You will need to adjust the Capsule cage to fit the new characters, but other than that, substitute the new character names in place of the Knight in the tutorial.

Conclusion

Congratulations on completing the two textbooks. You should have a good understanding of how 3d modeling works, the basic pipeline for creating video game assets from characters to environments. This was by no means everything there is to know about modeling. You now have your feet wet. Dive in and learn all you can about the various aspects. Try different modeling programs and various game engines. Most of all, I hope you enjoyed the process and can appreciate what you have accomplished.

Index